Stormie,

I'm happy to present my 12th house metaphysical life to you, where Jupiter rules natally.

With that said, I know enough astrology to know that all this craziness started when Uranus transited my 9th house.

Enjoy the read!

Jamahia

HERMETICALLY SEALED in ONE ORDINARY GAL

HERMETICALLY SEALED in ONE ORDINARY GAL

Part I

a memoir by
Jarnalia Jennings

Editors: Kimberly Damone & Nicholas Denton
Book cover designed by: Semnitz

This book is dedicated:

To the forgotten Egyptians who prepared our old bodies for their royal tombs, and to the mothers who opted to nurture our new bodies in their wombs, so that we might embrace life once again through the magic of reincarnation.

Contents

Acknowledgements

My most favorite person in the whole world, my son, who told me one day, *"I was not born just to keep hearing your crazy talk*!" Thank you, Beno, for taking that ride with me, and I love you immensely.

The "Sunshine State" for awakening me to me.

I would like to sincerely thank Mrs. Patricia Dressler of Angel & Guides and Margaret McElroy of Mrs. M&M Radio Show for their extraordinary gifts. This book would not have been possible without you, and I wish to work with you again in a future lifetime. To the one and only KareBear, who knew before I did that, I would write a book one day. KareBear, if you are holding this book, I finally did it! Darcy, Golden Rose, and Sandra, your enlightenment has been just as grand, and I could not have continued this saga without you, too.

The Universe for its abundance and beautiful wisdom, and to the Universal Forces for all of their support in my spiritual expedition.

Introduction

Music is life, so I use it to express myself in every way, and it's exemplified throughout this memoir. First, let me grab Tone The Beat Bully to get things started. Put on the track *Dreams and Nightmares Instrumental Version*. I specifically want to hear the piano melody along with the harmonics of the strings as I envision myself at an extraordinary concert with Chilly Gonzales at the helm and the Kaiser Quartett accompanying him. I love this intro, it's reminiscent of a soap opera my mother used to watch when I was a child coming up. Hold up, wait a minute, I do want Meek Mills to speak, for it's his song too! So, I will do it like this: Meek, you could speak to me as if you were my coach, informing me that training day is now over and your lines remain the same, "Ain't this what they been waiting for? You ready?"

I swear the biggest lie ever told to man is, "We die only to never be born again!" Now, that's a crock of shit! Have you ever seen that meme where a businessman is bent over, sweeping the word "truth" underneath the red carpet with a push broom? Oh, how that little depiction speaks volumes. In my opinion, I feel we are all living in a perpetual lie that's been cycling for thousands of years now. For some individuals, living in this deception can be very restrictive. We have to go along just to get along. Plus, if one of us brave individuals wishes to break from life's false perception and speak out about what is true, we are given shifty eyes and deemed *loco*!

Here is one truth about our Western civilization. We are under the school of thought that our life starts out as an infant with zero histories and life completely ends when we succumb to death. This is not completely true. What is the first Law of Conservation of Energy? Energy can neither be created nor destroyed; energy can only be transferred or changed from one form to another. Well, we are energy! Our souls are pure energy. Therefore, when we die, we change form, and our energy form had a long history way before we are ever slapped on the behind. It's right here in our science.

Winston Churchill said history is written by the victors. As a result, the victors intentionally left the subject of reincarnation out of the most referenced book in our Western society. Therefore, our Westernized Good Book is missing a lot of good, vital, and need-to-know information! Information like what happens at the very moment when we die? Where do we go? And, none of that heaven and hell rhetoric! What exactly is the light? What will happen if you don't go towards the light? What's the soul's family? Do we come back, and if so, do we have to? Certainly, this resourceful information was clearly left out of the "good book"! Except what human being can answer these questions correctly? Most of those toting the "good book" can only tell you how to live your life according to the laws of that little black *holy* book. So, if you want the answers to those questions that I have written above, which are all metaphysical questions in nature, well, you would have to ask the holy ghost herself/himself to convey those truths through you with the help of alternative means.

In all honesty, my book isn't about what happens to the soul at the moment of death, nor going with the light. My book is my own personal account about coming back from death again, and again, and again—on a cycle. Then, realizing the greatest lie ever told to man.

My Programming

In my adolescent years, I believed everything that everybody told me about God. Older people would recite the word of the Lord to me verbatim. They would talk about the dichotomy of right and wrong and heaven and hell. So as a child, I too would frown upon or shake my head at another if their beliefs differed from what I was taught about God and the "good book." Things changed briefly when I was a teenager; I no longer was concerned about the holy ghost! Between the ages of 13 and 14, my mother would send me to church unaccompanied. I would walk up to Mount Gilead Baptist Church by myself and sit there in complete boredom while Reverend Dean preached his sermon—I wasn't even listening.

After a while, my slick ass changed up the routine and unbeknownst to my mother, I started skipping church! I would go over to my friend Tia's house and hang out with her and her sisters. Then, I would leave Tia's house at an ample time and return home when my mother was expecting me to be walking through the door coming from church. I would head straight to my bedroom take off my church clothes, put on my play clothes, then head right back over to Tia's house for the remainder of the day. Part of me wants to believe my mom never suspected any foul play. But, on the other hand, mothers know everything!

Despite my deviant acts, I still believed in the Word, mainly because older Christian people were still volunteering their Christian views on me. Again, they shared information with me that was printed in the "good book" and I never questioned it or them. Everything that I was ever taught as a child coming up, well into my twenties, I never questioned any of it. I just accepted it, by conforming and trying to live the right way instead of the wrong way. Like most of us do. So, I say to you, did you ever question the religious beliefs you were taught by your elders? Or did you just run with their truth and believed it as your own?

I can honestly say, what I realized for myself later on down the road is that, for many years, the Christian faith distorted my perceptions of what truth really is. People listen to me, no matter what walk of life you come from, you have played all types of roles in this thing we call life. We keep living and dying shedding the physical form because it's part of the soul's evolutionary growth. We live out lessons that we have already chosen to learn as a soul. We even continue to learn when we return to the world of spirit when our life here is over.

My 3-Year Depression

After having all that religion professed to me since childhood by my mother, grandmother, grandfather, by the church and the "good book" and other religious people alike, I got very depressed once I realized the truth. Well, today I stand firm on this topic. **I will not have anybody preaching to me about saving my soul, and do not come to me, telling me that Jesus died on the cross for my sins.** ***What sins*****?** By 2011, I was already up to 10—minor past lifetimes before I walked into Egypt.

Spiritual Lesson #1

"The soul creates the flesh." –*Seth*

What is Reincarnation?

I'll share with you from my studies of metaphysical truths. After death, the soul leaves this physical plane of existence behind and then the soul returns home for a little R&R. The soul needs this rest because the human experience can leave you exhausted. How long does the soul need to rest? It varies per individual. In the spirit world, your soul will continue to learn and expand on its spiritual path, and sometime after your soul has rested up, you and your spiritual advisory team will begin to plot and plan your next mission. Let's say you look over what lessons your soul wishes to work on, or even remaster for its spiritual growth. For the record, we are here to learn spiritual lessons. Lessons on betrayal, confidence, compassion, greed, kindness, leadership, loneliness, love, trust, unity...I could go on and on. Once your lessons have been established, you then select your parents. Now, your parents have already agreed in the spirit world to play the role of your parents, way before they reincarnated to Earth themselves. With that said, everybody in your life has agreed to help you learn your spiritual lessons.

Following, you as the soul, pick the time and location. You pick the circumstances that will enable you to learn those lessons that your soul needs for its spiritual growth. You pick all your specifications, skin color, hair color, eye color, body type, talents, and the likes... whatever you specify is going to be the highest expression of the soul for that lifetime. Now, you are ready to reincarnate. You get a brand-new body full of vigor! You get a brand-new mind and a brand-new mission! Additionally, just like a soul can choose to have a brand-new abled body that works perfectly, a soul can also choose to have a body that is disabled, in whichever capacity. Whatever restrictions that soul has placed upon itself, it still comes to Earth on a mission of spiritual growth and to assist you with yours.

The Prelude to Jarnalia Jennings

Before I captivate your mind with my amazing tale. I want to throw out a disclaimer about myself. Just like everyone else, I started out normal. I was a fun girl and even an extrovert. I loved hanging out with my crew and I loved to be seen. Yes, I would say I was conceited as hell up to a point where I probably sickened some of my friends. My grandmother bought me everything and even paid for me to go to the hair stylist monthly. I used to hate it when she touched the finished product. On the home front, my mother made sure that I had everything I needed and wanted.

I wasn't eccentric at all, although I had had a handful of unusual experiences between the age four and 28. In my opinion, it was not spectacular enough to rattle me to the point where it altered my life's viewpoint. As you'll see, that changed once I moved to Florida. Granted, I guarantee you, that by the time you get into Chapter 6, you are going to think that I sound completely "cray-cray" as Kanye puts it. Furthermore, the story you are about to read is genuinely my own!

My life experiences are completely non-fictional, nor is it a twenty-first century exaggerated parable. Although I really do wish that I could report to you that my memoir is en masses factitious. But truth be told, I couldn't produce anything this *imaginatively bizarre* on my own accord! Everything that I have reported in this book has honestly happened to me. This is my real-life experience from my point of view. If we analyzed my book from Dr. Phil's expertise, it would be a book of loose associations. Lol.

At the beginning of my spiritual awakening, the Universe intentionally placed significant hints before my very eyes, as well as thought-provoking manifestations. This was followed by a redirecting, as a new method was used once I returned home to Virginia. My subconscious was playing out these extraordinary stories as I slept; that is, stories of ***you and me***.

What is this book about?

It's a majestic tale of Egypt's past. It's a homecoming for the most powerful, influential, notable, celebrated, and unforgotten Pharaohs and their Great Royal Queens of ancient Egypt. As well as a myriad of personal revelations about myself of the highest magnitude unveiled along the way.

Roll Call

If you made the first cut on the J-List, I feel that it is important for me to recite the words of Q-Tip to you, "I don't really mind if it's all over your head cause the job of resurrection is to wake-up the dead!"[1] Well, I'm here, dammit, like it or not, to reawaken and resurrect you modern day pharaohs and you modern day queens from your slumber and restore you to your sovereignty.

---

[1] A Tribe Called Quest, Jazz (We've Got You), track 11 on The Low End Theory, Jive Records & RCA Records, 1991.

1

Jacksonville, Florida (The Twilight Zone)

At last, Beno and I arrived in Jacksonville, Florida, May of 2007. I had convinced my son, Beno, that we were going to have a great time living in Jacksonville. I lied, telling him we would visit Disney World and Universal Studios regularly. I had to make the transition sound appealing to my kid since I was separating him from his father. Selfishly, my inner being had to get out of Virginia. I'd lived there all my life and I was ready to see the world, or at least a different state anyway. By nature, I am a person who is always on the go, rarely sitting idle. Even my imagination has traveled to St. Lucia 100 times without packing a suitcase or boarding an airplane. I want to travel the world. I guess you could say I have wanderlust.

4519 Melvin Circle West

We landed a place to rent on the west side of Jacksonville off 103rd Street. You see, I am a tactician by design. I must plan everything before making any serious moves. So, before uprooting to Jacksonville, Beno and I moved out of our apartment in Waverton Place in Chesapeake and temporarily moved in with my grandparents in Norfolk.

Are you wondering how one prepares to move four states away? At least, that's how Beno's dad puts it. Well, first I went on Rent.com and pored over properties in Jacksonville until I found one that piqued my interest. As I looked over some properties in Jacksonville, one in particular caught my interest. It was located on the northwest side of Jacksonville. My plan was to remotely fill out the rental application, be approved, and pay the security deposit all while still living in Virginia. Then we would move in as soon as Beno finished the second grade.

Lenox Apartments

The apartment complex that caught my interest was called Lenox Apartments. I telephoned the complex and requested that a rental application be mailed to me in Virginia. I explained that I wanted to have my living arrangements worked out upon arriving. The leasing agent sympathetically expressed to me that she completely understood my plan. She and I then went over my grandparents' physical address where the application was to be sent. I felt confident that the information I requested was coming to my address in several days and then I could fill out the application and send it back with a money order to secure a unit.

A full week had drifted by and no leasing application from Lenox Apartments. I got on the internet and had to look up the apartment complex telephone number because I didn't write it down the first time. I phoned Lenox Apartments office again. After the agent gave her telephone greeting, I began to ramble, explaining that I called last week and requested that a leasing application be mailed to me in Norfolk, Virginia. I added that I had been patiently waiting for the application to arrive in the mail for a week and a day and I hadn't seen anything yet. Then I asked her, "Are you sure that the application got mailed?"

The leasing agent politely asked for my name, then placed me on a brief hold. When she returned to the telephone, she said, "Yes, Ms. Jennings, I can see when the application was mailed out." She added, "Just give it a few more days and if it hasn't arrived by then, I'll personally re-send the application." In the following days, I routinely checked the mailbox and still nothing on behalf of Lenox Apartments.

Needless to say, I got on the telephone for a third time and dialed up Lenox Apartments yet again. I respectfully gave the leasing agent a few seconds to get out her greeting and thereafter, I went on another rant. I babbled on how I was coming from out-of-state and I wanted to secure a place before I moved down to Jacksonville and I had still not received the leasing application. Calmly, the leasing agent found a way to get a word in and expressed to me that she totally understood my concerns. At that point, she reassured me that she would personally re-send an application to my address in Norfolk, Virginia. Again, we verified the physical address for surety. Now, that's two different leasing agents, at two different times, and both mailed me a leasing application, to the same address and I had not received either of the two! Hmm?

Another week zoomed by and still no application from Lenox Apartments. I could not comprehend why I did not receive either of the two applications in the mail even though both leasing agents had assured me that they placed the application in the mailbox and sent them out to the address I had provided. I picked up the telephone and called Lenox Apartments again and this time, I was furious. I irately summarized all I had experienced with their company over the past three weeks. I was being extra dramatic by expounding on the fact that I was uprooting 692 miles away and I was trying to get my moving arrangements in order, and I had the money needed to secure their unit.

This time the leasing agent was benumbed by my rapid speech. However, she replied she too could not understand why none of the rental applications had not arrived. Trying to subdue my irritability, she suggested she send me a third rental application. I quickly denied her courteous proposal. Instead, I informed her that would not be necessary, for I was coming to Jacksonville in only a few short weeks and I was going to pick one up in person.

Just as I planned, I arrived in Jacksonville with the address to Lenox Apartments programmed into my GPS. But when I arrived at their door, their office was *closed*! Might I add, they were closed during operating hours! In my rationale, I wasn't putting two and two together. I didn't stop and question these flukes. Believe it or not, I just sat there and waited for them to open. Was I not destined to move into Lenox Apartments? As I reflect on my Florida experience, this is where the bizarreness began.

As fate would have it, I didn't move into Lenox Apartments. For one reason, their rent amount exceeded my housing voucher, and two, Divine Intervention. Had I lived on the northwest side of Jacksonville, it would have put me in the path of a different shopping mall altogether.

I continued to look for another rental property. It just so happened I was smart enough to grab a copy of the Jacksonville Section-8 Vacant Housing List from their office. Not long after, I became completely overwhelmed by the large selection of properties listed. I traveled far and wide to random properties in various parts of Jacksonville. I found myself in Arlington and the northside, then I was back on the westside and still I wasn't pleased with anything that I saw. So, I gave up. I just stopped looking altogether. I concluded that I would travel back down to Jacksonville at a later time to look again for a rental property.

A month later, I traveled back down to Jacksonville, with the vacant property list in hand. I saw 4519 Melvin Circle West under the Westside Region. I called and arranged to meet with the owner at this property. Slyly, the owner had co-blocked the viewing time. She scheduled another lady and me to view the property at the same time. The owner walked us through her vacant one-story, two-bedroom home. After the walkthrough, we were standing around talking outside of the vacant home. The homeowner had the garage door lifted and she had the garage's back door opened too. All of a sudden, the garage's back door slammed all by itself! We all were startled, yet we continued to talk. I thought, *Damn, what was that? Is this house haunted?* The homeowner asked the other prospective tenant when she could move in. She answered that she didn't have her housing voucher yet! The homeowner's facial expression was priceless. She looked at this lady like, "You've been wasting my time!" I immediately jumped into their conversation and blurted out, "I have mine right now!" And this is how I moved into the pink and brown house at 4519 Melvin Circle West.

If you know me personally, you know that I love the mall. The closest one to the westside of Jacksonville was out in Orange Park, appropriately named Orange Park Mall. It was less than 10 minutes away from my house. Taking Fireside Road all the way out, a few left and right turns put me right there. Orange Park Mall is located off Blanding Boulevard and Wells Road. Ironically, when I was a kid, I grew-up on Bland Street and Sewell's Point Road.

The very first time I visited Orange Park Mall, I entered through the food court and I must have got there too early because nothing was open yet. I remember walking past a shop that was painted all pink and brown. I remember walking underneath the sign and I turned my head up just to see the name of this store and it read: *CamiCakes*. Boy, was I happy this shop wasn't open. Reason being, I am a cake connoisseur. If I baked a box cake, I would eat the entire cake in one day. As I was walking away from that little shop, I thought to myself, why did they paint it pink and brown? I didn't think about it anymore. Weeks would pass before I made an unusual comparison, that little shop was the same color as the house I was living in, *pink and brown*.

After exploring this closed mall, I would have to say it did not get my stamp of approval. I had uprooted to a city with no Nordstrom's, no Arden B, no Macy's, no BeBe, and no-fly ass shoe stores like Aldo, Barefeet, DSW, or Off-Broadway Shoes. What was I going to do, commute to Orlando just to shop? However, Orange Park Mall had a Dillard's and some store called Belk. What is a Belk anyway? I'd never heard of it. I thought this place was so country. The next time, my son and I visited Orange Park Mall, the cake shop was open. This is when I learned that it was actually a cupcake shop. This little place had a variety of nicely garnished assorted cupcakes and they all looked delicious. I remember buying a banana cream pie cupcake for myself and I got Beno a chocolate classic cupcake. Undoubtedly, after the tasting of our first cupcake, we both were hooked! At this point, Beno and I became returning customers at CamiCakes and I became infatuated with those cupcakes. As a result, I started sampling all the flavors and gained 12 unwanted pounds. My favorite cupcakes were the banana cream pie, the peanut butter Reese's Cup, the pink cami classic, and the chocolate buttercream CamiCake. Honestly, in my opinion, the rest were not so good. Although not too long after the sampling of all those cupcakes, I started telling my friends and family back home in Virginia about this great little shop that only sold cupcakes. I told them that they needed to taste them.

July arrived, and my friend Michael flew down to visit with Beno and me while on vacation. Michael had just left Jacksonville back in May; he helped me drive a big U-Haul truck and even moved all my furniture into the house. When he arrived, the first thing I did was take him to Orange Park Mall for some CamiCakes!

While in the food court, Michael and I sat there with our CamiCakes in hand, and simultaneously we vocalized that a cupcake shop was definitely needed in our area in Virginia. After that statement, Michael didn't say too much more, as his taste buds were being titillated by the decadent baked good. I blurted out, "Michael, you should open one!" I was still feeling out Jacksonville and I wasn't sure if I wanted to become a permanent resident after my first year or not. About six weeks had gone by and I had read a book called *Girl Get Your Money Straight* by Glinda Bridgforth. In Glinda's book, she tells the reader to create a list of trade ideas that they could implement now to generate a few extra dollars or think bigger, start a real business. This was coupled with *The Ellen Show,* where Ellen spoke about creating a "bucket list" of activities to achieve before you croaked. Taking both ladies' advice, I did just that. I wrote out a list of ideas. Now I can't remember what I wrote for the first thirty-eight entries, but the thirty-ninth and final entry was to own a business.

A few more weeks passed. I was walking around my bed in my bedroom and an idea popped in my head: *"You should start the cupcake business back at home."* I immediately called Michael and told him about my new idea! And from that moment, my unnamed cupcake shop was born in a form of *a thought*.

Entering the Twilight Zone

July of 2007, I had found a job. It was a weekend position working with adults with intellectual disabilities in a group home setting, and this job allowed me to bring Beno with me to work. This was a plus because I didn't have a babysitter. When I received my first paycheck, I purchased a book called *The Secret* by Rhonda Byrne. And to be totally honest, I had no idea what the book was about, I just knew that it was changing people's lives.

One day, a few weeks into our dwelling in Jacksonville, I was talking on the telephone with my aunt who I call Mama, and I was walking throughout the house. For no reason at all, I moseyed on over to the window just to peek outside, and lo and behold, I saw a rainbow in my backyard. Now, I've never witnessed a rainbow up close and in person before. Sure, I've seen one at a distance in the Earth's stratosphere. And let me add, it was the beginning of the arch of the rainbow. I would have been remiss not to mention this beautiful spectacle to Mama. So, in an enthusiastic tone, I said, "Mama, there's a rainbow in my backyard!" Well, she didn't reciprocate in the same excitement, at least that's how I felt. Witnessing that rainbow in my backyard coupled with my aunt's apathetic attitude toward it had me frantically searching for my camera.

I found that camera, and luckily for me, that rainbow was still there. Strangely, a few weeks after taking the picture of the rainbow, I got a neon orange flyer in the mail with a leprechaun sliding over a rainbow to a pot of gold. It read: Golden Estates. At that moment, I did think that it was a little weird as I just saw an actual rainbow in my backyard but without the pot of gold. In light of this, I had no interest in the flyer, so I ripped it up a few days later and threw it away. As of today, I still do not understand the meaning behind that unusual connection.

Returning to when I had the epiphany that made me want to start up a cupcakery business back home in Virginia. I had decided right then and there that my stay in Jacksonville would only be temporary and I was going to take that year living there to formulate a master plan. I stopped by Books-A-Million in the Orange Park Mall and purchased a *Streetwise Business Plan Book* for some direction. I hurried over to the Camicakes' website and read up on the owner's backstory. I found out the owner of this cupcake shop was named Andra, which is remarkably similar to my closest friend's name Aundria Trouble. Not to mention, Andra was a sista, an African American woman. I just knew she would be pleased to assist me. I took the initiative and wrote her a letter on my favorite colored paper, yellow, and expressed to her my own personal backstory. In my letter to Andra, I explained I really loved her business concept and I wanted to take that same concept back to Virginia. I had high hopes that Andra would write me back. Weeks rolled by and she ***never*** responded to my letter. Given that, I called her on the telephone at her place of business. I introduced myself and asked if she received my letter. She told me she had, but she had been really busy and she couldn't respond. However, she told me to come up to her store and she would talk with me face-to-face. The day I ventured out to Andra's cupcake shop, I dropped Beno off at school and prepared myself to work with her. I also brought my *Streetwise Business Plan Book* with me because I had prepared some questions for her.

I got to the mall, so excited thinking Andra was going to teach me about making cupcakes and how to start a cupcake business. I arrived a little too early, the outside doors were still locked. While standing outside, I could see Andra in the front of her shop. I was so happy and excited, I waved at her from outside, trying to get her attention. She saw me waving and didn't wave back. Finally, when the mall opened, I walked straight up to Andra's counter and told her I was the person who had written her the letter and called. I expressed to her that I loved her cupcakes and I even gained 12 pounds. Andra told me she received my letter, but she couldn't help me—something about making her employees sign a non-disclosure agreement, so sharing her trade secrets with me wouldn't be right since it was illegal for her own staff to have the inside scoop. However, she could help me with my business plan.

Once I left her shop, I was so disappointed with her because I assumed she would be pleased to assist me, as well as show me the ropes about baking and running a small business. Plus, we were both women of color, and I thought that counted for something. *Wrong*! However, I didn't let her lack of assistance stop my dreams of becoming a cupcake shop owner, I had that entrepreneurial determination! Monthly, I would frequent Books-A-Million to pick up a *Success Magazine*, which delivered to me a great deal of motivation. Then, I purchased a subscription to *Black Enterprise*, which was incredible for providing inspiration to entrepreneurs. Eventually, I even visited the SCORE Office for a little help with my business plan. I was serious about this cupcake stuff. At the same time, I got on the grind in the kitchen too and taught myself how to bake cakes from scratch. On my son's eight birthday, I made my first attempt at making some homemade cupcakes. Sadly, they weren't great, but they turned out okay.

Not too long after my son's birthday, I began going up to the Jacksonville Library on 103rd Street every day. This daily trip allowed Beno to have some independence and some social interactions with other children his age. While B was busying himself in the kid zone, I was researching and printing cake recipes from different websites as well as thumbing through cake cookbooks on the bookshelves. Now, here is where I noticed my story started to become rather unusual. Cue the *Twilight Zone* theme song.

One evening at home, while on my personal computer, I was on a packaging supply website and was looking at some high gloss 4x4x4 pink boxes to place cupcakes in for my company-to-be. The ***very next day***, Beno and I visited Orange Park Mall, and as we passed CamiCakes, lo and behold, what did I see? ***The same 4x4x4 high gloss pink box looking back at me.*** I was shocked! It was just a single box on display. I had just decided to go with that specific set of high gloss pink boxes in my planning for my company- to- be just last night! Oh, I was so upset. In my fury and ignorance, I remembered thinking to myself, *She didn't want to help me and now she's using my supplies at her shop.*

I started looking into additional packaging supplies, such as larger food boxes to place six cupcakes in at a time. I was looking at a specific brown gable box with brown ribbons and brown ribbons with a hint of pink. I thought adding ribbons to the boxes would add a little extra cuteness to my packaged product. Yet again, I visited Orange Park Mall about a week or two later. I passed by CamiCakes, and to my disbelief, what did I see? ***The same darn brown gable box and brown ribbon looking back at me***! Baffled, yet again! I saw the brown box with the ribbons first, WTF!

Unequivocally, I was puzzled because I was recognizing my thoughts and ideas on display as they were materializing at *her* shop. Could this have been the power of *The Secret*, as I was reading this book at that time. My ignorance had me mad as hell. She was duplicating my ideas and I didn't share them with her! Not to mention, she was the one who had denied me help.

Let me state for the record, there weren't any individuals hanging around my house that could serve as a cupcake informant, that would go back and tell Andra what I was doing at my house. The only person who knew what I was up to was Beno, who was just a kid at the time. It couldn't have been him. After those two episodes with the packaging supplies, Beno and I visited the mall once again. We passed by CamiCakes, and this time I saw a book displayed on top of Andra's pastry case titled *Where Is My Money* by Twyla Prindle, and illustrated by Randy Jennings.

At that very moment, I was completely mystified. I was in an awestruck state of speechlessness when I saw my last name on the cover of that book—***Jennings*** and on display for me to see. I clearly felt "something" was vying for my attention. This wasn't the power of *The Secret* or the law of attraction at all. This was a predestined awakening unfolding right before my eyes and I found a way to tune in.

Shortly after, I became aware of an odd ability that I possessed—which was actually deciphering encrypted messages within a name. For example, one day I wrote out Andra's company name—CamiCakes. I deciphered this message in less than a minute.

C a m i C a k e s

2 Cs

2 As

and what's left is mike.

As I rearranged the letters and numbers, it said: ***C 2 a mike.*** With additional refinement, the encrypted message became a little clearer. It actually said: ***See to a Mike.*** I am acquainted with a Mike, I know him quite well! I thought to myself, *What does Michael have to do with this*? Not only did the company's name serve as a key holder, but there was another common denominator between CamiCakes and me. My address was 4519 Melvin Circle West, and CamiCakes's telephone number was 904-541-1095. If you look closely, you'll see 4519 **twice**! All these strange signposts of hidden messages were making me aware of something, but what exactly?

Equally important, at the same time, as I was going through my everyday life as a single mother raising Beno, I was experiencing a number of other synchronicities and oddities that weren't related to CamiCakes. For instance, one day, as I was taking the clean wet clothes out of the washing machine, I saw a dime left behind inside the machine. I reached in and picked it up. When I examined the coin closely, I noticed that it wasn't a dime at all! In fact, it was a Canadian coin that looked a lot like our American dime. I wondered where it had come from. I didn't recall receiving any foreign money back as change after any of my sales transactions. I put the coin up somewhere and didn't give it a second thought. Shortly after finding that Canadian coin, I saw a late-night PBS special on Queen Elizabeth II. As I watched the program, I didn't make any comparisons to my most recent finding of the Canadian coin with Queen Elizabeth II minted on it. As if odd could not get any odder, after finding that first Canadian coin in my washing machine, you would have thought I lived in Canada because nine more Canadian coins had made their way into my hand before leaving Jacksonville, Florida.

One fine summer day in July 2007, I was working at the group home and Beno and I decided to go out for our lunch break and explore the northside of Jacksonville. As we rode down Lem Turner Road, I passed a side street that had my surname posted on it. I thought, I should turn the car around and take a picture of that street sign. So, I did just that. I parked across the street from the sign, then crossed the street and snapped this picture. I was completely amazed because I had never in my life observed my last name on a street sign before.

Stay with me now, I have more compelling evidence of living in the "twilight zone." October of 2007, I had switched Beno from public school back to a private school. The private school I selected was in Middleburg, Florida, which was roughly 20 minutes away from our house on the westside of Jacksonville. I selected this school for its Abeka Curriculum and its price point. However, I was completely unaware of the school's physical location, although I was aware that it sat off Blanding Boulevard. Oddly enough and to my surprise, the school was at the intersection of Blanding Boulevard and Old Jennings Road. Uniquely, somewhere off Old Jennings Rd was Jennings State Forest.

What in the world!

Again, and again, the exhibition of my surname, and I would see these two signposts every day. I took it upon myself to take pictures of all this stuff, I guess for proof of my bizarre experiences at that time in my life. However, the young filmmaker, Beno, got a hold of my SD card and reformatted it. As a result, all my pictures were erased, and some of those images I needed for evidence. When writing Oprah for advice, I journeyed back down to Jacksonville just to insert some of those lost images into my letter to her. But I still can't get back that rainbow picture. Thanks, Beno!

But wait, I have even more compelling evidence of living in this mystifying world. After spending quite some time coming up with a name for my cupcake franchise, I had put together queen buttercup. Why queen, I'm not sure. Then one day, a month later, while in the shower, out of nowhere, the word "little" popped into my head, so I added the adjective to my company's name. After a small revision, my cupcake franchise was now known as little queen buttercup.

Several months had coasted by after naming my company. As I was exploring other communities on the westside of Jacksonville, as fate would have it, I came up to a stop sign. I stopped and looked up to see where I was. When I did, I was boldly smacked in the face by this street sign's name.

At that moment, I laughed. I laughed so hard only because the eccentricity of these synchronicities did not surprise me anymore. I had surpassed the shock and awe state. I had experienced unfathomable magic in my everyday life. By the end of April 2008, Michael flew down to Jacksonville again, and this time it wasn't for a vacation, it was to help me move out of the pink and brown house at 4519 Melvin Circle West and store my furniture back in VA. When he got there, we headed over to pick up my U-Haul truck and you know I got him some CamiCakes too.

At last, it was our last month living in Florida. This would bring us up to May 2008. Beno and I flew back into JAX Airport. I had left my car behind in Jacksonville, so I could transport Beno back and forth to school. My boss, Charlotte, with her beautiful heart, allowed my son and I to temporarily stay at her group home where I worked so my son could finish his last month of school. Since the group home was on the northside of Jacksonville and I now had to travel through Lem Turner Road and Dunn Avenue every day. Jennings Road is precisely nine blocks north of this intersection. And if my story can't be anymore inexplicable, there's this. If you mapped out my 90-minute daily commute, from Lem Turner Road and Dunn Avenue Intersection to Blanding Boulevard and Old Jennings Road, it would look like I was traveling between two coordinates of my surname: *Jennings*. Perplexing! It still puzzles me today. There was a clear message from the Universe being conveyed to me.

Oprah and The Barber Shop

I was in the process of moving back home to Virginia permanently, in May of 2008. I remembered watching television and I saw a preview of Oprah's upcoming show, the topic was: *Reincarnation* with Past Life Regression by Psychotherapist Dr. Brian Weiss.

I thought to myself, *I must watch that*!

When the episode aired, I found myself at the barber shop with my son around 4 o'clock. The barber shop was filled with African American men and my son's barber had not called him yet. I remember debating back and forth in my head, saying, *Either you are going to miss this show, or you could speak-up and ask if they can turn to Oprah*! I did not want them to judge me as a crazy person for wanting to engage in such a taboo conversation about past lives. Nevertheless, I gathered up the courage and asked if they would turn to *Oprah* about eight minutes past the hour. I wouldn't miss the show after all!

I felt the topic of past lives was intriguing, and unbeknownst to me at that time, ***I was living in my very own reincarnation narrative***. I can thank the Oprah Show and her guest co-host Dr. Weiss for remotely bringing my Florida experience full circle.

2

Returning Home

Returning Home to Virginia

It was the end of May and the early part of June 2008. I returned to Virginia 200% lighter—there was a sense of weightlessness about my soul and I had a beautiful outlook on life. I had also lost all that undesirable cupcake weight. Contained within me was a profound new truth, the power of my thoughts. I knew for sure that I could create my wishes on command, through the power of *The Secret*. I was hopeful, and I had love in my heart. Given all of this, I quickly detected that I could not be around negativity, deception, combustible people or *noise*.

Jacksonville's ambiance was very, very, tranquil. I never heard the sound of cop sirens. I never heard cars riding through the community violating the neighborhood's noise ordinance. I never heard the neighbors arguing in the street, nor in their front yards. And, most importantly, I didn't hear the neighbors slamming their doors, nor did I see or hear heavy foot traffic in and out of my neighbor's home. All in all, Jacksonville was a place of serenity and a place where you could hear your own thoughts.

Once again, Beno and I moved back in with my grandparents temporarily until I found us a new place. During this time, I noticed that everyone around me was extremely negative, I even keenly observed these unfavorable traits within my grandparents as well. Even though they were regularly attending church folk, they were still just as negative as my friends. At the same time, my family and friends noticed a real difference in my personality, they could probably tell I was reserved, distant and limited on idle talk. In the face of my changes, I always had a positive message to deposit in their lives, especially when friends and family were venting about other people or the woes of their life. I personally think my one-year stay in Jacksonville had *erased the 30 years of me.*

Prior to my Florida sabbatical, I was mean, argumentative, I loved to gossip, and I was very materialistic. In the face of my changes, I was humbled and very generous. I would say yes to just about everything. For example, if you asked me to borrow something of mine, I would say yes guaranteed. Because I believed in sharing what I had with others. Even my car. Upon returning, I really was not the same person who left my hometown a year prior and I think I had reached some kind of enlightenment in the Sunshine State.

I came back home to start a cupcake business. I was empowered by the spirit of entrepreneurship called ambition and determination. I had a completed business plan and my baking skills were superb now. One fortunate afternoon, I was reading *Success Magazine* and had the remote control in my other hand, channel surfing. I just so happened to stop at *Larry King Live.* He had two guests on the show, one of whom was a woman. Her name was JZ Knight. I don't remember what the topic was about exactly as my attention was wavering between the magazine and the television program. Several months coasted by, and I was watching a movie called *What the Bleep Do You Know*! Again, there's JZ Knight, except this time she was fatter. She was teaching and talking in a slightly masculine voice and her name was different too. This time her name was *RAMTHA*! Her name was just JZ Knight a few months ago! It really perplexed me that this woman had two distinctly different names.

The next day, I scurried over to the library, hopped on their computer, and took to Google. I Googled JZ Knight's name and oh boy, was I in for a life-altering expedition! I found out that JZ Knight channels a great being by the name RAMTHA, who is over 35,000 years old.[2] This information piqued my interest, since it was the kind of unconventional shit that I like. Not too long after, I got a hold of one of RAMTHA's books titled *RAMTHA: The White Book.*

After reading this book, my attention completely shifted from entrepreneurial pursuits to going on a metaphysical quest. RAMTHA says, ***the teacher appears when the student is ready!*** After reading *The White Book*, I cried. I cried because it was such a beautiful book of pure love. In fact, for one whole year I stayed in my new apartment reading tons of books on ancient wisdom, metaphysics, personal philosophy, and spiritual growth by authors like RAMTHA, Neal Donald Walsh, Dr. Brian Weiss, Robert Monroe, Edgar Cayce, Barbara Marciniak, Zecharia Sitchin, and Jane Butts. These books unequivocally awakened my mind and spiritual being *like no other.* Before then, my soul was suffering from malnutrition and dehydration. As a result, I felt like I could breathe again, as if inhaling a once familiar air.

After immersing myself in the subject of metaphysical truths, I was now receptive to the subject of reincarnation that Dr. Weiss had demonstrated on *The Oprah Winfrey Show* just two years prior, as well as my old college professor a decade earlier. After my own analysis of the subject of reincarnation, it left me with this: *if I've lived before, then I'll live again*. Along with that thought, I wasn't afraid *to die, nor live*!

Professor James Brown

Ten years earlier, before seeing Dr. Brian Weiss on *Oprah,* while in college, I had heard of the subject of reincarnation. I attended Norfolk State University (NSU) and had a professor named James Brown who taught African Studies. From time to time, Professor Brown would digress from the lesson and talk about reincarnation. I clearly remember the very first

[2] "Questions and answers about Ramtha, JZ Knight," The Olympian, July 16, 2006. Available at https://archive.is/20130204080730/http://www.theolympian.com/689/story/50048.html.

story he had ever disclosed to our class. Professor Brown is a white man with a bald head who easily reminds you of Mr. Clean. This is quite the contrasting image of the late iconic '60s pop singer James Brown, the Godfather of Soul. Professor Brown shared a few personal anecdotes about his very own past lives and the very first story I remembered him sharing with our class was the most captivating of them all.

Professor Brown said that ever since he was a little boy, he would have recurring dreams of himself being on a beach and swallowing sand. One day as a grown man, out of the clear blue sky, he received an unexpected phone call from an unknown caller asking him if he would like tickets to see Langston Hughes, who was speaking later on that day. Professor Brown took the caller up on their invitation. While Langston Hughes was speaking, he stated that when the slave captives came to take the Africans by force, moments before being hostilely taken aboard the ships, someone amongst the African people told everyone if they ate the sand, they would die! Professor Brown felt as if *a lightning bolt instantly shot through his head*! That chance phone call put him in the right place, at the right time, which explained his perplexing lifelong dreams. We can assume he was one of those Africans who ate the sand in an attempt to commit suicide. This Mr. Clean looking man, is fully aware that he played another role, in another lifetime, as an African of black descent. So, what does that say about race and racism?

In this lifetime, Professor Brown's travels have taken him back to the "motherland" several times. He even took up residence in Africa. In our African Studies class, Professor Brown seemed to be so proud of his time spent in Africa, he even brought in pictures to share with the class of his voyages to the motherland. Moreover, in one of those photographs, Professor Brown was wearing a Dashiki. Here are some questions to contemplate. Where does that nostalgia originate and why is Professor Brown so drawn to Africa, if not because of a possible lifetime lived there.

As I listened to Professor Brown tell his many stories, I thought they were compelling. But, what did they have to do with the lesson and why was he telling all of this to us? I ended up dropping Professor Brown's class at the very end of the semester. In retrospect, I am convinced that the Universe put me in his class just to hear his unauthorized teachings and unorthodox dialogue about evolution for the purpose of my future awakening.

From 2010–2012

After my analysis of the subject of reincarnation, the topic left me with this question: *Could I have possibly had a past life with the CamiCakes lady*? Because clearly there was some connection between her shop and me. A few years after realizing this mysterious connection between Andra and myself, my attention began to shift in the direction of music mogul Pharrell. Why him out of all people, you might be asking? Well, let me try to elaborate on my reasoning. When Beno would go off to his dad's house for the weekend, I remained home alone with nothing to do. Sadly, by choice, I had no friends to hang out with because I could not tolerate being around toxic people. And, unfortunately, those seemed to be the only individuals I knew.

I found it comforting just to chill in my own home, in my own space. I would parade around my apartment while rocking out to music, preferably hip hop. I would set the tone by playing all the melodic, instrumental beats produced by Pharrell, placing myself in weekend chill mode. Listening to Pharrell's instrumental melodies would send me into ugly crying fits. The tunes that would perpetuate my crying outbursts were *I Know* and *Excuse Me* both by Jay Z, *Luv You Betta* by LL Cool J, and *That Girl* by Pharrell.

The instrumentals of *That Girl* and *I Know* pulled at my emotions the most. You would have thought I was grieving over someone deeply near and dear. Odd, huh? It would take me two full years before I could listen to those songs without going into uncontrollable crying fits. However, the opposite is true for *That Girl*. Bear with me for a moment, I'm not a music engineer, so I don't speak in their language.

The musical properties of the song *That Girl* are so powerful, it sort of sounds like a string orchestra playing high-pitch frequencies off a tone generator. To me, it would be comparable to that high-frequency pitch in Kool and The Gang's *Summer Madness* song. The frequency is just too powerful for my ears to handle. Inexplicably, I feel Pharrell's musical compositions speak to me, as if there is life within his musical arrangements and I've dwelled there before. It also sounds intergalactic, as if I can travel on or within the notes throughout the cosmos. I definitely hear an intergalactic connection whenever I'm tuning into P's music. During this time, my consciousness was so suspended in the world of metaphysics, I concluded in my own logic that Pharrell and I must be connected in some non-human existence or something. Because I was understanding his language in the format of his amazing musical compositions. *Senseless Jarnalia,* you might say. And I would counter, *Maybe, maybe not.* Ultimately, it's what the music does to me.

Believe it or not, Pharrell and I also shared uncanny parallels, just like the ones that I shared with the CamiCakes lady. You see, in the early 2000s, I saw Pharrell at the brand-new MacArthur Center, a local mall in Norfolk, Virginia, in passing. I remembered entering the mall with little Beno in hand, but he had broken away from me and took off running. There were many people moving toward me, leaving the MacArthur Center. As I was casually walking to catch Beno, I spotted Pharrell! He was amongst the people leaving the mall. As a matter of fact, he was staring at me before I even noticed him, and as we passed each other, he was still gazing at me from the corner of his eye. I thought it was the "judging my parenting" stare since Beno had broken away from me and ran off, and I was casually walking to get a hold of him. This serendipitous encounter has never escaped my conscious awareness.

In hindsight, I think it was two old souls crossing paths once again and each energy essence transmitting a nostalgic, "Hello, I remember you!" As I come to know myself, I perceive this as a kismet experience giving way to my extraordinary awakening and my unbelievable life's story. The Universal Forces were working on my behalf, long before my Florida experience. The seeds were being planted, as one day my consciousness would elevate to a higher level of awareness, then draw upon that chance encounter with Pharrell at a later date in my future. After I saw Pharrell at the MacArthur Center, I realized that we had *two* trivial connections, but at that time, I did not know how to categorize it.

Let me illustrate some common denominators that I detected that could justify my outlandish statement of a possible shared connection. First, when I was a little girl, I use to live on Bland Street. The street directly behind mine was Hugo Street. Ironically Pharrell's co-producer's last name is *Hugo*. Secondly, when I was in high school, my best friend Christy and I would hang around one of her male friends whose name was Nate. One day, Christy didn't come to school. As I was rummaging through my locker, Nate came up to see me and chit-chat. I thought, *Wow he wants to hang-out with me without Christy.* Without a question I was flattered! I was just an overaged ninth grader and he was a cute, wild, and popular eleventh grader. Several years later, I was at a local concert in Portsmouth and I spotted Nate walking around. I hadn't seen him since high school. I told Piggy, the gentleman I was with, and he informed me that Nate is Fam-Lay, and he was performing in the concert. Nate/Fam-Lay is one of Pharrell's artist.

Once again, I was at the MacArthur Center, but this time I came across Chad Hugo. He was sitting outside a ladies clothing store called Arden B, and for this reason alone, I strolled into the store. While in the store, I was looking at some clothing and being nosey too. For the first few minutes, no one was around. Then, the next thing I know, a Filipino woman and the sales lady walked from the back of the store and came over to where I was standing in the front of this store. The two ladies were talking about a clothing item that was closest to me as I was standing near the clothes rack near the wall. The Filipino woman summoned her kid to bring Chad inside the store. As I was standing there looking at some clothing I couldn't afford, Chad is now standing next to me, within arm's reach, with his back turned. How bizarre was that?

One summer day in 2005, I had an Infinity rental car and was with my other BFF. MaryJane and I were cruising in this luxurious car with the windows down, chilling. We were headed back to my place in Chesapeake. I was on Battlefield Boulevard and got caught by the stop light. A car pulled up right next to us and stopped. Their windows were down as well. MaryJane and I peeked over because it was a big fancy black car. The driver was observing us too. Guess who it was? It was half of The Clipse, Malice. Now, if you know hip-hop music, I don't have to tell you that Malice is another musician associated with Pharrell. At that time, I really did not think anything of it. I just thought, *Damn I must be at the right places at the right times.*

3

The Year of the Cat

When My Paradigm Shifted

Eight years after my fateful chance encounter with Pharrell, four-years since living in the "twilight zone," and now I was looking up Pharrell's biography on the internet. As I expressed earlier, I have an eccentric gift to decode encrypted messages. There was clearly a major message being transmitted to me through my address at 4519 Melvin Circle West.

The address said, *"The Lion Lives in Me."* The number sequence 4519 and the street's name Melvin Circle West were vital for my awakening and self-awareness. The number itself represents LION—*to me*. Pharrell's bio on Wikipedia listed his birthday as 4-5-1973.[3] Another instance of 4519. Straightaway, this piqued my interest. It would be two more years before I eventually plunged a little deeper into Pharrell's background, and when I did, it was eyebrow raising.

Not too long after, I ended up discovering a theorist researcher on YouTube by the name of Michael Tsarion. In one of his lectures, he talked about an Egyptian goddess by the name of Sekhmet, describing her role as it relates to the pharaohs of Egypt. At that time, I believe I was multitasking, and I really wasn't personalizing the story, but I did hear the basis of it. Then, I found an animated YouTube video on Sekhmet and I watched it several times. In brief, here is what I gathered.

It was toward the end of Ra, the sun god's long reign, when he began to lose control over the Egyptian people. They no longer feared him, nor obeyed his laws and he realized that he needed to restore order. Ra went to the other gods for advisement. As a result, he decided to create an enforcer to stop his adversaries in their tracks by creating a lioness goddess out of his eye. His daughter's name was Sekhmet, and she was a killer! After a while, Sekhmet got so bloodthirsty that it was impossible to stop her carnage and the Egyptian people and gods complained to Ra that his daughter had to be stopped. Ra devised a plan of action. He intentionally mislabeled some wine barrels as blood to lure in his bloodthirsty daughter. When Sekhmet saw the barrels of blood, she got so drunk that she passed out. At that moment, Ra was able to manipulate his creation and made Sekhmet as a more peaceful woman.[4]

Two years later, now 2012, I was examining Pharrell's personal background from another online resource, and this time I saw that Pharrell has two brothers. One brother's name is Cato, the other brother's name is Solomon, and Pharrell's father name was listed too,

---

[3] "Pharrell Williams," Wikipedia, last edited May 9, 2019. Available at https://en.wikipedia.org/wiki/Pharrell_Williams.

[4] "The Eye of Ra: How Sekhmet Became Hathor," Youtube, 5:01, LetItBeOnigiri, 2007, available at https://www.youtube.com/watch?v=RDlfHTx-c0A&feature=youtu.be.

Pharoah (spelled correctly).[5] A little time went by and I was watching a movie called *Diary of a Wimpy Kid: Rodrick Rules* with Beno. A little girl in the movie stood up and said her name was *Patty Farrell,* and to the left of her in the background was a poster with ancient Egyptian faces.

At that very moment, everything came together in my mind and *I had an aha moment*! After putting together all the cryptic messages and synchronicities that were meant for me to ascertain in Florida, finally, the encryption, *"The Lion Lives in Me"* made sense! Pharoah—pharaoh, Cato—cat, and Solomon—sun and moon. Pharaoh represented an Egyptian ruler and the cat who has the sun over her head is Sekhmet the sun goddess. At that moment I thought, *Am I the reincarnation of Sekhmet, the Egyptian lion goddess,* that Michael Tsario talked about in that lecture?

I pondered if Pharrell and his family were part of that Egyptian story too. I also wondered why my free clairvoyant didn't tell me this. This specific encrypted message had plagued me for five years and now I understood what it meant! I went to Google to see if anybody else out there thought they were a reincarnated ancient Egyptian, and I found someone—a man by the name of Dr. Mitchell Gibson. Dr. Gibson made a YouTube testimonial video stating that he knew that he was *Imhotep*.

I set out to find a clairvoyant who would provide me with the answers that my free psychic never shared with me. I was compelled to find out if Pharrell and I had shared a previous life together, so I took action. The first lady I found, Atomarane, has the ability to read the soul's first origin and she provided a free service on YouTube by making videos for anyone who used her service. However, by the time I came along, she had completely stopped giving free soul origin readings as she had shifted her attention to writing books. As a result, I wasn't able to utilize her abilities.

The second lady I came across on YouTube has the ability to get

---

5 Katy Botnar, "Always Happy! Meet Pharrell WIlliams and his adorable family," Body Height Weight, September 2, 2017, https://bodyheightweight.com/pharrell-williams-family/.

into the Akashic Records. Sunshine Rose provided past life readings as well as soul origin readings. Just like Atomarane, she too made YouTube videos, then posted them under an established alias for her paid clients. I was totally impressed with Sunshine Rose's clairvoyant abilities, and the quality of the readings were well researched. I thought I could definitely use her services. When I visited Sunshine Rose's YouTube channel, there was a link that took you directly to her website. Once on her site, I looked over all her services. You had to do some additional navigating to get to her eBay store if you wanted to place an order for a YouTube past life video reading. Honestly, I felt like I was on a scavenger hunt. When I got to eBay, I found dozens upon dozens of other psychics offering past life readings, and way cheaper than Sunshine Rose's services. You see, at that time, eBay had a Metaphysical Corner and there were many clairvoyants who came with an A+ ranking by the eBay buyers. I thoroughly looked over the customer's comments and level of satisfaction before I selected a clairvoyant.

In the end, I spotted a reader who only charged $2.99 for a one-question reading. Two dollars and ninety-nine cents was hardly a drop in the bucket. Certainly, I could afford to risk losing $2.99 for a humbug reading. Ultimately, after viewing her other services, I decided to go with a three-question reading for a grand total of $6.99.

This was my first time paying someone for a past life reading. I was used to dealing with someone who provided free, brief, and vague past life readings on a radio show that was open to the public. However, on that show I *never* wanted to ask any questions about any celebrities in a public format for the sake of their anonymity. Although in the beginning, on one occasion I got so frustrated by the clues that were building up in my head, I had to abandon my integrity and reach out any way that I could, which happened to be in a public format. Undoubtedly, going forward, I felt a private email reading would be the perfect environment for full discretion and it would allow me the confidentiality that I needed to ask any question about any celebrity. As a result, I hired a lady and her guides to assist me: Angel & Guides.

How does this foolishness work, you might be asking? Mrs. M&M, who hosted the radio show, explained that you do not have to be face-to-face with an individual to give them a reading, for the energy can be read through an email, over the phone, or via Skype. Remember, everything is energy, even your soul! While looking for a gifted reader on eBay, I came across some readers that requested you provide them your full name, date of birth, location, and some even wanted a picture of you. I guess that helped them with honing in on the energy.

In my own experience, I've noticed that many of the gifted clairvoyants who possess mystical powers, actually have a great amount of assistance from higher energies in higher realms, such as celestial entities, spirit guides, and/or ascended masters. If you could work with a reader like this, they could report a multitude of stories about your soul's sojourners en masse, that would probably blow your mind. So, no, a clairvoyant does not have to be sitting across from the person that's requesting the reading.

An Open Letter to Pharrell

Dear Pharrell,

For years, I used to be so safeguarded with this sacred information that is contained within me. I often contemplated, why do I possess this knowledge? Why do "I" need to be cognizant of these truths? How does possessing this sacred knowledge help me today in my current existence? I searched high and low, looking for answers, and the one response that consistently showed up in my quest was that I am here to communicate metaphysical truths through speaking, teaching, and writing. So, if you are reading my words right now, then the prophecies were precise. I have committed myself to execute this writing project to bring you some personal revelations.

Forgive me in advance for shaking up your personal space, even your public persona, and your internal spiritual beliefs, for I do not mean any harm, nor do I wish to persuade you to abandon your core spiritual truths. I am presenting these sacred messages to you out of pure love. And if you are already aware of this profound wisdom, then let me co-sign this knowledge with a song by Leaders of the New School: "I know you and you know me, I know you and you know me, I know you and you know me."[6] But it's not about a car at all. It's really a "sob story."

In addition, I ask you to forgive me in advance for putting this content out in a public format, but what were my chances of spotting you again? Oh, maybe luck would have struck while having an Auntie Anne's pretzel at Lynnhaven Mall. Yeah right! Or while walking down College Park Blvd? Or while waiting to catch the #12 or the #15 bus? Although the likelihood could have been probable, so probable, in fact, that after knowing what I knew about our shared connections, here is what happened to me.

In brief, around May of 2012, after having my awareness restored about our shared connection, I was standing in my hallway and I was blocking the entryway to the apartments. Then, the door opened to my neighbor's apartment and someone left. Mind you, my neighbor only had women coming and going from her property. I turned around to see who was coming up on me so I could move out of their way. When I turned around, it wasn't my neighbor at all, nor was it even a woman. It was actually a man, and it happened to be Pusha T!

So, how about that, Pharrell? The Universal Forces have managed to position me in direct alignment with you and your squadron quite a bit, huh? However, as of today, I know who I am, and I know what I needed to ascertain before our official reunification. I heard a lecture by Les Brown and he stated that this wisdom came from Dr. Howard Thurman.

"The ideal situation for a man or woman to die is to have family members around their bed praying with them as they cross over. But imagine being on your death bed and standing around your bed 'the dreams' given to you by life, 'the ideas' that you never acted on, 'the talents,' 'the gifts,' 'the abilities' that you never used and there they are standing around your bed looking

6 Leaders of the New School, Sobb Story, track 8 on A Future Without a Past, producers, 1991.

at you with large, angry eyes, saying, 'We came to you! And only you could have given us life and now we must die with you forever.' And the question is if you died this very moment, what will die with you? What dreams? What ideas? What talents? What leadership potential? What greatness, that you showed up to bring, that you allowed fear or procrastination to hold you back?"

Pharrell, I carry this knowledge with me, day in and day out, and once I'm sleeping, the stored memories play out involuntarily. I pledged in front of my television with Les Brown that I refuse to die an unlived life! As a result, I'm telling my dreams! I choose to give *you all* a sacred message for your own soul's evolutionary growth! In the same way, when I'm lying on my death bed, before I choose to transition back to spirit, I will not have my dreams and my gifts accosting me by parading around my bed and probing me with their large, angry eyes asking me, "Why didn't you give me life?" I am certainly facilitating their wishes right now, openly, and at all cost.

Mr. Pharrell, without further ado, I have provided the actual copy of my past life readings that has everything to do with you.

An Open Past Life Reading to Pharrell

From: 2xQueen2xGoddess
To: Angel & Guides
Sent: Wednesday, January 04, 2012 8:56 AM

Hey Angel

1. Did I share a past lifetime with Pharrell Williams? He is a celebrity in this lifetime.

2. What relationship did we share in that lifetime?

3. If it was on Earth, what year and location. If not Earth, what planet?

Thank You,
Ms. Jennings

From: Angel & Guides
To: 2xQueen2xGoddess
01/06/12 at 12:08 PM

Hello,

Thank you for your questions.

Yes, you did indeed spend a former lifetime with Pharrell Williams. I see him as being a magician. And not the sleight of hand magician that we have now. A real magician but he hid his abilities behind a magic act. You were his assistant. He found out some secrets of the universe that he didn't even understand, and it led to his demise. You were quite a bit younger than he was. He was in his early 40s and you were in your 20s. For the time that I am seeing 1800s, this was not acceptable. You were always attracted to each other and hid your passion for each other by becoming his assistant. That way you had an excuse to be together.

Your mother did not want the two of you to be together and so you pretended to like someone else to get her off your back. But your mother wasn't so easily fooled. One of his "tricks" got out of hand. He didn't understand all the dynamics of what he was doing and someone disappeared for real. They accused him of murder but, of course, the body was never found. I just see a long tunnel where it went. I believe the person was transported to another dimension.

With the disappearance of that person, your mother began to see him as not only undesirable, but evil. I believe she is the one who killed him. He died in your arms.

I do believe it was on Earth, but I don't know the location—perhaps more towards the east coast, 1800s.

Many blessings,
Angel

Pharrell, KareBear doubled checked this reading and she said that much of the reading was good, but some of the details are incorrect. Can you see why I would go into crying fits over your music? For I was certainly grieving—you died in my arms! After the reading, I wrote the Angel & Guides a reply message, and I was quite pleased. Pharrell, the Angel & Guides added something else for you below.

From: 2xQueen2xGoddess
To: Angel & Guides
Sent: Saturday, January 07, 2012 8:08 AM

Angel,

THANK YOU !!! Thank You, so much for clarifying and helping me to remember our soul's history together. I thought our connection stemmed from ancient Egypt.

Angel, I really wasn't prepared to read/hear that response. I'm in awe! I know that I'm an amazing old soul and even a star seed. But hearing your response gives more validity to my inner thoughts. An assistant to an alchemist with great secrets about the universe...that's extraordinary! No wonder I tend to talk to and once heard a reply from Ascended Master Merlin.

And what's even more phenomenal, is Pharrell is connected to something far greater–maybe he is a grand wizard/sorcerer. The sacred knowledge, unearthly talents, and his gifts are still within him–possibly dormant. WOWZERS!!!

For three years, I wanted to have a past life regression and was finally able to have one on December 26, 2011 via Skype for the fee of $120.00–my grandmother paid for it on her debit card. I specifically wanted to see if Pharrell and I had a past incarnation together. However, the regression didn't work at all, but I was still being charged $120.

So, mentally/verbally I was saying I hope that the charge doesn't go through. Well, I received an email a few days later that the card declined...and of course, you know I was elated that the manipulation worked out for me. All I had to pay you was $6.99... for the same information. Damn, that's good.

I'm sharing my gratitude with you. There is this video called (redacted) featuring Pharrell (look it up on YouTube). This video it makes me sooooooo happy. See, (redacted) was my past life brother during the time when the cello first came out. And, of course, you told me about Pharrell. So, for me to see them together and entertaining me makes my heart smile.

Thanks, Angel....
Jenell

From: Angel & Guides
To: 2xQueen2xGoddess
01/07/12 at 9:20 AM

You are very welcome. And your lifetime with Pharrell could very well have originated in Egypt. My guides have a tendency to tell you a lifetime that you haven't heard about before. And I do feel that Pharrell is still very powerful, but he may not have figured it all out yet in this lifetime. Thanks for the feedback. I appreciate it!

Angel

Pharrell, that's all I have for the moment.
Jarnalia

My Egyptian suspicion still wasn't answered! Nevertheless, my reading was very impressive. I realized that I had to take a more direct approach and just spell out my question. I returned a few hours later, this time paying $10.99 for a five question reading.

From: 2xQueen2xGoddess
To: Angel & Guides
Saturday, January 07, 2012 3:49 PM

Hey Angel & Guides, round 2!

I was really impressed with my first reading, so now, let's turn up the volume.

1. Where does my soul originate from?

2. Do you see me as Sekhmet of ancient Egypt? If not, what is my connection to the Panthera genus/ Felidae/or cat family?

3. How many incarnations have I spent on Earth?

4. Question is censored.

5. Question is censored.

Thanks,
Jenell

As I anxiously waited for a reply, I checked my email account four to five times throughout the day just to see if I had something from Angel & Guides. A total of two days had whizzed by and I finally had a message in my inbox. I was so eager to have that validation. I opened my email and noticed that all five questions were answered.

From: Angel & Guides
To: 2xQueen2xGoddess
1/09/12 at 11:35 AM

Wow, love it, love it! Thank you for honoring me with your questions.

Your soul originates from a space that is all good. I see what appears to be a universe and there is a spiral of light in the heavens. To me, it means the cosmos, a place from all that is. When I ask for specifics, all I hear is, "Time. You came from time." I am not seeing things like planets, just the universe with a spiral of light.

I can easily see you as Sekhmet.

Bookmark this reading, it's imperative that I pause here!

Sekhmet, the Egyptian Sun Goddess

This picture was taken around Halloween of 2013, in Greenbriar Mall in Chesapeake, VA. This is me now, and this is me over 3000 thousand years ago in ancient Egypt.

After reading the response, I finally felt confirmed. After five years of being plagued by the encrypted message "The Lion Lives in Me" over and over and over again, little ole me had actually put these clues together all by myself. The pieces were all scattered about and I assembled them accurately. I was so proud of myself. I also felt a sense of self-assuredness from within, because my encrypted problem-solving technique could be trusted. This means, within Jarnalia there's a lioness that dwells within.

Who is Sekhmet of ancient Egypt?

According to Ancient Egypt Online, the name Sekhmet means the powerful one. She is a warrior goddess and a goddess of healing. Sekhmet is a lioness, she is the fiercest hunter known to Egyptians, and she was seen as the protector of the pharaohs and led them to warfare. She is the daughter of the sun god Ra, who was an ancient Egyptian pharaoh. Sekhmet is known as the sun goddess and bears the solar disk and the uraeus, which associates her with Wadjet and royalty. Sekhmet was created out of her father's eye, she is the "Eye of Ra," and she is the goddess of fire, war, and dance.[7]

Who is Ra?

Ra was the god of the sun of ancient Egypt. He is a man with the head of a hawk, and he has a solar disk on top of his head with a serpent.[8] "He was often considered to be the King of the Gods and thus the patron of the pharaoh and the central gods of the Egyptian pantheon. He was also described as the creator of everything."[9]

"To the Egyptians, the sun represented light, warmth, and growth. This made the sun deity very important, as the sun was seen as the ruler of all that he created.[10] The sun disk was either seen as the body or eye of Ra. Sekhmet was the Eye of Ra and was created by the fire in Ra's eye. She was a violent lioness."[11] Ra also created Bastet and Hathor.

"Ra was worshipped as the creator god among some ancient Egyptians, specifically followers of his cult at Heliopolis. It was believed that Ra wept, and from his tears came man. These cult-followers believed that Ra was self-created. Ra is also accredited with the creation of the seasons, months, plants, and animals."[12]

The Lion Lives in Me

Are you still wondering how the heck I concluded that the lion lives in me? Let me see if I can guide you to follow my logic. Every letter of

---

[7] "Sekhmet," Ancient Egypt Online, available at https://ancientegyptonline.co.uk/sekhmet/.

[8] Mark Millmore, "Ancient Egyptian Gods and Goddesses," Discovering Egypt, available at https://discoveringegypt.com/ancient-egyptian-gods-and-goddesses/.

[9] "Ra," Ancient Egypt Online, available at http://ancientegyptonline.co.uk/ra/.

[10] "Ra," Ancient Egypt Online, available at http://ancientegyptonline.co.uk/ra/.

[11] "The Eye of Ra: How Sekhmet Became Hathor," Youtube, 5:01, LetItBeOnigiri, 2007, available at https://www.youtube.com/watch?v=RDlfHTx-c0A&feature=youtu.be.

[12] Jenny Hill, "Ra," Ancient Egypt Online, available at http://ancientegyptonline.co.uk/ra/.

the alphabet is correlated to a number. So, "LION" would be L-12, I-9, O-15, N-14. Remove the repetitious number "1's" and you're left with 1, 2, 9, 5, 4. Two and five are essentially the same number flipped, so omit the number "2". What's left? 9, 5, 4, 1. And remember the house where I dwelled on the westside of Jacksonville? Well, the address was 4519 Melvin Circle West—in other words, the representative numbers symbolizing the word "lion".

Second, let us look at the name of the street. I disassembled the name Melvin. Me meant me, of course. I saw "lv" as lives, and "in" meant in. Then, I gave it this order: "lives in me." Once I discovered that 4519 meant Lion, I felt that I was on to something. So, I started saying to myself every day as I looked up at my street sign, "*The Lion Lives in Me!*" However, I was completely clueless about my new frame of reference.

In like manner, I realized that I lived on the lion's circle, and this was coupled with a picture sample for my company's logo. I took notice that the crown was round with a W appearance to it, so I started to envision a royal lion with a crown on its head. All the clues were within my full address. Equally important, the house was pink, so it must've represented a female lion.

Bear in mind, this was at the same time when I was putting together a business plan and looking for restaurant equipment and other items. When I would go into certain businesses, I would notice that they had a pastry case. I would go over and look at the manufacturer's name for a possible future purchase. But each time I did that, I noticed that the manufacturer's names I kept seeing were names like "Regal" and "Royal." I realized something was being expressed to me, but what it was, I did not know!

Before Florida, there could have been a clue pointing to the Lion dwelling within me. You see, I have an L carved into the side of my face; it's been there since I was a little girl living out in Oakmont North. When I was a little girl, there was another little girl who had long fingernails and she and I use to fight all the time. In one particular kiddie brawl, I got scratched on the side of my face by her long fingernails. At first, the scratch appeared as an upside-down capital T. Over the years as the skin repaired itself, it only repaired one line. By the time I took my photo for my learner's permit, I noticed that my embedded scratch read as a capital L. I've worn this battle scar on the right side of my face all my life.

Using Context Clues

Another key point I overlooked was in my birth name! I knew that the word **bacchanalia** meant to drink heavily, but I did not know where the word stemmed from. Bacchanalia were Roman festivals of Bacchus, the Greco-Roman God Dionysus, the god of wine, winemaking, grape harvest, freedom, intoxication, and ecstasy. The bacchanalia festival was a nightly celebration in Bacchus's honor.[13] Initially, it was a women's only festival until one high priestess wanted to bring her son, changing the celebration.

A bacchanalia sounds like a modern-day *Freaknik*! Now, let's analyze my name, JARNALIA. Can you see the same suffix in my name as bacchanalia? Remember the cartoon animation where Sekhmet was tricked by her father Ra into drinking barrels of ***wine*** that were intentionally mislabeled as blood?

Do you see any correlation?

Did you know that in ancient Egypt there were festivals to honor the sun goddess Sekhmet as well? These festivals were celebrated at the end of battle, so that Sekhmet's destruction would come to an end. During an annual festival held at the beginning of the year, a festival of intoxication, the Egyptians danced and played music to soothe the wildness of the goddess and drank great quantities of wine ritually to imitate the extreme drunkenness that stopped the wrath of the goddess.[14]

---

[13] Leonhard Schmitz, "Bacchanalia," Penelope University of Chicago, available at http://penelope.uchicago.edu/Thayer/E/Roman/Texts/secondary/SMIGRA*/Bacchanalia.html.

[14] "Provocative Yet Sacred: The Ancient Egyptian Festival of Drunkenness," Ancient Origins: Reconstructing the Story of Humanity's Past, February 3, 2016, available at https://www.ancient-origins.net/history-ancient-traditions/provocative-yet-sacred-ancient-egyptian-festival-drunkenness-005289.

Aha! There are some precise parallels between my name, Jarnalia, god of wine, Bacchus, the bacchanalia, Sekhmet's wine hoax, and Sekhmet's festival. I totally understood the message within the message for my awakening, and it was through that animated Sekhmet YouTube wine story that I got it. Apparently, the Universal Forces put this parable before me first.

More Clue Holders

Could my school's mascot have held a clue for me as well? The first elementary school I attended was Larrymore Elementary in Norfolk, VA. The school's mascot was a ferocious Lion. The middle school I attended, Rosemont, in Norfolk, VA, their mascot was a black panther. In my logic, I clearly saw a theme of big feline cats. Even today, the community where I reside in Virginia Beach, the property is owned by Larrymore Organization, and I went to Larrymore Elementary School in Norfolk. But, guess what, the two are not associated at all! The high school kids in this area attend Tallwood High School. And Tallwood's mascot is a ferocious Lion! The college I attended, Norfolk State University, is abbreviated NSU. Now, move that N behind the U, and as you can see, I actually attended the University of the SUN!

To all you Astrology Natal Chart readers out there: I am a Leo Ascendant, Sagittarius Sun and Taurus Moon. I was born on November 22, 1977 in Norfolk, VA, at 9:10 pm. I was born on Corprew and Majestic Avenue and I was conceived on E. 27th & Leo Street.

Another Reading

But what about Pharrell's family members?

I was at my friend Tyra's house, minding my own business, and out of all the conversations to have, she mentioned that someone told her about a guy she knows supposedly having a meeting with Pharrell. This guy's name is—Sporadiq. I immediately wondered if Tyra could have been my mother before, and if she murdered the magician. This event is what prompted me to seek out another reading, and this time it produced something more intriguing. (Note: I am not including the replies to questions two and three.)

Another Reading for Pharrell

From: 2xQueen2xGoddess
To: Angel & Guides
Sent: Thursday, August 16, 2012, 8:18 AM

Hey Angel & Guides...I've missed you all!

Well, I would like to dedicate my 3 questions again to the theme of Pharrell.

Question 1: By chance, do I have a connection to Pharrell's father, Pharaoh, and brothers Solomon and Cato, or were their names a catalyst for me to figure out I was an Egyptian queen and goddess? Very curious...

Question 2: Does my friend Tyra have something to do with my lifetime with Pharrell? If so, can you explain, please?

Question 3: Is there any past life connection with an artist under Pharrell by the name Pusha T? If so, can you explain, please?

Thanks,
Jenell

From: Angel & Guides
To: 2xQueen2xGoddess
Sent: Friday, August 17, 2012, 6:31 PM

Hello Jenell,

If you and Pharoah have a connection, it is so many lifetimes ago that I can't really pick up on it. So, it may indeed have been a catalyst for you. However, I do get a stronger connection with you and Pharrell. I believe you were brother and sister in one lifetime. In fact, you could have been twins as you look identical

> in size and age. You were very close, and he took flak sometimes for preferring to be with you than with his male friends. He was very protective of you and just didn't feel as close to anyone else as he did to you. You really were inseparable. I am seeing you are around the age of 10 and you really did do everything together. Around 16 I see Pharrell standing with a group of guys–like he has pulled away some and is devoting more time with them–but all the time he is in their group, he watches for you out of the corner of his eye, making sure no one is bothering you. It didn't matter if it was female or male if someone upset you, they were in big trouble with him. I see you being married but still extremely close to him. I am not sure if he got married as he really didn't want another female coming between the two of you.
>
> Your husband didn't seem to mind that the two of you were so close and so it worked out well for you. I do feel he was the first to die. It looks like a battle of some kind. He wasn't very old–early 30s. You were never the same. You kept telling others that you still saw him and heard him until even your husband thought you had lost it. So, you kept quiet after that when you felt him around you and became very sad. That sadness led you to not take care of yourself and you died of some contagious disease a couple years after Pharrell died.
>
> Many blessings to you,
> Angel

He died again, and before me!

That reading was so sad. I lost my twin brother! Then I lost myself! Poor me in that prior lifetime, as I do not know what it is like to lose a sibling this time around. Yet, I must've felt her devastation when I was listening to Pharrell's music around that two-year timeframe. All in all, this was a great reading, and a few things stuck out for me. For one thing, she said, "*he watches for you out of the corner of his eye.*" Well, back when I saw Pharrell in the MacArthur Center, he was staring at me, and when we passed each other, he was still giving me the side eye. For her to relay this specifically back to me was spot on! Wow, Pharrell and I were twins! Could that explain that deeper communication I hear in his music arrangements?

The two readings revealed enough information that helped me understand why I felt Pharrell's music was communicating a message to me and why I would go into ugly crying fits over his music.

Unbelievably, Pharrell and his family members had absolutely nothing to do with my Egyptian lifetimes and these findings left me completely confused! There's a quote by Virginia Woolf that I love, "*Arrange the pieces that come your way.*"[15] This quote has truly exemplified its meaning in my life. Pharrell's brothers Cato and Solomon and their father Pharoah, their names just functioned as clues to my Egyptian puzzle. I wonder why it took their names specifically to arrange the pieces of the puzzle? I was raised by Horace, my stepdad, who had a mean-ass Shollie by his side named, Isis. Ahhh-mazing, right?

Pharrell, if you want to disprove my alleged allegations, then go have a past life regression with someone certified. I could even join you and they could regress us both. It could be a twin venture. P, I saw you in a video called *Reincarnation* by Karl Lagerfeld on the Chanel YouTube channel. I smiled due to the parallelism. Hey, Snoop, Pharrell and Stevie Wonder, thanks for California Roll. I felt the video message was made just for me.

Pharrell, I love you, my brother, and it's great to see you again. Kisses from my heart to yours.

"Attention, lost souls, we are all connected!" –Jarnalia

We are alive and well today and I'm back to write about it! Being a spiritual being is a beautiful thing; for death is only a temporary state of being, because you live again and again and again and again.

---

[15] Virginia Woolf, "Saturday 5 September," Woolf Online, availble at http://www.woolfonline.com/?node=content/contextual/transcriptions&project=1&parent=41&taxa=42&content=6303&pos=7.

4

Beauty has Returned

A Diamond in the Rough!

Let's return to my reading. Angel & her Guides even mention *Nefertiti*!

From: Angel & Guides
To: 2xQueen2xGoddess
01/09/12 at 11:35 AM

Wow, love it, love it! Thank you for honoring me with your questions.

Your soul originates from a space that is all good. I see what appears to be a universe and there is a spiral of light in the heavens. To me, it means the cosmos, a place from all that is. When I ask for specifics, all I hear is, "Time. You came from time." I am not seeing things like planets, just the universe with a spiral of light.

I can easily see you as Sekhmet. Even Nefertiti. It was/is a very powerful time for you. It feels like it served as a doorway for you between all that is and all that was. It provides a pathway between other universes and this one. I can see you teleporting yourself through a shaft of light to another galaxy. It looks like you are standing in a small area and a shaft of light shines through but there is no window, no way for the light to shine. But when you beckon your family or ancestors, a beacon of light appears. You have such vast knowledge that even then you had to limit what you passed on to us. You really did/do have a vast knowledge of the universe, much of what can now be given to you in your present physical state. As the earth energies become higher, that will change though.

When I ask how many incarnations you've had, I get the number 22. I sense there are more–possibly 37, but they offered the number 22 as an indication that you have been a master in more than one lifetime.

Many blessings,
Angel

(FYI, I know I've lived more than 37 lifetimes because I have many, many stories to tell you all.)

***Queen Nefertiti*?!**

What are they talking about? I *so* did not believe her nor them! Because that's not what the Universe was showing me! Although, if it were true, how did I miss that? Then, instantly, I had a mental flashback. I said to myself, *What about that time when you were in college*?

Ten years earlier, way before uprooting to Florida and before my spiritual awakening, I was attending Norfolk State University. In one of my core psychology classes, Dr. Boyd, the professor, was calling students to the front of the room to pick up their papers. Individual after individual went up to retrieve their work, until she asked for two girls at the same time. One girl's name was Barbara and the other girl's name was Nefertiti. I remember aggressively confronting the two girls as they returned with their papers in hand. I said, "*Whose name is Nefertiti*?"

The second girl replied timidly, Me.

Why did I get so upset with that girl about her name?

Could that have been a sign then?

Also, why did I brand my company's name as little queen buttercup? Why queen? What about all the Canadian coins bearing the face of Queen Elizabeth II on them?

After the paid clairvoyant answered my questions, I took it upon myself to challenge her findings—I sat out to prove her wrong! I took my inquiries to other for hire eBay clairvoyants and asked them the same question but rephrased it a little.

If I was the Egyptian goddess Sekhmet and Queen Nefertiti and I am here, *then could it be true my husbands Ptah and Pharaoh Akhenaten are here as well*? I pondered this with great intent. I was inundated with thoughts of *who is he?* and *where is he*? I started to think of all the mentally strong and smart men in my life. The only two men who came to mind was the ex-jailbird and my (now deceased) absentee biological father.

Queen Nefertiti / Me
This picture was taken around October of 2013 at Greenbriar Mall.

I thought of the ex-jailbird because he and I had an incredible twin-like connection. So, I went to the second eBay Clairvoyant and asked her, "Was the ex-jailbird—Pharaoh Akhenaten when I was Queen Nefertiti?" She replied the ex-jailbird and I were not married when I was Queen Nefertiti, however, he did serve me then. That's a yes confirmation. But I did not believe her either. As you know, the Universal Forces are always listening and working behind the scenes in your favor. The answer showed up and delivered me a *big one.* So, brace yourself!

When I left Jacksonville, Florida, the magic (the signs or signposts) in front of my very eyes had completely stopped. Instead, the signs had chosen to manifest through my dreams. Three years post Jacksonville, magic started to show up in my dream state.

"Listen to your dreams, for they are revealing to you your soul's history." –Jarnalia Jennings

5

Salute to Egypt!

You are about to step into the corridors of time, as I resurrect these late pharaohs and queens from their tombs behind the sacred walls of the Valley of Kings. I am not an Egyptologist. I am Queen Nefertiti and I have reawakened in this majestic day and time to announce that we are all here!

Watch your step.

"The eighteenth dynasty of ancient Egypt, Dynasty XVIII, (c. 1550-c. 1292 BC) is perhaps the best known of all the dynasties. It is sometimes known as the Thutmosid Dynasty because of the four pharaohs named Thutmosis (English: Thoth child).

As well as Tutankhamen, famous pharaohs of Dynasty XVIII include Hatshepsut (1479 BC—1458 BC), the longest-reigning queen-pharaoh, and Akhenaten (1353—1336 BC 1351—1334 BC), the "heretic pharaoh," with his queen, Nefertiti.

Dynasty XVIII is often combined with Dynasties XIX and XX to form the New Kingdom period of ancient Egyptian history.

The pharaohs of Dynasty XVIII ruled for approximately two hundred and fifty years (c. 1550-1298 BC). Many of the pharaohs were buried in the Valley of the Kings in Thebes.

Dynasty XVIII was founded by Ahmose I, the brother or son of Kamose, the last ruler of the Dynasty XVII. Ahmose finished the campaign to expel the Hyksos rulers. His reign is seen as the end of the Second Intermediate Period and the start of a New Kingdom. Ahmose was succeeded by his son, Amenhotep I, whose reign was relatively uneventful."

Amenhotep I probably left no male heir, and the next Pharaoh, Thutmose I, seems to have been related to the royal family through marriage. During his reign, the borders of Egypt's empire reached their greatest expanse, extending in the north to Carchemish on the Euphrates and up to Kurgus beyond the fourth cataract in the south. Thutmose I was succeeded by Thutmose II and his queen, Hatshepsut. She was the daughter of Thutmose I, and soon after her husband's death, ruled for over twenty years after becoming pharaoh during the minority of her stepson, who later would become pharaoh as Thutmose III.

Thutmose III, who later became known as the greatest military pharaoh ever, also had a lengthy reign after becoming pharaoh. He had a second co-regency in his old age with his son Amenhotep II. Amenhotep II was succeeded by Thutmose IV, was followed by his son

Amenhotep III. The reign of Amenhotep III is seen as a high point in this dynasty. Amenhotep III undertook large scale building programs, the extent of which can only be compared with those of the much longer reign of Ramesses II during Dynasty XIX.[16]

And this is where my story begins…

To Egypt, we go!

Anubis, We All Made It to the Afterlife!
Thank You!

[16] "Eighteenth Dynasty of Egypt," Crystalink, available at https://www.crystalinks.com/dynasty18.html .

Pharrell says:

THE TRUTH WILL SET YOU FREE, BUT FIRST IT'LL PISS YOU OFF!

6

The Afterlife Is Now, The Resurrection of the Dynasty Family

The 18th Egyptian Dynasty
The Dynasty Family Tree

Pharaoh
Amenhotep III

Chief Queen
Tiye

Crown Prince
Thutmose

Pharaoh
Amenhotep IV/Akhenaten

Vizier
Amenhotep-Huy

Vizier
Ramose

Pharaoh Amenhotep IV Aka Pharaoh Akhenaten of the 18th Egyptian Dynasty

"Amun is Satisfied"/ "Effective for Aten"

Father: Pharaoh Amenhotep III

Mother: Queen Tiye

Wife: Chief Queen Nefertiti and other minor wives–no need to name them 😉

Offspring: Six daughters with Queen Nefertiti and a son who was known to the world as Pharaoh Tutankhamun with a minor wife and/or sister

Reign: 17 years

Buried: Originally buried in Amarna, but was relocated to The Valley of Kings (KV55)[17]

[17] Peter Dorman, "Akhenaten," Encyclopedia Britannica, available at https://www.britannica.com/biography/Akhenaten.

Amenhotep IV was a pharaoh of the 18th Egyptian Dynasty. He was the second son of Pharaoh Amenhotep III and Great Royal Wife Queen Tiye and *my past life husband*. Initially, Amenhotep IV wasn't supposed to inherit the throne as his father's successor. In fact, Amenhotep III and Tiye had an older son whose name was Thutmose, known as Crown Prince Thutmose. Being that Thutmose was the first-born son of Amenhotep III, he was predestined to become his father's successor and rule Egypt. However, Thutmose never became his father's successor due to an untimely death. He died before his father's reign had ended. Therefore, through divine intervention, this put my husband, Amenhotep IV, in position to inherit the throne as his father's successor and rule Egypt.

Co-Rulership

"It was theorized by some Egyptologists that there may have been a sharing of power with Amenhotep III and his son Amenhotep IV for up to 12 years and this created much debate amongst the Egyptology Society about a proposed co-regency."[18]

"In February 2014, the Egyptian Ministry for Antiquities announced conclusive evidence that Akhenaten shared power with his father for at least eight years. The evidence came from the inscriptions found in the Luxor tomb of Vizier Amenhotep-Huy."[19]

Why did Amenhotep IV change his name to Akhenaten?

In his fifth year of reign, Amenhotep IV took a journey out in the desert. This is where Aten communicated with him. Aten is a sun disc deity. Aten conveyed to Amenhotep IV: In this location, this is where

[18] "Eighteenth Dynasty of Egypt," Crystalink, available at https://www.crystalinks.com/dynasty18.html.

[19] "Pharaoh power-sharing unearthed in Egypt" Daily News Egypt, February 6, 2014, available at https://www.dailynewsegypt.com/2014/02/06/pharaoh-power-sharing-unearthed-egypt/.

creation began." The pharaoh was so spiritually transformed by this communion, my husband changed his namesake from Amenhotep to Akhenaten, which means "Living Spirit of Aten," "Horizon of Aten," "Aten is Pleased," and/or "Servant of Aten," to prove his complete devotion to the sun deity, Aten.[20]

The Era of the Amarna Period

Pharaoh Akhenaten completely abandoned the capital Thebes and moved 180 miles away to establish his own new city. He positioned his domain between Cairo and Luxor and this new city became known as Amarna. This was the same location where Akhenaten had his divine encounter with Aten. Akhenaten declared Amarna to be the new capital. In this new city, Akhenaten created a new religion—worshipping Aten.[21]

Ancient Egyptians believed in worshipping many gods, polytheism. However, in the capital of Amarna, Akhenaten eradicated that religious practice by introducing a new religious practice of worshipping of one god, monotheism.[22] ***All praises to the Sun!***

The Egyptian priesthood was very displeased with my husband Akhenaten's newfound religion. The main god of worship was Amun, and now Akhenaten was taking the focus off of Amun and putting the main emphasis on Aten.

As a consequence of Akhenaten making these radical changes, after his reign there was an "active campaign" to destroy and eradicate us from Egyptian history. The most compelling evidence of this, our faces and names were chiseled away on the reliefs on the walls in the tombs. Additionally, in the Temple of Abydos, Akhenaten's name was

---

[20] Peter Dorman, "Akhenaten," Encyclopaedia Britannica, available at https://www.britannica.com/biography/Akhenaten.

[21] "Pharaoh Akhenaten," Crystalinks, available at *https://www.crystalinks.com/akhenaten.html.*

[22] "Pharaoh Akhenaten," Crystalinks, available at *https://www.crystalinks.com/akhenaten.html.*

deliberately left off of the list of Kings published by Seti I. My husband, Akhenaten, would go down in Egyptian history as the heretic king.[23]

Who is Akhenaten today, in the 21st century?

With the powers vested in me, I resurrect my husband, Pharaoh Akhenaten, from his tomb (KV55). Today, he has incarnated as...

[23] "Amarna: Egypt's Other Lost City (SECRET ANCIENT HISTORY DOCUMENTARY," Youtube Video, 47:41, Gracieladavina516, 2016 available at *https://www.dailymotion.com/video/x3thir8*.

Barack Obama II

43rd and 44th
President of the United States of America

How did I receive this grand illumination?

I was in the process of racking my brain, trying to figure out who my husband could be in this day and time. Certainly, if I was here, I knew my husband was here as well. I could cross off the ex-jailbird from my list; however, he did serve me when I was Queen Nefertiti. Also, I could strike my absentee biological father Qulius from my list, because he was not a part of the 18th Egyptian Dynasty. Again, as you know, the Universal Forces are always listening and working behind the scenes. This time, they delivered me a *big one.*

The Intuitive Dreams

At this point, I started having dreams about the Obama family. I believe the first dream was just a flash of insight because I remembered seeing a picture of the family for just a quick second. Then there was a second dream, and that one featured Michelle Obama, but it wasn't too clear. The third dream was as vivid as the purple pajamas I am wearing right now! The dream was about former president Barack Obama II. The waking, conscious part of me, Jarnalia, ***never*** volunteers to have these experiences that I undertake in dream state. As you know, "you" are free to roam to any time or place, past, present, future, anywhere above, anywhere below, anywhere in between the in between, and anywhere beyond the limits of time. In the dream state, your consciousness, your soul, your essence, is *not bound by any laws, rules or jurisdictions.*

I found myself eavesdropping in on a meeting. My consciousness really was like a fly on the wall. The meeting was indeed a backroom deal, and I was able to view it from my own living room wall. There was a group of men at a table discussing who they've prepared to execute their agenda. On my left, I could see a continual series of cascading doors opening, and behind the final door was Barack Obama II, who was being manipulated like a puppet by a puppeteer.

When I woke up that morning, that was the day I decided I was no longer going to participate in voting in elections because I believe from my own experience that the higher powers already have in position who they want to run their show. Even though I voted for Obama in 2008 and sat in front of my television on the day of the inauguration, crying just as hard as the next black person, I did not participate in the 2012 election, which was due solely to my out-of-body experience (OBE). I was completely unaware that this new president and I had a legendary past life Egyptian connection.

The Universal Forces at Work

One day, I wanted to visually meditate to a famous picture of Akhenaten and Nefertiti with their children, praising Aten. Just thinking about that now warms my heart. At the same time, I wanted to listen to a song called *Golden Time of Day* by Frankie Beverly and Maze. As I looked for a picture on Google images of the royal family, I found a picture of former President Barack Obama II infused with Pharaoh Akhenaten on the cover. I thought, *What the hell*?! Literally, within a fraction of a second, my two dreams instantly came up from out of the back of my head and made their way to the center of my mind to say, "***Remember us***?!"

I clicked on the photo, and it took me to a page with an article and other comparison pictures of Akhenaten and Barack Obama II, as well as a picture of Michelle Obama being compared to the Pharaoh's mother, Queen Tiye. I thought, *WHAT*!!! Suddenly, I got so emotional because I did not understand what was going on. At that time, I thought these people were overseeing the country and I was living in poverty. I started to assess and analyze myself. I thought, *I'm not Ivy League smart, nor do I have anything going for myself this time around, yet it appears as if I have played very powerful roles in other lifetimes*. I called up Michael to tell him of my discoveries and I got so emotional trying to explain my findings, I just started crying. I cried because I felt like I was a part of something much larger and deeper than what I could understand. I couldn't understand why in this current incarnation I am limited and powerless.

I am so thankful to the person who created this infusion!

Our Shared Connections

When I was 24 years old, I left Norview and got my first apartment out in Chesapeake, VA. The apartments are strikingly similar to some old apartments I used to live in when I was a little, little girl out in Norview called Lakeland. Beno and I lived here in these apartments up until the night our house was broken into. On this particular night, my then 3 year old Beno spent the night with my mother, thank goodness. I was home alone, and I was standing in my living room on the telephone with Aundria, when someone knocked on my front door. I shouted, "Who is it?" as I looked out my living room window to see if I noticed any cars, which I didn't. The building was a four-unit apartment complex. I lived downstairs and the hallway light downstairs was broken, but my apartment itself was well lit.

The voice audibly whispered, "*Let me in*!" Through my door, and in a sassy rebuttal, I yelled back, "I'm not letting you in!" Then the masculine voice pleaded with me, "*Someone's after me*!" I said, "Oh well," as I looked again out my window. However, this time around, I saw a young man crossing my street—Yale Court, and he was about to step up to the curb. I could see him toting a large, shiny, silvery handgun in his hand. I didn't know if the young man had known that the guy, he was hunting down was in my hallway and at the front of my door. My fight or flight impulses were firing off. I wondered if he was coming to my house too! The intruder shouted, "*Here he comes*!" The intruder bust down my front door in three attempts. When he came in, I was standing between the living room and kitchen, still on the telephone with Aundria. Outraged, I screamed, "What are you doing!?" The intruder was a short heavy-set guy, whose face I'd never seen before out in that neighborhood. As I was exiting my back door, the intruder politely closed my front door behind him and calmly expressed to me, *"Ma'am the guy was after me,"* as if it was justified.

That was some crazy shit! I moved the hellup out of those ghetto azz apartments after living there for 15 months. That home invasion gave me legal grounds to break my lease and that's when I moved to Waverton Place. I say that to say this, Former President Barack Obama II and Former First Lady Michelle Obama, both who went to *Harvard University*. The name of that apartment complex where I once lived was called *Harvard Apartments*.

In Perfect Alignment

I used to work for a paratransit company called MV Transportation. This company provides a wonderful pick up service for the mentally/physically disabled and elderly population. The day was September 4, 2012, and this was a very honorary day for the Hampton Roads area because President Obama was visiting Norfolk State University. Yes, the same college where I heard Professor Brown's reincarnation stories;

yes, the same college where I encountered the girl named Nefertiti; and yes, the same college I graduated from. Superficially, I felt my pharaoh was looking for me, *his queen*. I felt his presence in my town was a non-verbal sign from the Universe. The Universal Forces were now signaling to me to step up and step out to the platform. I had already traversed three different cities, so I was tired—with an attitude, and ready to go home. My last client was getting off from work and she did not live too far from where she worked. Ironically, the client's first name is my middle name. I picked this client up somewhere between 2 p.m. and 3 p.m. The streets were calm and free of traffic congestion. I drove down Azalea Garden Road and noticed that on the Interstate's overpass, which is visible from the street, a Norfolk police car and cop at a standstill.

As I rode down Windermere Road, I turned onto Norvella Avenue or Texas Avenue. I rode that down one block and then made a left on Johns Street. Much to my surprise, I could clearly see a cop standing in the middle of Johns Street, about a few hundred yards away from Norview Avenue. He was standing there, blocking my access, with an orange cone placed in the center of the street, prohibiting traffic. I proceeded anyway. I drove down the street wondering what he was doing there and why he was blocking this street. As I drove down Johns Street, the cop came walking swiftly toward my car. His body language told me he was agitated with me. He raised a single hand out, telling me to stop. Then he came up to my window and demanded in an authoritarian tone that I turn around. I asked why the street was blocked. His response was to tell me to turn the car around. I was pissed off, of course. I was ready to get the client home and go home myself. I had been driving all day. I just wanted to avoid any evening rush hour traffic, as any industrious person would feel after a long day's work.

I gave in and complied with the officer. I put the car in reverse, backed up slightly, but then I stopped. I had caught something in my peripheral vision and stopped moving just to watch what was going on. About 75-100 police officers on motorcycles were riding down Norview Avenue and entering the Interstate. Several more cars followed that police escort—primarily three distinguished identical black town cars with presidential flags on them. I immediately understood why Johns Street was off limits.

I am from Norview. I went to Norview Elementary, Rosemont Middle, and Norview High School. I've traveled up and down Norview Avenue all my life, and now the president is in my neighborhood—traveling down the same streets I came up on. *How bizarre*! Out of everything I had experienced in my eccentric life up until that point, nothing trumped that.

As the entire motorcade completely and successfully entered onto the Interstate, the cop who was standing in my way moved the orange cone and granted me access to pass through.

I thought to myself:

What was the message for me in that chance encounter?

Was my past life pharaoh looking for me?

Was it symbolic?

Why did the Universal Forces coordinate this alignment and why did they put this in my path?

I questioned everything.

President Obama had visited the fire station on Norview Avenue. When I saw him and the motorcade, he was just leaving the fire station, a few steps away from Johns Street. Not only that, but the Norview Fire Station is on the same grounds as my old neighborhood Lakeland, and that neighborhood looked similar to Harvard Apartments.

More compelling evidence of this bizarreness. Norfolk State University is located in a different part of the city of Norfolk and it's not even close in proximity to the Norview area, as both are within the same city. As I am sitting here right now, filling in the street names I navigated through that day, I noticed ***Texas and Johns***. I was born 11-22-77 (all master numbers), exactly 14 years after John F. Kennedy's assassination. President Kennedy was assassinated in the state of Texas and his first name was John. Inexplicably, I found myself positioned in a transversal alignment to Texas Avenue and Johns Street and positioned in direct alignment with President Obama, our current president. Interesting, wouldn't you say?

An Open Letter to my Pharaoh Akhenaten/Mr. Obama

You built Amarna just for us. Even today, I partially carry it in my own name. Through the field of Egyptology, I am allowed to travel back to ancient Egypt to observe our love story, the power play, and I just marvel at the beauty of it all. I can see our shared love for each other, our six daughters, and the sun. I would call it the "Golden Time of Day." I was your queen then and you were my pharaoh.

Today, I am so thankful to have the sun still a part of my life. If it did not shine its rays on my soul daily, I would perish due to its absence. It is the sole source of vitality for all living things here on this Earth. Even though that time has passed us by, I would bask in the rays of Aten's glory with you. Praise in the rays of Aten's glory with you, and I would worship in the rays of Aten's glory with you, again and again. That is, in any lifetime. Thank you for showing up in this present day and time and reflecting back to me, my own greatness as well.

Mr. Barack Obama II, do you have a penny for my thoughts, because I have one more tidbit for you. You were also Abraham Lincoln, the sixteenth president of the United States of America. This was announced twice, on two separate intuitive radio shows, by two of my trusted clairvoyant's, Mrs. M&M and KareBear. In that lifetime, I was a male and an escaped slave. I fought in the Civil War and survived! Thank you for emancipating us!

Amarna Forever,
Jarnalia Jennings

Queen Tiye
Great Royal Wife
of the18th Egyptian Dynasty

Father: Yuya

Mother: Tjuyu

Husband: Pharaoh Amenhotep III

Notable Offspring: Pharaoh Akhenaten and Crown Prince Thutmose

Other Kin: Grandmother of King Tutankhamun, either Pharaoh Aye's sister or cousin, and Queen Nefertiti's mother-in-law.

Reign: 1390 BC to 1353 BC

Buried: The Valley of Kings: KV35 Thebes, KV55 Amarna and/or WV22[24]

Queen Tiye was a very powerful woman of the 18th Egyptian Dynasty. She possessed an incredible amount of administrative power over her husband's reign, as well as her son Akhenaten's reign. Queen Tiye was

[24] Joshua Mark, "Tiye," Ancient History Encyclopedia, July 18, 2011, available at *https://www.ancient.eu/tiye/*.

wise, intelligent, strong, and fierce. Foreign leaders were willing to deal directly through her. She was the first queen to have her name recorded in state official acts, and her dignitary position gave way to her becoming her husband's trusted adviser and confidant.[25]

Tiye's father, Yuya, was a non-royal, wealthy landowner from the Upper Egyptian town of Akhmim, where he was a priest and commander of chariotry. Egyptologists have suggested that Tiye's father was of foreign origin due to the features of his mummy and the many different spellings of his name, which implies his name was non-Egyptian.[26]

Tjuyu, Tiye's mother, was involved in many religious cults, as attested to by her different titles including Singer of Hathor and Chief of the Entertainers of both Amun and Min, [27] which suggests that she was a member of the royal family.

Tiye also had a brother, Anen, who was Second Prophet of Amun. Ay, a successor of Tutankhamun as pharaoh after the latter's death, is believed to be yet another brother of Tiye, despite no clear date or monument confirming a link between the two. Egyptologists presume this connection from Ay's origins (also from Akhmim), because he is known to have built a chapel dedicated to the local god Min there and also inherited most of the titles that Tiye's father, Yuya, held at the court of Amenhotep III during his lifetime. [26]

Queen Tiye was married to Amenhotep III in the second year of his reign. Their children include Thutmose Crown Prince, Akhenaten IV, Sitamun, Iset, Henuttaneb, Nebetah, Smenkhkare, The Younger Lady, and Baketaten.

---

[25] Joshua Mark, "Tiye," Ancient History Encyclopedia, July 18, 2011, available at *https://www.ancient.eu/tiye/.*

[26] O'Connor, David, and Eric H. Cline. Amenhotep III: Perspectives on His Reign. Ann Arbor: University of Michigan Press, 1998.

[27] Joyce Tyldesley, *Chronicle of the Queens of Egypt,* (London, Thames & Hudson, 2006), 115-116.

QUEEN TIYE

With the powers vested in me, I resurrect Pharaoh Akhenaten's mother and my mother-in-law, Queen Tiye, from her tomb KV35, KV55 or WV22. Today, she has incarnated as…

Michelle Robinson

Former First Lady of the
United States of America
and Wifey of
Former President Barack Obama II

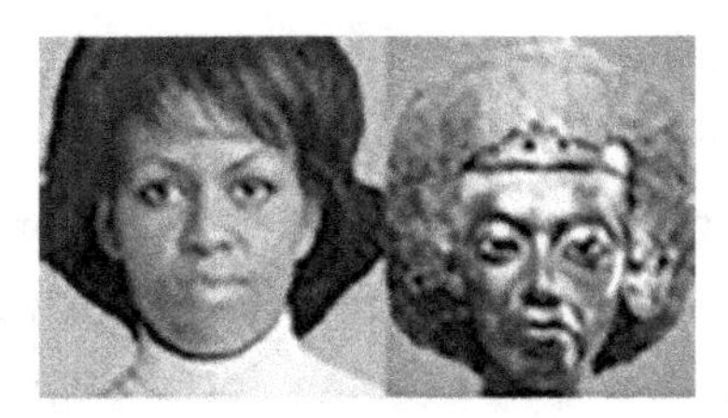

Michelle now and Michelle when she was Queen Tiye in ancient Egypt

Again, I'm sending out a great amount of gratitude to the person who created these comparison photos of the Obamas then and now. You have helped me greatly and through you, I was able to instantly understand something that was hidden within myself.

Can someone please tell me why I unearthed this information during election time? I was so overwhelmed during that time by the continuous campaign commercials that ran every day, all day, of former President Barack Obama and Michelle Obama.

In a distant past lifetime, Michelle took up a very powerful role in Egypt. In light of this, it comes as no surprise that she has incarnated back to help her past life Egyptian **son,** now husband, to run the most powerful nation in the world. Mrs. Michelle Obama is built for leadership. She is very much queen today as she was then in ancient Egypt. I raise my cup to Michelle Obama aka Chief Queen Tiye, for I remember your Egyptian greatness.

What am I saying? (Spiritual Lesson #1)

The soul of Queen Tiye has returned to Earth as Michelle Robinson. Michelle has chosen to reincarnate with some of her same family members once again. Attention, novice YouTube theorists: you have made up some deceptive concepts about my family. You have some of the people right, but you have the process totally wrong. I feel that you are misguiding your audience with these damaging misconceptions. *We are not clones*! I repeat, we are not clones! It's called reincarnation!

Let me explain. The soul will temporarily dwell within a physical body or a physical vehicle and live out lessons for its spiritual growth. Some may say that these lessons are Karmic Lessons.

When the soul "chooses" to vacate the body through the process of death, the soul returns to Spirit (home) for some much-needed R & R. Following much-needed rest, the soul continues to learn and become more enlightened over on the other side, then the soul will move into a new process, the return. In this process, the soul meets with its spiritual advisors or spirit guides to prepare for its next incarnation. We are all doing it! From the preacher preaching about damnation to David Duke, all souls are evolving and reincarnating on this spiritual journey.

My Dream Connection

My first dream was about the family, and really, it was a flash of insight, just a picture of the whole family. I rationalized it as my mind filtering through something I had seen on television earlier that day or something. Then the second dream, was about Michelle Obama for sure. Again, I do not know what she was doing in my dream because I forgot the details, but she showed up right before I woke up. However, when I woke up from that dream, I got out the bed and went to lay on the floor in my living room. As I was laying there, I turned on the television and just wasn't satisfied with what I was watching, so I began to channel surf. I came across a channel that had some people working out, then I turned to a different station and caught a glimpse of Michelle Obama before skipping to the next channel. I found myself fumbling with the remote, trying to get back to that television program. This happened within a few minutes of me turning on the television. That was indeed mystifying to me! I remembered thinking, *I just finished dreaming about her, this is weird*! I wondered what message was trying to be conveyed to me.

I got up immediately and went to my #1 resource, Wikipedia, in the hopes of finding a hidden message within the message. While looking over Michelle's bio on Wikipedia, I didn't notice any tale-tale signs. I didn't see anything at all really. I believe I noticed some small similarity between Nancy Regan and Michelle Obama, but nothing connecting her to me.

An Open Letter to Queen Tiye/Michelle Obama

I want to thank you for showing up and reflecting back to me my own greatness. I dreamt of you once again in 2016. This was around the time when there was a canard perpetuated that you were going to run for office after you had clearly stated several times that you were not. I dreamt someone was after you! Oddly enough, you were out here in College Park where I live today, and you needed to go into hiding. First, you took cover in the back of a laundry mat, but then we had to flee. At that point, you and I were walking down the sidewalk as I was attempting to have you take cover at a Jewish nursing home facility. LOL! Craziness! Queen Tiye/Michelle, I saw you as a courageous woman, for you stood there tall and strong against the assailant and you refused to keep running and hiding. I stood in front of you, guarding you. Little ole me, 4'11.5. Although I felt you really didn't need my help, I was going to protect you anyway from any combat.

Queen Michelle, to me, you represent power, strength, and fearlessness. With that said, even though you are a powerful, valiant queen who doesn't need my support, I want you to always remember, I always got your back, Mrs. Michelle!

Now, here is my very first reading from Golden Rose. I often return to this reading whenever I need to lift my spirits, mainly when I feel like my life has no purpose.

Sincerely,
Queen Nefertiti *(your ancient Egyptian daughter-in-law)*

An Open Past Life Reading

From: 2xQueen2xGoddess
To: Golden Rose
Sent Date: Apr-23-12 16:19:09 PDT
Subject: Psychic E-mail Reading (1 Question)

My name is Jarnalia Jennings and DOB is 11-22-77.

This is not a joke!

I have discovered some inconceivable facts about my soul's validity.

So be honest, thank you.

Hello, I have a question about my pastlife when I was Queen Nefertiti in Egypt. Since I was told this by 2 other eBay psychics, I've been trying to figure out who my husband was, Pharaoh Akhenaten aka Amenhotep IV. However, over the past month and a half, President Obama and his wife have been showing up in my dreams and I didn't think anything of it until I saw Michelle on a commercial right after the dream; which was my second dream of them. This happened on Sunday. So, I got up and looked up Michelle Obama's bio on Wikipedia and I didn't see any spot-on facts that we shared, not like I normally would see. So, I stopped searching. But yesterday, I wanted to listen to a song about the SUN and I wanted to meditate to a picture of Queen Nefertiti, Pharaoh Akhenaten and Aten (Sun). I found the picture I was looking for and I also discovered a picture of Pres. Barack Obama on the cover of Time Magazine infused with Pharaoh Akhenaten's statute and Michelle Obama as Queen Tiye, the Pharaoh's mother. I dismissed it for a split second, then I realized that my dreams about the Obamas may have a direct indication.

So, I'm starting to suspect that President Barack Obama was Pharaoh Akhenaten and Michelle Obama is his mother Queen Tiye.

Is my suspicion accurate? I can handle it.

Thx,
Queen Nefertiti

From: Golden Rose
To: 2xQueen2xGoddess
Apr 24, 2012 at 11:26 PM

Hello Jarnalia,

Thank you for having a reading with me.

It is a pleasure to connect with your energy. 

First of all, I am getting a lot of tingles with your birthday. As this is being shown to me as a powerful soul number. So, the way this comes through is that it's important for you to trust your insights and intuition. Because you have been given a gift of insight, and the ability to see between the veils. And that means the ability to pick up on past and future lifetimes!!! The connection you feel to Obama and Michelle I feel is directly related as you have mentioned. So, I am getting a yes with this. I also get that you have a lot of power and knowledge from this past life being Queen Nefertiti, and it's important to tune into this, and bring forth your gifts into this lifetime. Because it provides clues to your life purpose and how you will help other people. And it's also interesting how Obama and Michelle take up roles of leadership in this lifetime, as they did in a way in the past life in Egypt. So I also get that you have the same role for this lifetime, but in your own way. You are born to be a leader, and I feel the bigger message with this, that Obama and Michelle want to get across to you, is make an impact and inspire others for this lifetime. Because that is your birthright. So they are coming in now to remind you of how amazing you are, and to go for it. You have what it takes to lead and inspire large numbers of people, and your birthday is so spiritual. I feel you came to do it in a spiritual way! So consider this a gift (the dreams and synchronicities), as sign posts along the way to really get out there and shine! You are a lightworker who came to usher in paradise on earth. Lead the way!

I hope this is helpful.

GOLDEN ROSE

Taken at Madame Tussauds Museum, August 2013.

18th Egyptian Dynasty's Queen Tiye, Queen Nefertiti and Pharaoh Akhenaten.

And still leading the way. Today, we are Jarnalia Jennings and Barack and Michelle Obama.

Just in case you were wondering. No, Michelle Obama was not Mary Todd Lincoln, she was actually Ann Rutledge. KareBear shared this on her radio show many years ago.

Spiritual Lesson # 2

I suppose for me to speak of such a revolting relationship between the former First Lady Michelle Obama and former President Barack Obama would be considered blasphemy! Metaphysically speaking, souls can play out any role with each other in this drama that we call life. A soul could be a mother today, wife tomorrow, or a child in another incarnation. With this in mind, love is expressed and experienced in a number of ways as it relates to relationships.

As you can see, souls see each other again! We sign right back up and agree to assist our loved ones in brand-new incarnations. To put it another way, if you've lost a close relative, 10 times out of 10, you will reincarnate with them again, but the roles in the next journey will be different.

Here are two examples. Your young lad today could cycle round and take on the role as your parent in a future lifetime. Or your recently departed grandparent or parent could reincarnate as your son or daughter, or even as your children's off-springs. I've read that we tend to incarnate back into the same families because it's just easier to reemerge through the same lineage. Humorously speaking, as a soul, we get preferential treatment.

Not only do our souls tend to incarnate back into the same families, even civilizations reincarnate together. Is this not beautiful, people? We are never really separated by death.

Pharaoh Amenhotep III of the 18th Egyptian Dynasty

"Amun Is Satisfied"

Father: Pharaoh Thutmose IV

Mother: Queen Mutemwiya; a minor wife.

Wife: Chief Queen Tiye and other minor wives.

Notable Offspring: Pharaoh Akhenaten and Crown Prince Thutmose

Other Notable Kin: Pharaoh Tutankhamun was his grandson and Queen Nefertiti was his daughter-in-law.

Reign: 38 or 39 years

Buried: The Valley of Kings (WV22)[28]

Amenhotep III was the ninth pharaoh of Egypt. He was born around 1388 BC to Thutmose IV and Mutemwiya, a secondary wife. Amenhotep III was crowned while still a child, perhaps between the ages of six and twelve. He was a member of the Thutmosid family that ruled Egypt for

[28] Joshua Mark, "Amenhotep III," July 15, 2011, Ancient History Encyclopedia, available at *https://www.ancient.eu/Amenhotep_III/*.

almost 150 years since the reign of Thutmose I. Amenhotep III needed a stronger tie to the royal lineage since he was a child of a minor wife; therefore, he married Queen Tiye in the second year of his reign.[29]

Amenhotep III and Queen Tiye had several children. One of their offspring was Crown Prince Thutmose, who predeceased his father in an untimely death. The second son, originally known as Amenhotep IV, would ultimately succeed his father Amenhotep III to the throne.[30]

Amenhotep III and Tiye also had four daughters: Sitamun, Henuttaneb, Iset, and Nebetah. They appear frequently on statues and reliefs during the reign of their father and also are represented by smaller objects, with the exception of Nebetah.[31]

And who has Queen Tiye's husband returned as?

---

[29] Joshua Mark, "Amenhotep III," July 15, 2011, Ancient History Encyclopedia, available at *https://www.ancient.eu/Amenhotep_III/*.

[30] Joshua Mark, "Tiye," Ancient History Encyclopedia, July 18, 2011, available at *https://www.ancient.eu/tiye/*.

[31] Joshua Mark, "Tiye," Ancient History Encyclopedia, July 18, 2011, available at *https://www.ancient.eu/tiye/*.

Amenhotep III Bust At the British Museum

With the powers vested in me, I resurrect Queen Tiye's husband, Akhenaten's father and my father-in-law, from his tomb WV22. We are all waiting. Today, he has incarnated as….

Shawn Carter aka Jay-Z

When Kingdom Come, he's ready!

Jay-Z is one of the most influential hip-hop artists of the late twentieth and early twenty-first centuries. I remember the first time I heard of Jay-Z. I was watching BET in the wee hours of the morning and it was a brand-new video by this artist. The lyrics went like this, "I'm out for presidents to represent me."[32] In hindsight, he certainly was spot on with that! While watching the video, I thought the song was dope, and just in case he was a one-hit wonder, I remembered his name. HA! Today, Jay-Z's name is synonymous with the word hip-hop.

During the late twentieth century, I was a young, young, lady, probably 20, just getting the taste of Similac off my breath. And at that time, there was an infamous rap battle surrounding Jay-Z and Nas. Quite frankly, I liked Nas over Jay because he spoke knowledge in his messages—that is, lost knowledge—and Jay's lyrical content was all about living how you get it and I couldn't relate to that kind of lifestyle. But I could relate to those Swizzy Beats though. Remember *Money Cash Hoe's, Money Cash Hoe's,* featuring DMX? The song that actually had DMX rapping when he said, "DMX and my dog's bite, Jigga my Nigga, rhyme all night!"[33] Oh my gosh, that song went (HAM) hard ass a muthafucker!

Let me tell you about the time Jay-Z came to my town, Norfolk, VA. My then best friend MaryJane got a phone call from a former co-worker, Ron, a much older man who was crazy about some MaryJane. Most men were. Rick James didn't even know my BFF and he wrote a song about her! MaryJane was Filipino with soul. Anyway, he called MaryJane and told her that Jay-Z was headed up to DJ's Music on Tidewater Drive. Oh, is that where you know me from? Yes, I used to work there with MaryJane. Although by that time, Jane and I had both just recently resigned our employment with DJ's. MaryJane and I did not have any children yet, so I'm going to say Jay came to Norfolk around spring/summer of 1998.

---

[32] JAY-Z, "Dead Presidents," Dead Presidents, Roc-A-Fella Records & Priority Records, 1996.

[33] JAY-Z, "Money, Cash, Hoes," Track 6 on Vol. 2...Hard Knock LIfe, Def Jam Recordings & Roc-A-Fella Records, 1998.

When we arrived, DJ's parking lot was surrounded by folks. There was literally a human fort built around DJ's parking lot and it slightly extended out to Lafayette Boulevard. I had never seen this type of turnout at DJ's before, everyone wanted to get a glimpse of Jay-Z. MaryJane and I couldn't even get into the parking lot to link up with Ron, so he could get us in for the meet and greet. We were forced to stand on the opposite side of Tidewater Drive, at the corner of Lasalle Avenue, and take in the view from afar. When Jay arrived and got out of the car, all I could see was a tall masculine figure with a navy-blue ball cap on. The crowd went ballistic and it was sheer pandemonium after that. It was much like an outdoor block party. Why was I standing only at a short distance away from Pharaoh Amenhotep III/Jay-Z and ultimately blocked by a human shield? Were the Universal Forces against our reunification at that time? Did they not want any mustard seed of Egypt brought to my awareness in my earlier years? You know that everything happens for a reason.

Now, let's fast-forward through 15 years of my life, stopping at 2013. All this time later, this man was showing up in my dreams. "*WTF*?" There are two very specific people of high notoriety who I thought I had no past life connection with. However, just when I thought I was in the clear, I was shown differently—these parties are not outside of me, they too are very much part of my epic tale. I am specifically speaking about Jay-Z and his wife. Trust me, people, I would have loved to have steered clear of this prominent couple, but it appears that I can't. Not only that, but it goes beyond them, as you will see later. But for now, let me present my case and unravel this past life connection.

The Most Bizarre Dreams

I've had this same dream on three different occasions, except they were actually out of body experiences, meaning my consciousness was fully aware that it was far from my apartment in Virginia Beach. I found myself on a tour bus having a helluva good time with Jay-Z and a lot of other men. We were gambling, playing cards, big money was passing through my hands and being passed around. This may come off as a little peculiar for you, but I believe I might be a man in these dreams because it's all men at the table gambling and having a blast. I questioned, why I was tuning into this. Why was I holding and passing Jay's money around with his permission? It couldn't be my money, because I'm broke! Then I thought there must be a deeper reason behind these dreams. Following my intuition, I had a reading. I went to see if Matter of Fact Sandra could help me analyze this odd position I found myself in. I asked about two entertainers, but for now, let's focus on Jay-Z.

From: 2xQueen2xGoddess
To: Matter a Fact Sandra
08/05/13 at 5:51 PM

Hey Mrs. Sandra,

I went on vacation for the first time in many many moons and internally I'm happy and I realized I want to change my mundane life.

I was sitting here contemplating these two men who are entertainers. I've been with them many times in dream state and I just wanted to know if there are any messages that I should know about us that may possibly have some validity to me.

Could you tell me if I have any connection to Jay-Z aka (Shawn Carter)?

Thanks,
Jenell

From: Matter of Fact Sandra
To: 2xQueen2xGoddess
08/05/13 at 7:52 PM

Hi Jenell!

Thank you for your purchase. I'm glad to hear you had an enjoyable vacation. It's so important to have some downtime with this stress-filled world we live in.

Jay-Z–As I touch in with his energy, all I feel is a very cold energy, so I don't feel that this person has a significant role in your life. As I look at past life connections, again, there are no intersections between the two of you, so I would say that this individual does not have any serious consequence for you.

Much love and many blessings,
Sandra

If you've got me pegged by now after reading my words throughout these past six chapters, then you would know I was completely dissatisfied with Matter of Fact Sandra's explanation.

I wasted no time and ran over to KareBear's radio show just to ask her the same question. KareBear explained that I was a spiritual teacher for Jay-Z in spirit. What teacher in spirit gambles with the student? That's not part of my work as a spiritual teacher! After KareBear shared her insight with me, I just left it alone, although I really wanted to understand my out-of-body rendezvous with Jay-Z. Feeling slightly disappointed, I determined that I would just have to wait for more information to unfold. That notion would pay off because I had a fourth odd ass out-of-body experience, and this one also included another Brooklynite, *Livie Lux.*

One early morning, I had an out-of-body experience where Livie and I were in a high-rise building and he was getting ready to take a meeting with Jay-Z. I desperately wanted to spend some more quality time with Livie Lux, but I had to go, this meeting with Jay was of high honors. Livie's slick ass was now walking me out of the building. I found myself walking down a long sidewalk, Livie escorting me out to a car. Right before getting into the car with a driver, I noticed a lot of construction going on in the adjacent lot with a fence that had an "Under Construction" sign posted on it. I got into the backseat of the car and the driver told me his name was Oliver. I was extremely saddened when we drove off because Livie had promised to spend some time with me, but he had put business before me once again. Oliver drove me straight back to my bed in Virginia Beach because I woke up and it was morning.

Livie called me that day, and I told him about my surreal dream. He was so hung up on the fact he was going to take a meeting with Jay. Liv asked if I thought they would be friends or get along. He mentioned the neighborhood where Jay-Z came up in Brooklyn wasn't too far from where he, Livie, came up in Brooklyn. Livie also told me that Jay-Z named himself after the subway train Jay. I'd never been to New York before and I really wouldn't know what Livie was talking about until many years later.

Although Mr. Shabazz has given up on our friendship, I still troll his Facebook page. Livie always said I was a sleuth! Well, while sleuthing, I noticed he posted a picture of himself standing at the top of some stairs, his back slightly posted up on the side of a building, and to his left was a sign that read Jay St—MetroTech Station R, NW corner of Jay St and Willoughby St. Above Mr. Shabazz's head was a 79 cents Deal Store in the frame of the picture. But peep this, I could also clearly see a street sign that read "Lawrence" in the background of the photo too.

At that moment, instantly I saw two connections between Livie and Jay-Z. The first connection, Livie is representing, or paying "homage," as he would say, to Jay-Z, and the second connection, Livie used to live in Lawrenceville and the word Lawrence is captured in the picture where Livie is paying homage to Jay-Z. *Hmm…the symbolism.*

Back to My Dreams

I just thought I was dreaming of Jay for (GP) general purposes, which wasn't like me at all because my dreams are clearly intuitive. I was clearly receiving higher knowledge—wisdom that was for me and me alone, and not my gifted seers. Over the course of a few years, those random OBE's would unfold more and more. I wasn't watching continual YouTube videos of Jay-Z before going to bed to help induce my dream experience or anything like that. These experiences would just unfold a story like the rest of my intuitive dreams. Despite the lack of information my sometimes helpful, clairvoyants shared with me. As a result, of my continuous Jay-Z dreams, I started to believe again that Jay and myself had shared a past life together or we are connecting in a parallel reality. Which leads me to another dream two years down the road from the last one.

In this particular dream, the environment is real to me. It's as if I live there right now, though parallel to this world, and I think it's in Florida. In this parallel world, he and I are walking down the street together. Jay's friendship feels like he is my muthafuckin boy (best buddy), but I'm a girl. I can clearly see that he is between 17 and 19 years old. When I stepped out of that world and back into this one, I disregarded the dream once again because I was not being confirmed by someone else. The Universal Forces observed my actions as well. I was completely ignoring my own intuition and surrendering to what someone else said was true for me. All of a sudden, I was hit by an avalanche of dreams in September of 2016, featuring the black Bonnie and Clyde team!

I finally reached a boiling point from being completely overwhelmed by my nighttime rendezvous with the duo. Not heeding the message within the message, I ran back to someone else for help. I emailed my most trusted intuitive consultant, KareBear, who had previously told me three years earlier that I was just a teacher for Jay in Spirit.

From: 2xQueen2xGoddess
To: KareBear
09/17/16 at 9:07 AM

Hi KareBear,

Can you please tell me that my subconscious is just running wild!

KareBear, I can't stop dreaming about Beyoncé and Jay-Z, it's getting on my last nerve now! One minute it looks like we are friends, then the next minute it looks like Jay-Z is trying to be my man and telling me I'm going to have all the pretty dresses. WTF!!

I've had five dreams since Sept. 1st about the couple for no reason!

I also dreamt of them two nights back to back!

I am not a fan, nor a fanatic.

They won't stop showing up in my dreams!

And, to put the icing on the cake, September 1st, several hours after the dream, some random man turned his car around to come introduce himself to me as I was walking home. I glanced at him and he resembled Jay-Z, then he got out of his car and introduce himself as "Jay".

What is going on?

Poor Me,
Jenell

From: KareBear
To: 2xQueen2xGoddess
09/19/16 at 6:49 PM

Hi Jenell,

LOL. This made me laugh. You are releasing past life memories (from more than one lifetime) with both Jay-Z and Beyoncé. Some lives they were both a part of, other lives just one of them or the other was. Just know it is your past life stuff being released, and the dreams about them will slowly fade away. I have had dreams like this too, and they can feel so real. I had to laugh because I have totally been there (with a few different celebrities). I had one dream where I was hugging (redacted) and he was crying to me like I was his mom. It was very strange, so strange I knew it had to be a past life! These dreams are a great way for you to work through past life energy even while you sleep :)

Love,
Karen

Say what now!

So now KareBear is tooting a new tune?

Her response left me completely confused because just three years ago she told me I was just a teacher for Jay-Z in spirit! Even Matter of Fact Sandra said no, Jay-Z and I did not have a past life together. At that moment, I learned something that I believe to be true: what's for you is for you! I even came up with my own theories. In some cases, not even the greatest clairvoyant can always see specific insight that's only for you to receive. Additionally, I now believe some insight could also be on a time lock, and again, not even the greatest clairvoyant has the key to unlock that lock until the time lock has been lifted.

After reading KareBear's email, I thought to myself, I knew it!

One thing about me for sure, I am an intuitive dreamer. I would not be dreaming of this man if there wasn't a deeper message being communicated. I knew what I was seeing was insight just for me! Unfortunately, I couldn't run back to KareBear for more details, for she no longer provides intuitive email readings. Although I could always email her for moral support. I had to now seek out another gifted clairvoyant who could help me, and I knew who to ask next.

I returned to Golden Rose. I had been to her once before with an Egyptian question and she had proven to be very helpful. So, I drafted up an extensive email putting in all of my frustrations. I told her about all the dreams and how I ran to other gifted clairvoyants for their input. I added, that I was told by the others that there weren't any past-life connections with Jay-Z and I, but then, my KareBear turns around and shares that we, in fact, did share a past lifetime together. As you can imagine, it took me a great deal of time writing out my email to Golden Rose and I left it in the draft box. A few days later, I was listening to my binaural beats and doing a little automatic writing with my spirit guide, Dorrian. I happened to ask Dorrian who Jay-Z was. Dorrian spelled out Amenhotep III! I was shocked, because for years I assumed MLK was Amenhotep III. How could you not be a pharaoh when your last name is King and you died in Memphis? This new source of enlightenment brought my awareness back to one of my dreams, and it made much more sense now than ever before. Specifically, that dream with Livie Lux taking a meeting with Jay-Z, for I certainly knew who Livie Lux was from the 18th Egyptian Dynasty.

I went back to the prepared draft and didn't erase a thing. However, at the very top of the email, I came straight out of the gate with my question for Golden Rose.

From: 2xQueen2xGoddess
To: Golden Rose
12/26/16 at 11:04 PM

Golden Rose Good Day,

After writing all that's listed below, Dorrian who's on my spiritual team tells me that SHAWN CARTER aka Jay-Z is the 18th Egyptian pharaoh Amenhotep III. Is this true?

If so, it explains all that's listed below.

Golden Rose, can your awesome spider senses give me clarity?

Do Shawn Carter AKA Jay-Z and I, Jarnalia Jennings, have a past life or any past lives together?

Thank You,
An Egyptian Goddess

From: Golden Rose
To: 2xQueen2xGoddess
12/27/16 at 12:38 PM

With regards to Shawn. I do get that he was 18th Egyptian pharaoh Amenhotep III and double checked with my pendulum to confirm this. However, I generally do not comment on other readings given by other readers. As everyone is coming from a different level with where they provide information. And so, it can get rather confusing at times if there is too much input in this way. So, I always tell people to take what they resonate with from any source and move forward in this way, letting things unfold naturally. As there may be some valuable tidbits from each source to contemplate, however, if the timing is not right to have everything come together or be revealed. It all may not make sense right now. And so, I feel part of this process for you is of 'discovery' and your guides ask you to trust your inner guidance on this, and you will have even more dreams and insights. As well I always tell people that the person who has the dreams should go with their first impressions as they are the most accurate, more than any other outside source. Which may be why you feel a little confused at some of the input. So, with your excitement, I just see that you have a deep and strong connection to many of these souls, and they are being revealed to help you discover more about yourself and your past lives at this time. And unfortunately, I cannot interpret all of these dreams in 2 questions, nor would I want to. As there is so much going on here on so many levels and lifetimes. But the main message I want to relay to you today is to go with what you feel strongest about in your gut and heart. As this is your inner guidance system of truth, and so I feel what is most accurate here is what you are getting and feeling. By connecting all the dots, some magic is unfolding here, and I honestly don't feel any one reader can give you all the answers you are looking for at this time. As you will also have more dreams, and a few of the pieces are not ready to be revealed yet and cannot be given to anyone but YOU! So, stay true to your power, and keep shining!

I hope this helps!

Sincerely,
GOLDEN ROSE

I had a dual reaction to the reading. On one hand, Dorrian was right! And, on the other, this meant Jay-Z and Barack Obama II were father and son in ancient Egypt! Fascinating!

Initially, I wasn't going to add the dream that I had on September 1, 2016, featuring Beyoncé and Jay. However, I stumbled across the story on TMZ's YouTube channel. When I saw the title, I was taken aback. The TMZ video had already been up for a full year when I got around to viewing it. Here is a brief description of my first dream involving the happy couple.

Their house was being foreclosed on and I house sat for them. As I was watching out for the foreclosure person, I went outside and spotted the person who had been harassing them. He came rolling down the driveway's incline on a Segway and once he came up and approached me, I cussed his ass out badly. Then I found myself sitting in the back seat of a car, directly behind Jay, and I was telling Beyoncé, who was in the passenger's seat, how I cussed out the foreclosure person. End of dream.

Several hours later, I met someone who looked identical to Jay-Z, and he too goes by the name Jay. This situation was freaky as hell, but it was confirming on so many levels! As of today, I've had countless dreams featuring Mr. & Mrs. Carter. And, in my conclusion, we three are the best of friends.

An Open Letter to Amenhotep III/Jay-Z

Wow, you were a hard person to pinpoint. Even when I was crying my eyes out over your producer Pharrell while listening to your song, I had no idea. Pharaoh Shawn, it gives me great honor to have found you now and to bring to you this enlightenment, as I have restored you to your divine sovereignty! I've found your land (Thebes), wife (Michelle/Tiye), sons (Barack/Akhenaten IV), and viziers. I've saved you a great deal of time, as you discover more about who you really are, and you can thank me by introducing me to your friends Gwen and Chris–*wink-wink*. Jay, I do have another reading that I would like to share with you in person or you can read it in a future book.

Hey Jay, I even found your chain!

Pharaoh Amenhotep III

King Hova,

I copy!

Your past life daughter-in-law,
Jarnalia Jennings *the Egyptian Resurrector*

A monumental statue of Amenhotep III and Queen Tiye.
Resurrected today as: Shawn Carter and Michelle Obama.

Jay-Z's current wife was not part of the 18th Egyptian Dynasty, but the plot does thicken! *So, stay tuned.*

Crown Prince Thutmose of the 18th Egyptian Dynasty

Father: Pharaoh Amenhotep III

Mother: Queen Tiye

Title: Prince of Egypt

Other Notable Kin: Amenhotep IV aka Akhenaten was his younger brother and he was Tutankhamun's uncle.[34]

Crown Prince Thutmose was the eldest son of Amenhotep III and Chief Queen Tiye, and he was given this title when he was a child, with the hopes that he would be his father's successor. Thutmose never was able to leave behind a legacy as ruler of Egypt because he died an untimely death.[35]

Prince Thutmose served as a priest of Ptah in ancient Memphis. His full royal titles are on the sarcophagus of his pet cat: Crown Prince, Overseer of the Priests of Upper and Lower Egypt, High Priest of Ptah in Memphis and Sm-priest (of Ptah). Thutmose is most remembered for the limestone sarcophagus of his cat, now in the Cairo Museum. The schist statuette of Thutmose is inscribed on three sides with this text:

"(right)...*the king's son the sem-priest Djhutmose*; (left) *I am the*

---

[34] "Thutmose (Prince)," Up/Closed, available at *https://upclosed.com/people/thutmose-3/*.

[35] "Thutmose (Prince)," Up/Closed, available at *https://upclosed.com/people/thutmose-3/*.

servant of this noble god, his miller; (front) *Incense for the Ennead of the western necropolis.*"[36]

The cat sarcophagus of Prince Thutmose establishes that he was indeed the eldest son of Amenhotep III since it stated his title of crown prince. Prince Thutmose died sometime during the third decade of Amenhotep III's kingship. In his place, his younger brother Amenhotep IV, better known as Akhenaten, succeeded to the throne.[37]

With the powers vested in me, I resurrect Crown Prince Thutmose from his Egyptian tomb. Today, he incarnated as...

[36] Aidan Dodson, "Crown Prince Djhutmose and the Royal Sons of the Eighteenth Dynasty," Journal of Egyptian Archeology, 1990.

[37] Aidan Dodson, "Crown Prince Djhutmose and the Royal Sons of the Eighteenth Dynasty," Journal of Egyptian Archeology, 1990.

“Prince” Roger Nelson

1958–2016

Crown Prince Thutmose incarnated back with the same title, *Prince*. He must have wanted us to know that he was here. Even the symbol that we all have come to identify him by looks strikingly similar to the Egyptian ankh! In this incarnation, Prince brought with him a wide range of musical talents, and he held the world spellbound. I can clearly see that Prince was searching for a deeper truth, beyond what's fed to us as truth.

How did this come to me?

I looked in this direction prior to February of 2017. For the past five years now, I have been researching the 18th Egyptian Dynasty and I have come across the name Crown Prince Thutmose several times. I remember wondering if I could connect Prince the singer to the ancient Egyptian Crown Prince Thutmose. The name Prince tells you that he's royalty and stands apart from the others, but upon further investigation, I couldn't see any other tell-tale signs beyond the obvious one.

Now, let's zoom in on February 10, 2017. It was a Friday and I was home watching Chris Tucker on *Steve Harvey*. During the interview, Chris Tucker shared that Michael Jackson used to take him to see Prince! His exact words were, *"The King took me to meet, the Prince*!" Chris's statement had piqued my curiosity quite a bit—it was uniquely articulated just enough to arouse my antennas. I would read right into a hidden and deeper meaning within that statement. Ironically—no, it's never ironic—at that very moment I was actually working on this chapter, specifically Chief Queen Tiye's ancient Egyptian legendary story, and I had written her son's name, Crown Prince Thutmose, a few times already.

A few days passed and it was now Monday, February 13, 2017. I was watching *Entertainment Tonight's* Grammy review. I saw Pharaoh Amenhotep III holding his current daughter, and the narrator had made a reference to what Jay-Z's little girl was wearing at this event. A pink prince tuxedo outfit in honor of the late great Prince.

Amenhotep III was sitting with the personification of his past life son, while his current daughter is also paying homage to his past life son. That was no coinkydink, there was a profound message right there, waiting for me to see it. I felt that I needed to revisit my initial assumption about the Purple Reign Prince. I could see if one of my clairvoyants would confirm this for me or I could just ask Dorrian myself. However, it wasn't always a guarantee dealing with my spirit guide Dorrian, for he could easily utter what I hate to hear the most from him: "Dorrian, can't tell you that!" Nevertheless, I needed to know if Prince Roger Nelson was the 18th Egyptian Dynasty Crown Prince Thutmose, the son of Pharaoh Amenhotep III and Queen Tiye.

Eventually, I drifted over to my spirit guide Dorrian. I put on my headphones and played my binaural beats to communicate with him through the process of automatic writing. I asked Dorrian, if Prince Roger Nelson was ancient Egypt's Crown Prince Thutmose. Dorrian spelled out "Yes" in cursive through my hand and pen. Internally, I was elated and thought, *I knew it, I knew it*! I had not experienced any dreams cluing me into the Purple Reign Prince, I just read further into the clues that were right before my face. Ultimately, this sacred intel was intended for me to ascertain.

In my writing project, I am presently resurrecting the first royal Egyptian family, "The Dynasty," and as you can clearly see, this ancient wisdom was not going to be overlooked. Even though I put two and two together and resurrected a dormant ancient prince by myself, I felt I still needed some more compelling evidence, such as an official intuitive reading. Considering this, I went knocking on Golden Rose's cyber door with my question.

From: 2xQueen2xGoddess
To: Golden Rose
Mar 27, 2017, at 6:38 AM

Greetings, Golden Rose!

I'm writing a book, so I'm on a mission.

Can you confirm the musician Prince of the 20th century was

Crown Prince Thutmose of the 18th Egyptian Dynasty, it just came to me back in February.

I mentioned it to Dorrian and he confirmed that my findings were accurate.

And do you think Prince knew who he was? He seemed to have understood that there is much more going on with life than what is told to us by mainstream media.

Thank You,
Jarnalia Jennings

From: GOLDEN ROSE
To: 2xQueen2xGoddess
Mar 28, 2017, at 12:55 PM

Hello, Jarnalia (Nefertiti),

Thanks for having another reading with me. I hope that I can help again.

Now as far as the musician Prince of the 20th century, I get really sparkly and sizzle sensations when connecting him to Crown Prince Thutmose of the 18th Egyptian Dynasty. So, I also get a yes with this! And there is also a very powerful energy coming through around this. Because he was very influential in this past life, as well as the most recent one. And such a strong energy of making an impact. That I feel he knew of his connection to this past life and actually used some of his past life influence to both naturally and consciously affect the world. As there is much more to him than that which meets the eye, and I see he did delve into the spiritual or magical at times in the most recent one. Which only enhanced his charisma and ability to tap into source.

So, I hope this helps to validate your questions today and provide further enthusiasm on your journey.

Sincerely,
GOLDEN ROSE

Amenhoptep-Huy Egyptian Vizier of the 18th Dynasty

Father: Heby

Mother: Unknown

Ruling Pharaoh Served Under: Amenhotep III

Burial: TT40

Amenhotep-Huy was the high steward of Memphis and vizier of Amenhotep III in the 18th Dynasty. With this title, he was one of the highest officials at the royal court. Amenhotep-Huy was also director of Upper and Lower Egypt and overseer of all the works of the king.[38]

Amenhotep-Huy, was a member of an influential family. His father, Heby, was mayor of Memphis. His brother, Ramose, was also a vizier under Amenhotep III and Akhenaten, as evidenced by his tomb. His son, Ipy, was high steward under Akhenaten. The family's accomplishments are one of the rare cases where an influential family kept its high position under the latter king.[39]

With the powers vested in me, I resurrect Vizier Amenhotep-Huy from his tomb TT40. Today, he has incarnated as...

[38] "Amenhotep, son of Hapu," available at https://www.britannica.com/biography/Amenhotep-son-of-Hapu.

[39] Anneke Burt, "Amenhotep Huy," page by Anneke Bart, available at https://mathstat.slu.edu/~bart/egyptianhtml/kings%20and%20Queens/Amenhotep-Huy.html.

Seeker ShabazzAllah

I wished our introduction could have started out like an Eric B and Rakim song. It would have gone like this: I seen him in the subway on my way to Brooklyn; he said, hello good lookin is this seat tooken... On the A-train, he was picking at my brain, he couldn't get my number, he couldn't get my name. But our reunification did not start off like that at all. You see, I have a cousin who is on a long hiatus at Penn State—*wink-wink*. My cousin would call and chop it up with me on the telephone regularly. As a result, it was becoming quite costly for my cousin to stay in touch with his family and friends. He told me that one of his boys on the inside with him had a hook-up on a phone plan. Under the circumstances, he needed me to give this dude some of my information the next time we spoke.

The next time I conversed with my cousin, Papa Doc, he said the guy was standing by and that I needed to give him that information now. So, Papa Doc puts this guy on the telephone and the dude said, "*Peace*!" When I heard his voice, my whole existence came to a complete halt. It was happening again! Now, I've had this experience once before, in my algebra class back in high school. A classmate was trying to get help with his math problem from our teacher, Ms. Halley. He was acting as if he already had the knowledge to the information he was seeking. Ms. Halley grew agitated with the student and yelled, "I've graduated three times!" When I heard that, it was as if the Universe was speaking directly to me, because later on in my educational journey, I too graduated three times.

Again, the guy said, "*Peace*!" I was mesmerized by this kismet experience and I felt like I was on a 10-second delay. My inner consciousness was reading the familial connection. After we took care of business, he put my cousin back on the telephone. I immediately asked Papa Doc, "Who is he?" And my cousin responded, "That's my man Shabazz!" Then, unknowingly, I told Papa Doc he was on my level. I asked my cousin what he looked like? Papa Doc said, "I don't know!" Like I was crazy to ask him to size up another man like that! Pushing for a response, I asked what celebrity he looked like? Papa Doc was growing slightly irritated with me. But finally, Papa Doc gave me something, I could work with. He said, "Shabazz reminds me of Mos Def." I told my cousin to tell Shabazz I said, "What's up?"

The next time Papa Doc called me, he put Shabazz on the telephone, so I could personally explain to him what I meant by him being on my level. He also wanted me to personally give Shabazz my contact number directly.

In late 2004, Shabazz sent me a short letter or card in the mail due to our business transaction. I remember it being Christmastime, but it couldn't have been a Christmas Card because Seeker studied under the Elijah Muhammad. So, maybe the brief letters said, Happy Holidays or Happy New Year! I really can't remember anymore. It's been well over 15 years now, and every letter and card that Seeker ever sent to me over the course of our nine year friendship when he was locked up became embers in the September wind.

By 2005, Shabazz and I became quite chatty over the telephone. Mr. Shabazz has many names, and one of his monikers for himself is Livie Lux. It stands for Living Luxuriously. He called me his gal-pal and we would write each other all the time. When he wrote me, it felt like Christmas! This man had such a way with his words. I had never been so emotionally swayed by any man before until I met Livie. Mr. Shabazz's personality is smooth as a *mutherfucker*! He's wise beyond his years, witty, politically astute, and he has a deep innate wisdom. Then again, Mr. Shabazz's personality reminded me of someone else I knew. Someone I preferred to keep the hell away from—my biological father, ***Qulius***.

During this time in my life as Seeker's gal-pal, Beno and I were busy bees. We were always on the go, we were social creatures then, and we had a life outside of our home. Even if it snowed, I would be out driving in it, going somewhere or another. That changed. I became so infatuated with Livie, I started waiting around the house just to receive his calls. My aunt, Mama, had even taken notice that I was hanging around the house more just to wait for a phone call from a nigga in jail.

One day, Mama was at my house and I must have told her that I was waiting around for Livie to call. When he called, she wanted to speak with him. She got on the telephone and said something to Livie about me paying for his phone calls. Knowing Livie, he probably said, "Rest assure, lady, I pay for all my calls!" I then heard my aunt say, "Oh," and she softened her tone. As a matter of fact, over the course of our nine-year friendship, Seeker often sent me money and he ***never*** asked me to reciprocate the gesture.

Eventually, I journeyed up to Virginia's Penn State to meet Mr. Shabazz in person. I remembered seeing him and thinking to myself, "*He doesn't look like much*!" He was short, but I thought about his grand personality over the telephone, coupled with his brilliant and intimate words on paper…this is what had warranted my visit. During that visit, Livie and I talked, and laughed, and took a picture together. At the end of our visit, he kissed me before we parted ways. It was weak too! He tried to stick his whole tongue down my throat! Yucky, desperado! But it did not take away from a strong feeling that I was experiencing after the visit. While driving home, I was bumpin' *De La Soul's Greatest Hits* CD and I felt a euphoria emitting from my being. The feeling was distinctive. I felt energized. I felt charged to the max!

Livie was the first man to have ever called me a queen. At that time, I thought it was a sweet little sentiment and thought it was customary for a Muslim man to outwardly give respect toward their female counterparts. This assumption would prove to be inaccurate, because in the ninth year of our friendship, I was betrayed, deceived, and hoodwinked by the *bazzhole*!

In the beginning, Mr. Shabazz and I were tight on paper and in the airways, as he used to put it. One thing for sure, you couldn't call him a gentleman. He referred to himself as a Diplomat. As I interacted with Seeker Shabazz, I learned Penn State housed some extraordinary men. In my opinion, these men have the potential to run corporations as CEO's. I was so proud to be acquainted with Mr. Shabazz. So much so, I would tell certain people that Livie was my main man. LOL!

In hindsight, I was a fool! I was telling people I was dating a nigga in prison and these same people would try to tell me that prisoners lie to women all the time. I thought, not my Livie. He and I had an understanding. Shabazz had about seven years left on his sentence. In that time, we stayed in contact periodically.

Through those years, one thing that was obvious, we had a very strong twin-like bond. I remembered him telling me we were more like twins then him and his own twin sister. For example, when I moved to Jacksonville, Livie and I exchanged letters irregularly. However, on the morning of March 6, 2008, Beno and I were involved in a car accident with a crane operating truck. We both walked away unscathed, but we were emotionally shaken up. The next week, I received a letter from Livie written on the same day of our car accident. I was shocked! It was like he knew something was up.

When Livie used to call me, he would tell me all this lovey dovey shit and I would experience something really unusual. I could actually feel him walking down to the bottom of my belly, invading a space to where only I could go. I remember telling him to stop it because I couldn't take the love and I didn't want to feel that feeling. I think it must have been that twin flame love.

Now, it's around 2012 and it's confirmed that I was Sekhmet and even Queen Nefertiti. I immediately zeroed in on Seeker Shabazz as I was trying to piece together if he was Amenhotep IV or the creator god, Ptah, Sekhmet's husband. Livie was certainly a charmer, someone who can captivate his audience, and he had a sense of greatness about himself and deep wisdom. I used to frequently tell him he was a wise old owl. In my quest to understand who I am or was, I wanted to know if Mr. Shabazz was my Akhenaten, for he certainly could foot the bill. Again, I went and found another reader, different from the first reader who told me I was Sekhmet and Queen Nefertiti. It wasn't the *Maury Show*, but the results were in. Again, the reading brought back three confirming declarations: I am Queen Nefertiti, Mr. ShabazzAllah was not Akhenaten, *but he served me in that lifetime*!

In my search for Akhenaten, I would tell Livie of my unusual findings and he would actually listen. Our friendship was solid. I could tell him anything. I was totally confident in sharing my true self with him. Even when I discovered Akhenaten was President Barack Obama II, I articulated my findings to Livie. He said, "I could see that." During those years, when we were friends, he never judged me. He might have said, I was wired weird like him. I just thought that was his cute way of showing me that it's okay that I'm different.

My Deciphering Technique

One day, I used my trusted deciphering technique on Livie Lux's legal name to see what I would find within his name. I deciphered something quite majestic! I actually found Amenhotep-Huy, an Egyptian vizier. I was like, *Damn, that was easy,* as I hit my imaginary red Staples button. The following day, I was watching television and I saw a clip for an upcoming nightly talk show, that was featuring a little short man name Chuy! I viewed that as immediate confirmation because I saw the name Huy in Chuy.

I found out that Amenhotep-Huy was a scribe. Interesting, because I would always tell Livie that he was a great writer, great at wordplay. He is a very clever man and could make up phrases to make you think or smile for miles. Seeker was a phenomenal person and many people took advice from him; he is swift with a gift. Amenhotep-Huy was vizier to Amenhotep III—*Jay-Z*! So, I printed out Amenhotep-Huy's information and his picture and mailed it to Lawrenceville for Livie to read all about his past self, for I knew without a shadow of a doubt that Livie Lux was who I resurrected him to be without any clairvoyant telling me beforehand.

Egyptian Connection

Remember Livie's moniker is Livie Lux. Amenhotep-Huy governed Luxor in Thebes.

Our Shared Connections

Livie and I had more twin connections than anything else. When I first started talking to Livie, the neighborhood I lived in was called Waverton Place, and Livie was living in Waverly, VA. Also, Livie was from Brooklyn, and I lived on Brookland Drive.

An Open Letter to Mr. Bazzhole

You deceived me so badly. I would have never expected you to mistreat me the way you did, and in front of others. I guess I was got by one of the four horsemen, huh? I was under the impression that we were honest with one another and mature enough to keep it 400. I didn't care about you moving on to the next woman because she had the house, the cars, the money, and the security.

Im'ma use some supreme mathematics of my own. You 8 with me over the telephone for nine years; you came home and 8 me in five months. Without any delay, you 8 with someone else. I was devastated. I see you finally got what you wanted! A congratulations is in order on fatherhood. Your young lad will have a remarkable man to look up to. Despite me being bent over us, my spiritual essence respects you enough to hold space for you, as I totally understand that you have to experience living your life in the way you chose to experience it for your own soul's growth.

Liv, you always had a friend in me and you should not have ever cut that friendship cord. Spiritually speaking, I'm the closest person to you on this planet, although I should be super elated that I was saved from your personality disorders. Listen up, because I am in your face. I am a gift from the Gods and a male suitor must be "ordained by those Gods" to be with me. And, Bazzhole, ***I see it wasn't you*!** Livie, you told me I was a queen and I told you that I was a goddess!

Initially, you had Option #1 in the palm of your hand and you fuckin' 8 it for the convenience of Option #2! Now look at me. Maybe you should have rethought your options! By birthright, baby, I'm always going to be in your "supreme mathematics," –Knowledge-Knowledge, Wisdom-Wisdom, Goddess-Goddess!

PEACE

Livie's Open Past Life Readings

From: Matter of Fact Sandra
To: 2xQueen2xGoddess
Sent: Mon, Feb 20, 2012 10:28 pm
Subject: Your Email Reading with Sandra 2/20/12
Jarnalia Jennings DOB:11-22-77 Local Virginia Beach VA

Question 1: Well, I started to see the connections that we have between the two of us and I found out he was a husband in a past lifetime. I know I was Sekhmet in ancient Egypt and I was told that I was also Queen Nefertiti. So, I am curious to know if Shabazz was Sekhmet's husband, Ptah, or Queen Nefertiti's husband, Akhenaten, or both or neither? And if he was a husband of mine in a lifetime before that is not related to ancient Egypt, then what type of relationship did we have?

Greetings Jarnalia!

What a beautiful name. I am pleased to make your acquaintance. I hope you are well. Thank you for your purchase. After reviewing your information and questions, I feel that this format is best for getting you the information you want to know. I receive my information through visions and auditory messages from my Spirit Guides. I will explain what I am seeing or hearing, but if you have questions, please feel free to ask for clarification. Let's take a look at your questions: I do feel that you and Shabazz share a past life, however it is nothing so grand as that of the

Egyptian Neteru. And you are probably aware that Akhenaten was not so keenly spiritual as Nefertiti. I am sensing that you were connected in that lifetime; however, I feel that Shabazz was a member of the priesthood of Amen Ra, and that the two of you connected on that spiritual level. Because Akhenaten believed in only one deity and tried to wipe out the Ancient Paganism, that is, multiple gods and goddesses, you, as Nefertiti, had to meet in secret–often on the Astral or Aetheric level of existence–to practice your true beliefs, much in the same way as you and Shabazz are doing now. So, you were not married, but you did have a very close and important spiritual connection.

Sandra

After this reading, I had a second reading done by Angel and Guides. Also, I forwarded this reading to my trusted intuitive consultant KareBear to double check its contents. She said, everything was correct except for the "Greek God" comment.

From: 2xQueen2xGoddess
To: Angel & Guides
Wednesday, June 06, 2012 7:14 AM

Angel and Guides: Bonjour!

There is this man named ShabazzAllah.

He is the only man on this planet that I cherish dearly.

I met Shabazz through my cousin while both were incarcerated together.

I found Shabazz "instantly" intriguing and he reminds me of my birthfather Qulius so much. Shabazz is very very wise; beyond his 37 years. He's ancient in his wisdom. Shabazz is a Muslim.

However, I think this is the way he channels he's spiritualism, because he is very very spiritual, on a much deeper level. Shabazz and I are dynamic together, we have conversations without a telephone and we have a very strong unique bond like– we are two particles of energy with instant communication.

My Shabazz knows when something is minor or majorly wrong with me before I can tell him.

It's like twin communication.

Shabazz is a twin, but not mine. He has conveyed to me that we connect more so than his actual twin sister.

Recently, Shabazz visited me twice mentally! I heard him in my head telling me, "Hey, Baby," as I was about to fall asleep; but, now that I think about it, I sent him a message–I wrote him something in the sky and I'm thinking he just responded. I guess!

Prior to me finding you, Angel, I asked the free clairvoyant about Shabazz: she said there is a "strong bond there" and he was my husband and I use to help him out, I guess with illegal stuff.

And, after you confirmed that I am the same soul as Sekhmet, I was trying to find out if Shabazz was Ptah (Sekhmet's husband). But, after some research on my part, I don't think Shabazz is Ptah.

So then, I asked another eBay psychic and she said she doesn't see us as married, but she sees us in Egypt when I was Queen Nefertiti.

Angel and Guides, I would love for you to tell me the real stories.

Question 1: What is Shabazz's role in ancient Egypt, when I was Queen Nefertiti?

Question 2: Why is our bond so strong?

Question 3: Did we spend any other lifetimes together? If so, details, please.

Namaste,
Queen Nefertiti

From: Angel and Guides
To: 2xQueen2xGoddess
Sent: Friday, June 8, 2012, 12:44 PM
Subject: RE: 7.99 special

Hello Nefertiti,

How exciting. I agree that you and Shabazz were not husband and wife in ancient Egypt. But I do believe he served you. I am hearing the word scribe but I am not sure that is the correct word. He was a scholar then and served as an advisor and personal counselor. I think he gave you legal advice as well as spiritual advice. He was tapped in during that lifetime as well as now. You trusted him unconditionally and he read you very well. You had an unbelievable connection then as well. You kept it professional. But I see you waking up in the middle of the night because he had connected with you in your sleep to warn you about impending danger. Due to that, you were able to escape harm. His energy in that lifetime was similar to one of the gods that they believed in. I don't know the name, but he would just smile and deny it when he was asked. He was warm, personable, very discreet but SOOOOOOO knowledgeable. Even then he appeared to have ancient wisdom. I honestly believe he was one of the Greek Gods reincarnated. So, the way that you describe him and your connection is absolutely right on.

You have chosen to keep this bond for many lifetimes. As you describe it–two particles of the same energy basically. Each is a part of the other–not always in a romantic capacity–but sometimes as husband/wife, student/teacher, etc. You have always brought peace and comfort to each other as well as sharing wisdom. It will continue in other lifetimes as well. Just in different capacities.

One other lifetime that I am being shown, Shabazz appears to be your father. You are a male in that lifetime. You don't get along very well as you don't understand him, and you want to live your own life rather than what he expects you to do. You don't want to walk the same path he is and so you become rebellious. There are many conflicts and you get very angry as you feel you aren't even allowed to live your own life. You were very athletic. I feel you were in the Olympics then–and threw a lance or spear. You were very good. You wanted to be known for your own skills, but Shabazz felt you should have higher aspirations than being an athlete. However, as you got a couple years older you became a fierce warrior and helped defend him. He admired that ability and grew to love you and respect you for your abilities in that area. I see you holding him as he is dying as he was killed by enemies who infiltrated his home. You went on to become very famous for your ferocious fighting skills.

Many blessings,
Angel

On my 39th Birthday, I ventured over to KareBear for a birthday reading, and this time I just spelled it all the way out.

From: 2xQueen2xGoddess
To: KareBear
Sent: Saturday, November 19, 2016, 7:25 AM
Subject: Birthday Question

Karen, I hope this isn't an overreach and I'm not trying to take advantage of you, but I wanted the 2nd question to be a bit different.

I wanted to know if you could just say yes/no, by questions 1 and 2 with no explanation.

1. Was Dr. Martin King Jr. Amenhotep III?

2. Was Shabazz Amenhotep-Huy the Vizer to Amenhotep III?

Much Appreciation,
Jarnalia Jennings

From: KareBear
To: 2xQueen2xGoddess
Sent: Monday, November 21, 2016, 3:16 PM
Subject: Birthday Question

1. Was Dr. Martin King Jr. Amenhotep III? No

2. Was Shabazz Amenhotep-Huy the Vizer to Amenhotep III? Yes

Love, Karen

I still had no idea that Jay-Z was actually Pharaoh Amenhotep III when I had this reading done. However, that enlightenment would be brought to my awareness only within a few short weeks.

Mr. Seeker ShabazzAllah, I found the pharaoh you served under, Amenhotep III (Jay-Z), and I even found your ancient Egyptian past life brother who was a vizier as well. Enjoy the resurrection, Amenhotep-Huy!

Ramose
Egyptian Vizier of the 18th Dynasty

Father: Heby

Mother: Unknown

Ruling Pharaoh Served Under: Amenhotep III and Amenhotep IV

Notable Kin: Vizier Amenhotep-Huy

Burial: Thebes TT55[40]

Ramose was born into an influential family. His father was the mayor of Memphis, Heby, who was in office at the beginning of Amenhotep's III reign. The brother of Ramose was the high steward of Memphis Amenhotep (Huy).

This ancient Egyptian noble was vizier under both Pharaoh Amenhotep III and his son, Akhenaten. He served under Amenhotep III in his last decade of reign, then he served under Akhenaten in the beginning of his reign. Vizier Ramose appears on jar labels found in the palace of King Amenhotep III at Malkata, along with, Vizier

[40] "Tomb of Ramose (TT55)," Egyptsites, February 7, 2009 available at *https://egyptsites.wordpress.com/2009/02/07/tomb-of-ramose-tt55/*.

AmenhotepHuy. Both Viziers are also shown side by side in the temple of Soleb.

In the New Kingdom, the office of the vizier was divided between the geographical region of North and South. However, it is not entirely clear whether Ramose was the Northern Vizier or the Southern Vizier.[41]

With the powers vested in me, I resurrect Vizier Ramose from his Theban Tomb (TT55). Today, he has incarnated as...

[41] Arielle Kozloff, *Egypt's Dazzling Sun: Amenhotep III and His World*, The Cleveland Museum of Art, 1992.

Martin Lawrence

"Wassup, Wassup, Wassup!"

Mister funny man himself was a serious Egyptian vizier to an influential pharaoh.

My Intuitive Dream

On March 22, 2016, I dreamt I was walking on a sidewalk and saw Martin Lawrence, who was walking toward me. I said, "Hello, Mr. Lawrence." He laughed, then said hello back. When I spoke, I was veering off the sidewalk to get to my car, which was in an open parking lot. I noticed that Martin was with his two sons, they were small, and they were lagging behind. Martin looked back at his children and said, "Come on," in a very kind and patient voice. When I woke up, I had no feeling about the dream. However, I knew I had to write it down, just in case I had to draw upon it later.

It was now late 2016. I was sitting in the Kolache Factory, having my usual breakfast before going into work—a chicken enchilada dredged in chipotle tabasco sauce. When I walked into the Kolache Factory, the television was playing a very old episode of *Martin*. On this episode, Tommy Davidson made a guest appearance, and his character's name was Varnel Hill.

I used to think Mr. Shabazz (Chief Vizier Amenhotep-Huy) resembled Tommy Davidson from the pictures he used to send me from Penn State. Occasionally, I would tease him by telling him so. When I sat down to eat my kolache, Varnel Hill was sitting down in the studio being interviewed by Martin. Each time Martin asked Varnel a question, Varnel would embellish on how good his life was as a response. My analytical brain started churning, evaluating this scene to the letter. I just knew within the background context of this scene there was a major clue waiting to be seen.

When I use to write Mr. Shabazz at Penn State, I sent the letter to Lawrenceville, Virginia. Keyword; Lawrence. Just like Lawrence in Mr. Martin Lawrence. Once again, Tommy Davidson put me in the mind of Mr. Shabazz. In my cerebral cortex, I was actually seeing Martin

Lawrence sitting with a replica of Mr. Shabazz. I was almost certain that I was registering something exceptional within that fictitious interview between Varnel Hill and Martin.

At that point, I still was under the assumption that MLK was Amenhotep III. Then I realized Martin Lawrence shared MLK's first name, so I thought that was slightly significant. In retrospect, I really wasn't clear on what I was witnessing that morning. Nevertheless, it was certainly noteworthy, and I wrote it down as a clue.

When I was a teenager, Martin Lawrence got married in Norfolk, Virginia. Well, at least that's how I remembered it. His wife then was a beauty queen who was crowned Miss Virginia, and she herself was from Chesapeake, Virginia. I remembered everybody and their mommas running out to the Marriott Downtown Norfolk just to get a glimpse of Martin. But not me or my momma! In retrospect, that was symbolic! You see, in my mind, with Martin's then-wife being crowned as Miss Virginia, I saw the symbolism connecting Martin Lawrence to royalty. In addition, one of his daughter's names has a very close semblance to our ancient land Amarna, just remove the N.

Around the same time, I found out that the ancient Egyptian crown prince was the 20th century "Purple Rain"/ Reign Prince. I wondered if Vizier Ramose was Martin Lawrence. This thought came to me after looking into Martin Lawrence's backstory. This was also coupled with a picture Mr. Shabazz posted of himself on Facebook. After analyzing that photograph, I could not dismiss the green Lawrence street sign in the background. Even though that street sign was a very minute part of that picture, it screamed the loudest.

I now knew Amenhotep III was Jay-Z. I also already knew Mr. Shabazz was Chief Vizier Amenhotep-Huy. Taking all of that into account, I grabbed my headphones and pulled up my binaural beats on my computer and struck up a conversation with Dorrian. I wrote, "Dorrian, was Martin Lawrence the 18th Egyptian Dynasty's Vizier Ramose?" To my surprise, Dorrian answered with a yes! I then posed the question differently, as I was trying to trick Dorrian. This time

I would asked if Martin Lawrence was a vizier for Amenhotep III? Again, Dorrian answered with a yes. I took Dorrian's confirmation into consideration, yet I still took it to Golden Rose.

From: 2xQueen2xGoddess
To: Golden Rose
Mar 27, 2017 at 6:29 AM

Hello Golden Rose, I'm back with more!

Can you confirm that Martin Lawrence the comedian was Ramose, vizier to Amenhotep III in the 18th Egyptian Dynasty?

I believe he was because the other vizier, Amenhotep-Huy (Mr. ShabazzAllah), is in a photograph today and he is posing with a subway sign that reads: Jay St Metro, in honor of Jay-Z, and in the background, I can see a street sign that reads Lawrence. Too, back in Nov/Dec 2016, I was watching an old episode of Martin the TV sitcom and Martin was sitting down with someone who I used to say Amenhotep-Huy (Seeker) resembled. For me, it was a very defining moment watching them two in the same frame, as if the Universe was giving me a clue at that very moment.

My spirit-guide Dorrian, said I'm right. And if I am, I have resurrected all of Jay-Z's (Amenhotep III) : closet viziers and I've resurrected two brothers of the Egyptian Dynasty! I'm gifted!

Thank You,
I Am Nefertiti

From: Golden Rose
To: 2xQueen2xGoddess
Mar 28,2017 at 12:55 PM

Hello, Jarnalia (Nefertiti),

Thanks for having another reading with me. I hope that I can help again.

With regards to Martin Lawrence. I get goosebumps with this energy, connection and sharing. So definitely get a hit that he was "Ramose," vizier to Pharaoh Amenhotep III in the 18th

Egyptian Dynasty. As the connection feels very strong, deep and synchronistic as if getting your attention to confirm what needs to be made known. Of this truth. In all that you are being given. And so I get a yes with this!

So I hope this helps to validate your questions today, and provide further enthusiasm on your journey.

Sincerely,
GOLDEN ROSE

An Open Letter to Martin Lawrence

Where do I start with you?

First, thank you from the bottom of my heart for showing up and entertaining me when I was an adolescent. You made my days a little more bearable while living in my mother's house. As I reflect over my life, you helped in creating some good memories for me through your comedy.

In 1993, Aundria and I must have been around 16 years old. I remember she had spent the night at my house, and we watched *You So Crazy,* and we laughed our young assess off. Then, we would go on and recite the crazy shit you said in your stand-up. The main one that got us were the jail poses. That shit was laugh out loud funny, and she and I could relate to that story even at 16 years old. Then, it was your eponymous show, Martin. I loved the fictitious love between you and Gina. But the show went away, and it felt like I couldn't go on without *Martin*.

Many years later, I had a baby boy whose name is Beno. Let me tell you how you influenced him too. When we lived in Harvard Apartments, Beno was two years old, and he would watch *Life* literally non-stop. Then there came *Big Momma,* and this show would play non-stop for many years! When I say non-stop, I mean it even played as background noise while he played, ate, and slept. Since Beno was a little tiny boy, he always wore costumes, even if it wasn't Halloween. Any day of the week, I would take him to the mall, and he would be dressed in a Spiderman costume.

However, as he grew older, around nine years old, he started to wear his Big Momma costume. He would wear an old lady wig, this was given to him by my grandma, his old Christening gown and whatever else he could find, then he would stuff himself with extra clothes in the front and back. Beno loved you too, Martin.

One day, we were at my cousin's house with my aunt and her beau, when Beno ran upstairs to put on his Big Momma costume. When he came back down the stairs, he was dressed as Big Momma and in his hand was his old lady stick too. The little boy had also changed his voice in an effort to emulate a much older woman. He said, "I'm Big Momma"! My son thought he was going to get a reaction out of my aunt's man friend. Of course, my aunt and I were entertained by Beno's Big Momma persona. However, my aunt's man friend did not even look at Beno, he didn't think my son's girly act was funny at all. As a result, my son has never ever put that Big Momma costume on again.

Mr. Lawrence, thank you for your continued work. You've influenced my generation, as well as my son's generation. As a gift to you, I'm sharing with you your past, and you don't even have to thank me. I just ask that you hold space for me and please forgive me for conjuring up a story that sounds completely absurd. For me, your story is my life, it's my purpose this time around. Even if I tried to turn my attention away from these stories, they will not let me live them down because they must be told–*by me*. I am a key holder and the Egyptian Resurrector!

Sorry I had to "RunTelDat",
Jarnalia

Spiritual Lesson # 3 Meanings and Terms

What is a Twin Flame?

"A twin flame is a very special soulmate connection. You share the same immediate over-soul. In order to create polarity consciousness on 3-D Earth, your over-soul chose two separate expressions of itself, one male and one female, each perfectly balanced and complementary to the other. The two soul aspects may incarnate together, or one may remain on the Other Side (next dimensional level) while the other descends into this level of consciousness. You and your twin flame are perfectly complementary, like two sides of the same coin. These two individuals, possessing the same soul, are intuitively aware of each other, and spend a lifetime looking for the other."[42]

What is a Soul Mate?

This term often gets confused with true love. But soul mates are people who consist of your soul family, and this could be anybody you keep reincarnating with. Soul mates are here on earth to assist you with your spiritual growth. Not only are they assisting in the development of your soul's growth, but you are assisting them as well. Even animals can be your soul mates.

What is a Soul Family?

"Your soul family is the spiritual equivalent to your birth family here on earth. They may take the form of a relative here on earth or could be anyone in your life. When you meet them, they feel like your siblings, parents or children. You and your soul family share the same over-soul, so you are all aspects of the same soul."[43] For example, there is a very famous man who I have had 35 lifetimes with, and it has been stated that he is in my soul family. Stay tuned for that book!

---

[42] Poonam Bhartie KyronIndia Channel, "Soulmates, Soul Family, Soul Groups, Twin Flames," LinkedIn, December 17, 2016, available at *https://www.linkedin.com/pulse/soulmates-soul-family-groups-twin-flames-kryonindia-channel.*

[43] Kim Hutchinson, "Soulmates: Soul Family, Soul Groups and Twin Flames," in5d, November 21, 2014, available at *https://in5d.com/soulmates-soul-family-soul-groups-and-twin-flames/*

What are the Akashic Records?

The Akashic Records are the energetic records of all souls about their past lives, the present lives, and *possible* future lives. Each soul has its Akashic Records, like a series of books with each book representing one lifetime. The Hall, Library, of the Akashic Records is where all souls' Akashic Records are stored energetically. The information is stored in the Akashic field, also called zero-point field. They also contain our collective wisdom.[44]

[44] Akashic Records, available at *http://www.akashicrecordsofsouls.com/.*

7

The Afterlife Is Now, The Resurrection of the All Eyes on We Family

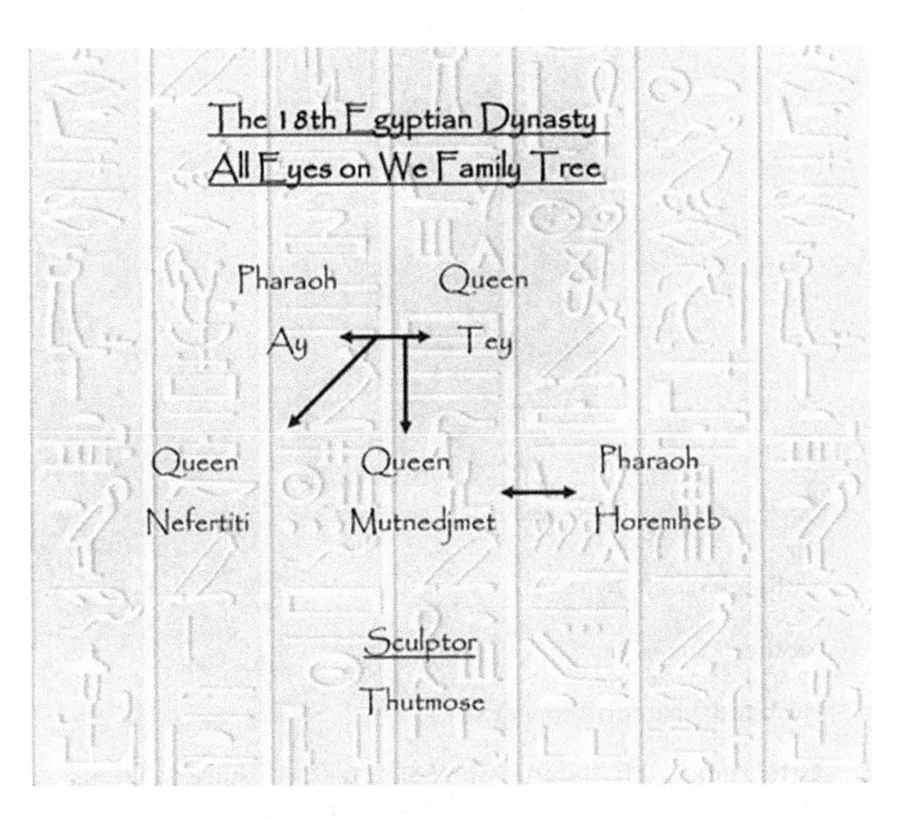
The 18th Egyptian Dynasty
All Eyes on We Family Tree
Pharaoh
Ay
Queen
Tey
Queen
Nefertiti
Queen
Mutnedjmet
Pharaoh
Horemheb
Sculptor
Thutmose

Queen Neferneferuaten Nefertiti King's Great Royal Wife of the 18th Egyptian Dynasty

"A Beautiful Woman Has Come"

Father: Pharaoh Aye

Mother: Queen Tey

Husband: Pharaoh Akhenaten

Offspring: Meritaten, Meketaten, Ankhesenpaaten, Neferneferuaten Tasherit, Neferneferure, and Setepenre. In addition to our girls, there was one son who was produced by a minor wife, known as King Tut.

Other Notable Relatives: Mutnedjmet's sister

Reign: 17 years

Buried: Unknown

I've read that Queen Nefertiti was one of the most mysterious and powerful women of Egypt. Historians don't quite know where Nefertiti came from, although they do believe she was born in Thebes. Nefertiti was the daughter of Pharaoh Aye/Ay and Queen Tey, but there still seems to be some controversy surrounding the true maternity of Nefertiti. In ancient records, Tey went down as Nefertiti's "nurse," or wet-nurse.[45]

Egyptologist have analyzed Tey's title for almost a century now and they have concluded that if Tey was the mother of me, Nefertiti, then her title would have read: *Mother of Pharaoh's Great Daughter* instead of *Nurse of Pharaoh's Great Wife.* From my perspective, anyone's boob I'm suckling from will be deemed my mother. Nefertiti also had a sister who was known as Mutnedjmet/Mutbenret, but I'm going to call her—Mutnedjmet and Sweet Mut throughout my story.

When Nefertiti was born, her father, Aye, was not pharaoh yet. However, he was working for the Egyptian government. In time, Aye ascended the ranks of the Egyptian military, from overseer of the horses to grand vizier working under his son-in-law, Akhenaten.[46] In addition, my father Aye also worked under our son King Tutankhamun as his grand vizier. Eventually, my father, took the Egyptian throne and he too became pharaoh of Egypt.

Nefertiti's family is made up of a king and three queens who lived in the wealthiest and most powerful Egyptian Dynasty, the 18th Dynasty. Here's to Queen Nefertiti's father, Pharaoh Aye, her mother, Queen Tey, and her sister, Queen Mutnedjmet!

Nefertiti and Akhenaten's Family

Nefertiti, "The Beautiful Woman Has Come," became a queen by marrying Amenhotep IV (former president Barack Obama II), who later changed his name to Akhenaten. I loved my husband, and just his name alone makes me blush today. It is speculated that I married him

---

[45] Joyce Tyldesley, "Nefertiti," Encyclopeadia Britannica, available at *https://www.britannica.com/biography/Nefertiti.*

[46] Arianna Sacco, "Opportunity Knocks: the kingship of Ay," Ancient Warfare Magazine, available at *https://www.karwansaraypublishers.com/awblog/opportunity-knocks-the-kingship-of-ay/.*

when I was 15 years old. Oh dear, that's awfully young! In our union, we gave birth to six lovely daughters, and I present to you our princesses in my Romper Room voice. I see Meritaten, Meketaten, Ankhesenpaaten, Neferneferuaten Tasherit, Neferneferure, and Setepenre. Now that's a lot of heads to comb. Oh, that's right, we kept ours shaved low! I, Queen Nefertiti, did not physically produce any male heirs to the throne, only heiresses. Even today Akhenaten has daughters, and guess what, in this lifetime, I birth a male heir. *Yay Yay*!

Although I, Nefertiti, wasn't Akhenaten's only wife. Yes, I was the chief queen, but he had other minor broads in his life, and one even popped out Tutankhamun, the notorious King Tut. Now, I wouldn't say that Tutankhamun is my stepson just because he wasn't my blood son. I would like to say he was my son produced by a surrogate, giving it a modern-day flair.

My Official Titles as Queen

In my legacy, I had many titles such as, "Hereditary Princess, Great of Praises, Lady of Grace, Sweet of Love, Lady of The Two Lands, Main King's Wife, his beloved, Great King's Wife, his beloved, Lady of all Women, and Mistress of Upper and Lower Egypt. "[47]

The King and Queen in the Beginning

According to my findings, Akhenaten and I ruled Egypt from either 1353 BC–1336 BC or 1351 BC–1334 BC. In the beginning of our reign, we dwelled in Thebes for several years and my husband went by his family's namesake, Amenhotep IV. In Egypt, it is customary for pharaohs to build statues and temples in honor of the gods. In Karnak, the main god of worship was Amun. Initially, my pharaoh husband followed the customs of his predecessors before him by making

[47] Wolfram Grajetki, *Ancient Egyptian Queens: a hieroglyphica dictionary,* Golden House Publications, 2005.

improvements to older temples in Karnak, however, he did not build any temples to satisfy Amun. My husband constructed and erected temples in honor of an unknown god—Aten. Soon, Amenhotep IV would break away from Egyptian tradition and we would completely abandon the capital Thebes altogether.

The Beginning of Amarna and the Worship of Aten

When Amenhotep IV changed his name to Akhenaten to show his loyalty to Aten, my name even received an upgrade as well. I was now known as Neferneferaten Nefertiti, which means Beautiful are the Beauties of Aten and Beautiful Woman Has Come. Oh my, what a mouthful!

As a result of my husband's new spiritual enlightenment, Akhenaten left the city of Thebes against the Egyptian priesthood's guidance and moved the capital 180 miles north of Thebes. Akhenaten erected a new city called Akhenaton, in honor of our new god, Aten. Pharaoh Akhenaten declared this location as the new capital of Egypt, and it would be called Amarna. As his wife, I, Queen Nefertiti, was right behind my man. I've read I am often depicted standing behind my husband Akhenaten, in offering scenes because it shows the role of the queen is in support of her husband.

Now in Amarna, Akhenaten changed the traditional religion from polytheism to monotheism. The Egyptian people had never heard of the practice of worshipping just one god, nor had they ever heard of this new god, Aten. As king and queen, we had the honor to bask in the magnificence of Aten's presence, and praise and worship in all of its glory. Aten was the mighty one, delivering to us the keys of eternal life. The rewards of Aten were handed down from Aten to us, and from us we handed down to the Egyptian people. ***All Praises to the Aten!***

I AM LEGEND

I first appeared in Thebes in the damaged tomb of the Royal Butler Parennefer (TT188), the new king Amenhotep IV, accompanied by a lady who is believed to be an early version of me. The pharaoh and his queen are worshipping Aten. I can also be found on the tomb of the vizier Ramose. I am shown standing behind my pharaoh husband Amenhotep IV in the "**Window of Appearance**," with Aten depicted over us while performing the rewards ceremony for viziers.[48]

Legend has it that Nefertiti was perhaps one of the most powerful women ever to have ruled. Her husband went to great lengths to display her as an equal. In several reliefs, she is shown wearing the crown of a pharaoh or smiting her enemies in battle. Despite this great power, Nefertiti disappears from all depictions after 12 years. The reason for her disappearance is unknown.[49]

This is a depiction of me/Queen Nefertiti smiting a female captive on a royal barge on a limestone relief. On display at Museum of Fine Arts, Boston.

[48] Anneke Bart, "Nefertiti," Ancient Egypt, available at *https://mathstat.slu.edu/~bart/egyptianhtml/kings%20and%20Queens/Nefertiti-inscriptions.html.*

[49] "Nefertiti," Biography.com, available at *https://www.biography.com/royalty/nefertiti.*

Iconic Bust

Where is the Iconic Bust of Nefertiti today?
Neues Museum Berlin, Germany
Who was the artist of this Masterpiece?
Sculptor Thutmose

There was a campaign to destroy everything Amarna, and yet my famous bust ***emerged from the ruins***. This sleeping beauty can't be eradicated from history, for she is Egypt's history. Queen Nefertiti resumed her position and she still commands your attention today.

My Letter to The People of Egypt

Come here, let me tell you something.

Come closer. Are you close enough?

Here's my secret, my soul is directly connected to a cosmic divinity. Within my being, I possess a tremendous amount of sacred wisdom that I wish to share with you in this day and in this time. These truths are within my soul's memories and they hold a message for you today. I can only assume wherever evolution is going, I must have a position in its transit.

I HAVE RETURNED FOR YOU.

I HAVE RETURNED TO REAWAKEN AND ENLIGHTEN THE IMMORTAL EGYPTIANS WHO HAVE LONG FORGOTTEN THEIR TRUE DIVINITY.

NOT ONLY THE EGYPTIANS, BUT I HAVE RETURNED TO ENLIGHTEN HUMANITY OF THEIR TRUE DIVINITY AS WELL.

THIS IS MY MISSION.

To Janelle Monae,

Yes, my crown is too heavy, I am Queen Nefertiti.

Dr. Gibson's taking back his pyramids and I'm trying to free Memphis City (Thebes).

Thanks for the recognition and I will preach!

Queen Nefertiti, the Egyptian Resurrector

The Sun and Me

The sun is a supernatural deity who is connected to an otherworldly god, and we are very familiar with each other. It is important to remember that in one lifetime, I was once the daughter of Ra, the sun god of ancient Egypt. In that life, my father wore the sun disc on his head, and I, his daughter, Sekhmet the lion goddess, wore the sun disc on my head as well. In another lifetime, I came back as Nefertiti, and I was paired up with a king who was transformed and inspired by another sun deity, Aten. My husband was so enlightened by the transmissions from the sun, that he went on to establish a new city, a new religion all around the sun deity, where he and I would bask in the glory of Aten's rays. I have a pretty persistent association with the sun god. In the words of Roy Ayers, "***Everybody loves the Sunshine***!"

What Burial?

They really don't know where I came from, and they don't know where I'm buried. Egyptian historians think I died circa 1330 BC in Amarna, Egypt.

No Sarcophagus, ha-ha!
No Mummy, ha-ha!
No real evidence of my death!

Eulogy to Nefertiti found on the boundary stelae of Akhenaten
And the Heiress, Great in the Palace, Fair of Face,
Adorned with the Double Plumes, Mistress of Happiness,
Endowed with Favours, at hearing whose voice the King rejoices,
the Chief Wife of the King, his beloved,
the Lady of the Two Lands,
Neferneferuaten-Nefertiti, May she live for Ever and Always.

Thank you, Pharaoh Akhenaten aka Pharaoh Obama II!

With the powers vested in me from the gods above and within, I resurrect myself and I bring myself forward. However, this queen goddess needs music. I desire the tune of GZA, Beneath the Surface Instrumental. Play this on a loop and I'll rise.

Today, I am…

Jarnalia Denise Jennings

Emerged from the ruins,
just to resurrect the souls of Egypt!

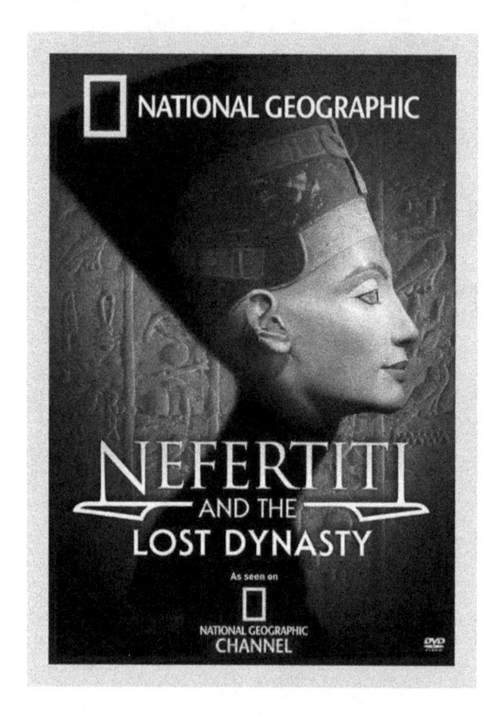

"*I'm not lost!* I found myself, my dynasty and I will resurrect them one by one."

Jarnalia Jennings, the Egyptian Resurrector

Why do I claim to be the late great Queen Nefertiti?

Why do I think I've lived as the most beautiful woman of the Nile? The icon for the ancient Egyptian brand. Are you saying it's preposterous? I can hear your thoughts from over here in Virginia Beach!

In the beginning of my self-discovery, I ran all over the internet just to disprove the enlightenment of the first whistleblower, only to have this grand illumination reaffirmed by many clairvoyants over and over again. With this reassurance, how could I refute them all?

Here's the 50-million-dollar question: why don't I remember this information for myself?

Spiritual Lesson #4

Here's something that I've learned from the teachings of Ramtha. When the body dies, the memories are stripped by the light. Having said that, when Queen Nefertiti died, my then brain/memories died with my then body. Meaning everything I did in that lifetime died with Queen Nefertiti's brain and body. Although my soul or oversoul houses all the memories from all my lifetimes—past, present, future, and parallel. You see, Jarnalia Jennings is just another face of my extensive oversoul.

I, Jarnalia Jennings, have concluded that I must be the version of my soul whose role it is to perform the task of resurrecting the forgotten souls of ancient Egypt through the process of writing a book. This past knowledge is ***hermetically sealed*** within me. I too am researching my own distant past life stories as I reveal myself to you. Thank you, to all the Egyptian historians for documenting our Golden Time of Day.

It's okay by me if you can't except my story or my new identity. But really think about what I am implying here beyond my own story and what this could mean for you. Even though you don't remember, you too have lived before in another time, in another land, and you subscribed to other belief systems in your past life. This is exactly what I've been conveying to you since the beginning of this book.

Posers

In the words of the late great Heavy D, "Many will come, but the chosen are few!" Everyone wants to be me, Queen Nefertiti! Haven't you notice that everyone seems to make the claim of being Queen Nefertiti reincarnated, but none of them can point out the other great royals from that same timeline!

Have you ever heard of a lady by the name of Nileen? Ever since she was a kid, Nileen had dreams of that time—when Queen Nefertiti reigned, and she just knew she was Queen Nefertiti in a former lifetime. Nileen was so compelled by her exploration she went out and surgically altered her face just to look more like her ***assumed*** once self. Even though when I was growing up, I didn't have any dreams about ancient Egypt at all, when I reflect on my life, I can see how Egypt has always been infused into it.

An Overview of Jarnalia

The absence of Egyptian dreams changed once I returned from the Sunshine State. Again, there's a quote by Virginia Woolf that I came across upon my return from Florida. I just love this quote. She says, "*Arrange the pieces that come your way.*" Can you believe I found myself doing just that? I call these pieces "encrypted clues," and they all came my way. I first took notice of them in Florida. At that time, they really did not make any sense to me at all. They were just enigmas. In hindsight, these encrypted clues were signaling two different Egyptian incarnations. One lifetime as Sekhmet; the Eye of RA, and the other—well just keep reading my ***magnum opus***!

From 2009 to 2011, Mrs. M&M never gave any insight into my

many incarnations in Egypt. I was only given stories of non-Egyptian lifetimes. My higher-self or the Universal Forces saw that this method wasn't cutting it and found a way to help me remember my ancient legacy as I walked into Egypt. It was around spring or summer of 2011 when I had an out-of-body-experience while sleeping.

My First Fully Conscious OBE

I, Jarnalia Jennings, found myself sitting in a lobby waiting for someone. The lobby was a small circular waiting area, and in the center of this lobby's waiting room was a round desk with two men standing there like they were attendants at a customer service desk. (Years after this OBE, I saw a commercial that's quite reminiscent of what I viewed—the Air Emirates commercial, where Jennifer Aniston is drinking at the bar on the plane.) The person I was waiting on and who came to assist me was an old boyfriend of mine named Ivory. When Ivory realized he was going to assist me, he was delighted with the honorary position that was bestowed upon him. He was selected to serve me—to take me up! However, Ivory had to put on a special blazer in order to be my escort and all his instructions were being given to him by the two agents at the desk.

I was walking up some stairs with Ivory and the stairs appears to be padded with red carpeting. The ambiance of the staircase reminded me of royalty. As we were going up the staircase, it reminded me of Nicole's townhouse. Nicole was a friend of mine when I was a teenager. She lived in a set of townhomes called Cedarwood. As I was going up the second flight of stairs, I could see three closed doors with a long black banister directly in front of them. When I got to the top of the stairs, the black banister had enough space where I could walk in between it and the doors. I walked past the first door that was labeled with the name of a country. I think it was Greece. Then I moved on to the next door and it too was labeled Rome or Persia. I said, ***"Wow! I got to remember this!"*** When I got to the third door, it too was labeled with a country, but I can't remember which.

Once I moved passed all of the closed doors, there was a fourth door that was wide open. The door had a label on it, just like all the others, and it was labeled EGYPT. This door was positioned off to the right of the first three doors like I was walking directly in its path the whole time.

Without any apprehension, I walked into the room and there were Egyptian artifacts on the shelves on the left side. (Back in 2015, I watched an old '80s video of Madonna's. In the video for "Who's that Girl" she walked into a room with different artifacts, some Egyptian. Well, my experience was very similar to that.) I was really flattered to be in this room and having this experience. I remembered picking up some of the artifacts, analyzing them and then putting them back in their place because I got distracted by Ivory. Ivory was going through a metamorphosis.

Flabbergasted, I could see all the stages of Ivory's metamorphosis, his experience was occurring right before my very eyes! Ivory transformed from blood to skeleton, back to himself, then to Livie (Amenhotep-Huy), and it was all happening really fast. I remembered there was a small window in this room a few feet away from me and it was sunny outside.

When I woke up, I was a little confused because I had been out of school for eons now, and Ivory of all people just so happened to pop up in my first fully aware astral travel. I had stopped considering Ivory a friend. I believe he was the culprit behind something that took place in my life, but I can't quite prove it was him for sure.

It was senior hook day, but I was no high school senior. It was the early '90s and I was just in middle school. My friends Christy and Tia and I were all skipping school and hanging out at Ivory's house on this particular day. While having a great time, Ivory's relatives came home, and we all hid. I believe I hid in the closet with Tia. Ivory's little cousin spotted him in his hiding spot and said in his preschooler's voice, "I see you, Ivy." That shit was too funny! Eventually, Ivory's relatives left, and we all came out of hiding. I clowned Ivory after the ordeal was over.

By this time, the school day was now over, and I walked home with my friends.

I was home alone around five o'clock when the school's absentee telephone notification came through. I thought I had gotten away with my crime of truancy. Later that night, someone placed a call to my mother and ratted me out. It was a boy who called.

Our mother/daughter relationship was already strained, and with Ivory interfering, it only created a more volatile situation for me. My mother got an orange extension cord and beat me with it. Then she started beating me with her bare hand. I reacted and hit her back. My mother ended up putting me out of the house at 14 years old around nine o'clock at night. I then walked to my grandparents' house, who lived about 10 minutes away by car. When I got there, it was 10 o'clock. In my personal opinion, I think my mother's reaction to the phone call was an overreaction. Of course, I was wrong for hitting my mother back, but I think my programming then was set to fight. Sorry, Mom! I ended up living with my grandparents for roughly eight months.

So, to see Ivory in this dream, extremely happy to guide me "up there," baffled the hell out of me. Ivory never knew the ramifications of his actions. He actually added lighter fluid to an already burning fire.

Why did I see Livie in Ivory's metamorphosis? Ironically, they both happen to share the same legal surname and they don't even know each other.

Hours later, I was at my temp job stuffing envelopes into duffle bags, and across from me, I happened to notice another female worker who was a few feet away, performing the same dull repetition as I. First, we assembled the Anthem membership papers in order. After we created the bundle package, we put them in a very large mailing envelope. Last, we took the membership packages and stuff them into a duffle bag for shipment. Simple. As I was in the flow of this boring routine, I just so happened to look up at the woman and noticed she had on a red t-shirt! The red t-shirt had the image of a human skeleton printed on it. I was shocked once my brain nudged its own memory. Seeing that red t-shirt,

I immediately had my validation that my out-of-body experience was completely 100% genuine.

I was completely bewildered. I didn't know what all this mess was about! Remember, this was my first out-of-body experience where I was completely aware of my presence somewhere outside my bedroom and I was aware of every minute detail of this dream. It all made no sense, and ultimately it wouldn't be understood until several months down the road, well into 2012.

After I got quite familiar with Angel and her Guides, I got around to asking them about my old boyfriend Ivory. It was now 2012. I had not seen Ivory since 2006 when I worked for Hertz at Norfolk International Airport. For Ivory to manifest in my astral travels six years later was quite puzzling to me. I thought he must have some significance to my story. So, I wrote out this entire story then asked Angel & Guides for their insight.

From: 2xQueen2xGoddess
To: Angel & Guides
Sent: Tuesday, June 26, 2012, 8:41 PM
Subject: $7.99 special Question 1

Question: I need to know what role Ivory plays in my life. Is Ivory connected to me and Egypt?

If so, who was he to me?

Thx,
Queen Nefertiti

From: Angel & Guides
To: 2xQueen2xGoddess
Sent: Friday, June 29, 2012, 10:21 AM

Good to hear from you, Ivory comes across as being a companion to explore things with in this lifetime. He supported you in ancient Egypt and will continue to do so in this lifetime. He will help you remember who you are/were. One of his biggest roles in your past life as well as this life is to guide you to places where you will learn. That includes mentally, emotionally and spiritually. He also comes across as a protector. Not in the sense of being a guard, but as someone who can help you identify danger and stay clear of it. So, he helps heighten your awareness. Then and now.

Angel

Companion? *No way*!
Protector and supporter? *You're shitting me*!
This reading was quite interesting, but it did not fully satisfy me.

Here are some stories of my experiences throughout my entire life?

Story #1: Eating Lunch in the Lion's Den

In 2006, I was employed with Norfolk Public Schools as a substitute teacher. One day, I took an assignment to substitute at Larrymore Elementary. As a matter of fact, Larrymore was the first elementary school I'd attended, and it was the school where I found myself unable to excel in my earlier school years. I was really excited about subbing at Larrymore, the home of the Lions, because I remembered they kept a collection of archived group photos in the library.

As a substitute teacher, I was now privileged to access the teacher's lounge, and on this particular day, I was in the teacher's lounge with a table full of friendly Caucasian women and we all were about to eat our lunches. My goal was to get my hands on the archived photo albums and thumb through it before I left Larrymore this day, and I was certainly sure being amongst this group, they could lead me in the right direction. I asked the group of teachers if they knew where the archived class photo albums were kept. All the teachers said, "No." As I ate my lunch, I wondered what they did with the archived group photo albums.

About 10 minutes had passed, and out of nowhere one of the teachers says to me, "You really are beautiful, you know!" I responded with a thank you! I did not think, *What the hell is wrong with this lady*? or *Where the hell is this coming from*? My thoughts were completely caught up on who to ask next about the photo albums.

Sometime after 2012, as I was taking inventory of my life, I reflected back to this time. I wondered if that teacher who complimented me was a clairvoyant or intuitive. She surely possessed some type of extrasensory perception! But why didn't she pull me to the side and enlighten me? Granted, I probably would have thought she was a little cuckoo for Cocoa Puffs initially, but eventually I would have mentally matured. This teacher would have planted a seed in my head, just like Qulius did decades back. A planted seed, just waiting for hydration to sprout.

Story #2: The Inauguration of President Barack Obama II

In 2008, yes, I voted for Barack Obama just because he was black. I'm not ashamed to admit it!

At that time, I did not know that President Obama was once my Akhenaten; I didn't even have knowledge of myself yet. However, I had just begun studying the subject of metaphysics and the subject of reincarnation was not a concept that I understood just yet. In my mind, I was still trying to comprehend the manifestations that unfolded right before my very eyes while living in The Sunshine State. I was still on some type of Florida high.

On January 20, 2009, Beno and I watched this historical moment together in my bedroom—he was out of school due to inclement weather. I remember the television sitting on top of a filled cardboard box, from the move six months earlier. Beno was lying on the floor and I was sitting on my bed. When Barack was getting sworn into office, I was crying. I was so elated for him. I didn't want Beno to see me crying, so I fought back the tears as much as I could. But he still saw me shedding tears of happiness. Do you know why I was crying? I was crying because I felt like black people were finally getting ahead; for we have come such a long way. As I watched on, I remember seeing Malia and her family standing behind a glass window as they were observing a parade in their honor. I guess you could call it the "window of appearance," in a sense. I remembered Malia taking her thumb and pinky fingers and motioning them back and forth, replicating a Hawaiian Shaka to a younger female who was a participant in the parade. Even this made me cry, for I was filled with jubilation for the Obama family that they received such a warm reception.

Four years later, January 20, 2013, was the second inauguration. At this point in my life, I was extremely overwhelmed by all my unearthings throughout 2012. The veil had been lifted from my eyes and the doors of infinite wisdom opened and everything Egypt and beyond began to flow in at once. On top of that, I was bombarded by Barack's 2012 television campaigns that ran on television non-stop during that time.

I totally ignored the inauguration ceremony and all of its formalities playing out on my television as background noise. As if being invaded by President Obama on my television screen and having this knowledge restored wasn't enough, I ran right into him and his motorcade that same year. *Fan-freaking-tastic*!

Story #3: The Worst Day of my fucking life—no coronation ceremony needed!

The worst day of my fucking life was on December 20, 2013, but let me back up just a little bit. A few weeks earlier, on Thanksgiving Day, my neighbor, Ms. Verna, invited me to join her, along with her family, at her sister's house for Thanksgiving dinner. I obliged, and I really enjoyed myself in her family's company. One of Ms. Verna's relatives suggested that we play a game called Taboo. As we were playing, a card came up that had the word "ASP" printed on it. I remember being a little embarrassed because I didn't know what the word was or its meaning. Ms. Verna's daughter, Sabrina, who was sitting next to me but on the opposing team, said, "It's the snake on the crown." I replied, "Oh, that's the Wadjet!"

Twenty-two days later, I was home alone watching a movie called *White Tee* and wanted a strawberry banana smoothie. I went into the kitchen and took out my Monin Banana Puree and blended it with something strawberry flavored. I returned to my loveseat and continued on with my movie. About five minutes after drinking the smoothie, I was hit with intense stomach pangs. I moved from the couch and sat on the floor. Within another minute, the cramping intensified even more. I walked, slumped over, to the bathroom and sat on the toilet.

Back in 2012, when our solar system was shifting into the fifth dimension, or the Photo Band, I physically felt the changes on our planet. I had the worst case of vertigo. And it wasn't just me—I observed other people complaining about feeling dizzy around that same time as well.

I closed my eyes because I thought the vertigo was kicking in at the wrong time. When I closed my eyes, the next thing I knew, I was alone in the darkness and I felt *no* pain. I called out, "*What is going on here*?" I thought I must've dreamt of that pain. At this moment, my awareness was fully coming back, and I questioned why I was lying on the cold floor? Where did this blood come from and why is the metal wastebasket completely crushed? I was totally confused.

I stood up quickly and I was mad at myself because my body had deceived me! I looked in the mirror and blood was rushing down my face from the top of my head, and my lip looked like it had been hit with excessive force. It was protruding out two inches more than normal and I even had two teeth marks imprinted on the back of my philtrum and my two front teeth were sore. As I was trying to figure out what the hell just happened, the stomach pangs kicked into sixth gear. I grabbed a towel and put it to my face to catch the blood.

I sat back down on the toilet and told myself this wasn't a dream, I passed out from the pain. After actually using the bathroom, my belly felt so much better. I was debating if I wanted to go to the hospital or not and let them see about my head injury.

I decided that I should go and get medical treatment because I didn't know where I was injured, nor did I know how deep the injury was. I called my grandmother and she got to my house straight away. When she reached me, she transported me to Sentara Leigh Hospital, and they ran an EKG on me immediately. After the EKG, I then spoke with the admitting nurse and he asked me what happened? I told him I was using the bathroom and I passed out! He said it sounded like Vasovagal, but to wait for an official diagnosis from the doctor.

I had experienced IBS Vasovagal. In a few words, I fainted from trying to take a crap! Medically speaking, Vasovagal has something to do with the heart rate slowing down and you losing consciousness; that's just how much pain I was in! I believe my body went forward, then my body weight crushed the metal wastebasket and my head hit the ground first. As a result, I busted my forehead and I received three stitches at the top of my cranium. As you can see, it was 22 days later, that I would come to have my own asp! Today, I stand before you with a permanent dent in the center of my forehead, so theoretically, my permanent marking is my "snake" of protection.

After this terrible ordeal, I ran to KareBear to share with her what I was experiencing in my eccentric life. I explained the same story to her, but I added a question.

From: 2xQueen2xGoddess
To: KareBear
01/10/14 at 2:01 PM

After my stitches were removed, I realized that I now have a dent in the center of my forehead–right where the snake sits on Sekhmet and Nefertiti.

And Karen, that light purple spot (Amun Ra), is now coming closer to my face/peripheral vision.

I found an old movie called Space is the Place (1976), a fictional story on Sun Ra, last week on YouTube. And then, that same Sun Ra/Space is the Place soundtrack popped-up on a "current editor pick list" that I was looking through on MOG, an entirely different online program.

So, I'm now thinking (Ra) must be coming to communicate with me soon. I'm just speculating, but something's up!!!

So, my question is: am I a channel for Ra? Or is a channeling supposed to take place between my father Ra and myself?

But isn't that Carla Rueckert's job? I thought she channeled Ra.

If I am a channel for Ra, I really would believe that I'm here on Earth for a spectacular mission as you stated months ago!!!

This is getting very interesting.

Thank You,
Jenell

From: KareBear
To: 2xQueen2xGoddess
01/11/14 at 12:07 PM

You are a channel for Ra. He works with very many channels on the Earth plane, each one with a different purpose. Your accident in the bathroom, although terribly unpleasant, actually assisted in opening up the third eye. Often Spirit will use a physical accident/aliment to catalyze the spiritual development process. Carla Rueckert is also a channel for Ra, as are others. Your job with Ra will be very specific and is very much aligned with your book! But, you have already figured that out :) Ra is firm but gentle and will lead you to the information you need to read/understand. Your job with him will be to connect others to the true history of Egypt and Nubia, not simply what has been written. It is with his energy, that you will be able to bring forward the true story of Africa's advanced civilizations. Your connection with Ra will develop slowly over time, and he is a very high level Ascended Master. He is adept at working with many channels simultaneously, and he knows how much energy to bring in at any given time. Simply be patient and allow him to guide you. Another signature of Ra's energy is the smell of cumin (especially when there is no reason for it).

Blessings,
Karen

My life is quite intriguing. I don't know what the hell is going on, but I know *something's up*! And for the record, ultimately, I think IBS will probably be the cause of my death because I have a poor diet and I love sugar. Oh, can someone out there please tell me what the hell that swooshing and ringing noise in my ears was once I came to after losing consciousness?

Story #4: Can you believe I have no tattoos?

I don't have any tattoos on my body, not a one. Although I ventured out on three different occasions to get myself one. At the tender age of 18, believe it or not, I wanted a sun tattooed around my belly button just like the singer Raja-Nee. Today, as I reflect on my first tattoo selection, it actually puts me in the mind of the Aten with its extending sun rays.

In my first attempt, my friends and I journeyed all the way up to Williamsburg to get tattoos. At that time in the Tidewater area, it was prohibited to operate a tattoo shop. When we got to Williamsburg, the shop was closing within the hour. I was told that the work I wanted would require more time. Therefore, no bueno!

In my second attempt, I was a little older and finally, it was now legal for tattoo shops to conduct business in the Tidewater area. So, I journeyed over to Ancient Art on Cleveland Street in Virginia Beach, near Krispy Kreme Doughnuts, and I was up there bright in early. When I walked into the shop, there was only one artist in the building. I pulled out a postcard and showed him what I had in mind. I had fallen in love with an image on a postcard I found in a store called Hot Topic. The image was of a bashful fairy. She has olive skin, long black hair, elf-looking ears, and she is sitting Indian style. (It would be roughly eight years before I discovered that the artist behind the image on the postcard was Margaret Keane, the lady associated with the *Big Eyes* paintings. Mrs. Keane, I love your work.)

After showing the tattoo artist what I wanted permanently inked into my skin, he drew out the image on paper first. The artist was an older man, and when he showed me his drawing, the damn thing looked like Betty Bop circa 1930s! I see why he was the first person in the shop that morning! In my opinion, he must not have been one of the more popular artists in that shop. I thought, *"Hell no,"* and grabbed MaryJane from the car, who concurred that I shouldn't get it done.

Again, no dice.

I made my final attempt not too long after my second attempt. This time, I trekked over to a little tattoo shop on Canal Drive in Chesapeake to get the bashful green fairy inked. When I got there, again there was only one artist in the shop and he already had a guy out on his table getting work done to his back. I showed him what I had in mind and he said it would be hours before he could get to me because he was working on someone who needed a lot of detail.

After three failed attempts, I gave up on my quest to stain my skin. Even before my spiritual awakening, if I noticed something happening in threes, I looked at it as a sign of some sort. I heeded the call.

Story #5: The Oddest Discussion

Joe, my uncle through marriage, lives out in Detroit and he and I talk on the telephone all the time. Uncle Joe is very knowledgeable about business issues. If you were sitting in a coffee shop chit chatting with him, you would probably think he operates several successful businesses since he is so educated about the ins and outs of business management. Even when I had the bright idea to open up my own cupcake shop, Uncle Joe was the first person I called to consult with each step of the way.

Uncle Joe and I are similar in a way, we both have a little quirkiness in our personality. I believe that is what bonds us, and sometimes we both can say the most peculiar things. Case in point, this random conversation that took place a little after 2008, but prior to my 2012 Egyptian awakening. I was on the telephone with Uncle Joe, and in that conversation, he told me if I wanted to get some easy money, all I had to do was tell the *National Enquirer* that I had a baby by the president, Barack Obama II. I believe Uncle Joe's point was that anyone could come up with the most disgusting accusation about our highly favored president and his adversaries would feed off the negativity by exploiting the storyline in an attempt to destroy his good name.

Unbeknownst to me, at that time, this foolishness would be my reality. If you are reading these words, I skipped the *National Enquirer* and just opted to put it into a novel. Not only would I say I had babies by the president, but I would fill it with more senseless stories, then profess that they are true and head straight to a book publisher! Uncle Joeby, I know after you read this you probably will put me on your prayer list. *Hallelujah, LOL*!!!

After this experience, I was convinced that our spirit guides can implant very specific messages through other people. These higher forces can and will grab your attention through an unlikely source. I truly believe this! How else can you explain this idiocy out of Uncle Joe's mouth? The Universal Forces and/or my spirit guides put those words in his mind and mouth and specifically addressed them to me.

Story #6: The Ring Master

Beno's dad and I took Beno to the Ringling Brothers & Barnum Bailey Circus when he was a toddler. I remember the ring master personally came over to our family, and paused when he got to me, staring at me as if he was mesmerized. He then shook my hand before he even touched my little Beno's hand. I get this reaction a lot from men, especially African natives. Even my gynecologist, who is a foreigner, gave me a hug after my paps smear. You might think that's a bit freakish, but I'm used to foreign men staring at me and people, in general, wanting to hug me. I took the latter statement up with the KareBear and she said, that I have a healing ability, and when people hug me, they get a sense that everything will be okay.

Story #7: Four Quick Encounters

I do not have a car, and I spend a lot of my time walking up and down College Park Blvd. As a pedestrian, many cars pass me by. However, I've had two encounters where I received some unusual special attention. One day, I was walking and a friendly Caucasian woman in an SUV was entering the driveway of Beth Sholom, a Jewish Nursing Home. She turned her head in my direction, staring at me with a big smile, then she put her hand up to her partially cracked window and waved at me. This experience left me a little puzzled because I was many feet away from her. I didn't stop in my tracks to be courteous to her, giving her the right of way; I wasn't even in her way at all. I felt like she went out of her way just to acknowledge me. I, in turn, politely waved back at the lady, who was physically happy to see my presence. As I continued on with my walk, I thought maybe she *really* knew me.

Another time I was walking down the sidewalk on Auburn Avenue, passing the other side of Beth Sholom, and a car sped past me. I could see that it was a Caucasian girl driving the car. Once she passed me, she abruptly stopped her car. I stopped and turned around because I thought we might have known each other from somewhere and I thought she was going to back up to say hey or something, so I stood there and watched her. I could easily see the girl turn to the passenger in her car and mouth something to them. She seemed like she was a little indecisive about what to do next. Ultimately, she continued on with her drive, but as she was driving, she waved at me from within her car before she stopped again at the stop sign. Odd, huh?

Then, there was this guy who was always happy to see me. He would always say something to get my attention when he saw me. So, one day, I gave him my telephone number and we talked over the telephone for a few nights. I just loved his accent; he was a Bostonian. One day, we met up and I remembered we were walking out of Rose's Department Store and were now headed toward Food Lion. This dude was a little amazed and overjoyed to be walking with me. He blurted out while looking at me, *"You a queen!"*

Even though I felt like a bum bitch, I smiled because I had been told this by three gifted clairvoyants already. This dude didn't know what he was saying…or did he? Turns out, this guy was no good. In fact, he was toxic, so I didn't pursue anything with him. However, come to find out through KareBear, I've shared 17 lifetimes with him! And yes, Egypt was one.

This next encounter took place around 2013 or 2014. One day, I was standing at the bus stop. When the bus pulled up and the doors opened. I immediately saw a man seated directly behind the bus driver staring at me. As I stepped up, I could instantly sense that this brother was loco. After I paid my fare, I turned around to find a seat. And right then, this crazy man stands up and slightly bows his head to me as I passed him by! Now, I could say he was being an old fashion gentleman, right? But once I sat down, the cuckoo bird stared at me the whole entire bus ride.

Story #8: My friend Clarence

When I was a little girl living on Bland Street, I had a male friend named Clarence who was in my second-grade class. Clarence was not my boyfriend, even though I really wanted him to be. He was so cute. He was the first bi-racial kid I'd ever seen. I would venture off to his house, but first, I had to go down this very steep pathway by my friend Jamie's house just to get to Norview Middle School's field. Clarence lived on the main side of the middle school. He had two older sisters who were always friendly and nice to me. By the time I was 12 years old, my mom and I moved to Oakmont North. I still saw Clarence in school, and by the time I was 14 or 15 years old, Clarence also moved to Oakmont North. As teenagers, we weren't close at all, but we were cordial with each other if we passed each other in the neighborhood or in the hallways in high school.

I never once saw Clarence when I was in my twenties or thirties. Around 2009, I saw Clarence's profile on Facebook. We added each other as friends then we shot each other a message and that was it.

Four years later, in another out-of-body dream, I found myself sitting on the floor with a book in my hand and the book had my full name across the front cover: JARNALIA JENNINGS. I was also sitting with a few others, and I think we're small, like little kids. We were sitting on the floor of the library in between some bookshelves, and the person in charge of us was Clarence. When I looked up, I was like, *Clarence, what*?! It didn't make sense, but I went with it. Being an elder in charge of the group, I couldn't question his authority. That's all I remember about that dream or OBE.

Due to the OBE/dream, the next day, I ventured onto Facebook to go to Clarence's page just to say hello again. When I pulled up his FB, he had a picture of Queen Nefertiti and Pharaoh Akhenaten standing in front of the Pyramids. Given that, I thought maybe Clarence was connected to my Egyptian lifetime or my spirit guide. I never did find out if Clarence had any connection to Egypt, but I did find out your Spirit Guide cannot be another living being, this is what Mrs. M&M shared with me. Although when I mentioned this same dream to KareBear, she said something about me going into the Akashic Records in the dream state and me spending a lot of time there with the spiritual work that I am doing for this book. KareBear added those other higher beings who work with me bring information out for me, too, and she also confirmed that it looks very much like a library because that's how I described it to her.

People, I don't know what is going on! I live a regular life just like most folks; however, I perceive things differently within the framework of life. Then, when I go to sleep, I'm literally sojourning to other places. I could write a fourth book on just some of the oddest dreams, OBEs, and transcendental encounters I've had in my nighttime slumber. You know what, maybe I'll do just that after I write books two and three. I'll make a note of it.

Around 2010 or 2011, I read *Seth Speaks*, and he said something quite interesting. Seth said people with simpler lives in waking consciousness tend to be quite busy on the other side or in the dream state. Given that, could you imagine the opposite? A very demanding life when you are in waking consciousness (daily life), then when you go to sleep, as your body is resting, your soul is working heavy things out on that side too! That's burning the candle at both ends. I can certainly attest to that statement made by Seth, for I have a very mundane life and yet this book is a product of the spiritual work I'm doing on the other side.

Canopic Jar

You know what I've always wondered, why does my name start off with "jar"? My first name is Jarnalia. My mother didn't name me, her eldest sister did. At first glance, when I examine my name, I can easily see "arna" from Amarna. But what does "jar" have to do with anything? At the beginning of my Egyptian research, when I was uncovering all the history as it relates to the celebrities of the 18th Egyptian Dynasty, I kept seeing the words "canopic jar." The Egyptian canopic jar is known as the protective spirits, and they are also referenced as the "Four Sons of Horus." Each of the four jars is represented by a baboon (Hapi), jackal (Duamutef), human (Imseti), and falcon (Qebehsenuef). Each of Horus's sons holds a different bodily organ. During the embalming process and mummification, the lungs would be taken out and placed in the baboon's jar. The stomach would be taken out and placed in the jackal's jar. The liver would be taken out and placed in the human's jar. The intestines would be taken out and placed in the falcon's jar. The jars are then placed inside the canopic chest before being placed in the tomb with the sarcophagus.[50]

That's interesting, right?

In this incarnation, I have declared myself to be the 21st century Egyptian Resurrector. I am here to wake up my fellow immortal Egyptians and yet my name has the word "jar" within it, just like the Four Sons of Horus canopic jars. I wondered if that has anything to do with anything. Not to mention, my stepdad's name was Horace.

---

50 "The Canopic Jar," Encyclopaedia Britannica, available at *https://www.britannica.com/topic/canopic-jar*.

Was Queen Nefertiti Black or White? It's Less Black or White, and More Egyptian.

I see this debate a lot, and here's what I have to say about it. Look at my people of Egypt today. Look at Hoda Kotb from the *Today Show*—she's Egyptian. Therefore, Queen Nefertiti was Egyptian! Although all the pharaohs, queens and viziers I've resurrected from the 18th Egyptian Dynasty are of African descent in this present day.

Look, they even put Queen Nefertiti on a postage stamp.
Now that's a stamp I'd lick!

Where is Queen Nefertiti buried?

If I knew where she was laid out to rest, I wouldn't tell you either!

Another great mystery about Queen Nefertiti.

With this in mind, let me direct your attention to something I discovered from my birthdate. I was born 11-22-77. If you go through the alphabet just like I showed you when deciphering the word LION, you may see something quite intriguing.

11 = K

22 = V

KV stands for Kings Valley. Now let's look at the year 77. Seven and seven could be divided, added, multiplied or subtracted from itself. So, the possibilities of my royal corpse could dwell in KV 1, KV 14,

KV 49 or KV 0, meaning nowhere. My birthday could certainly hold a clue! That's my theory. One more tidbit, in 1999 when I gave birth to Beno, I had him at 150 Kingsley Lane. That is: KINGS/LEY, where the kings lay.

A Gift of Enlightenment for a Very Specific Woman!

Nileen from the United Kingdom, this is for you, babe!

I couldn't understand how these gifted clairvoyants were telling me I was Queen Nefertiti, then I ran across an article of another woman professing that she was Queen Nefertiti too. Geez, I had a hard time believing my own legacy. Yet, in the back of my mind, I could name everyone associated with Queen Nefertiti from that lifetime, and even you, lady. I knew who Queen Nefertiti's father was, her sister, her mother, her brother-in-law, I knew who Queen Nefertiti's husband was, I knew who her children were, I knew who her in-laws were, I knew who the viziers associated with the pharaohs were, and I know her many other faces in Egypt and yet I never saw Nileen.

Therefore, I was more convinced that Queen Nefertiti's story was more my owns than Nileen's. I discovered that Nileen wrote a book under two different titles, as well as two different pen names, and I refused to order and read them while writing this book. I was compelled to include her story in my book for I knew that there would be a day when I would write my life's story and I needed to find out why Nileen was intentionally impersonating me!

It was now 2017 and I darted over to be a nuisance to KareBear for she no longer had a radio show, nor does she give psychic readings via email any longer. Although annually, she accommodates me when I request a birthday psychic email reading. But this wasn't my birthday. I needed to ask her a question before I finished this book and I only wanted to consult with her on this matter. I deposited a note in KareBear's inbox, and she provided this reading a few days later. Nileen, know thyself and know thy place.

From: 2xQueen2xGoddess
To: KareBear
May 31, 2017 at 9:12 AM

KareBear,

Hello, it's me again! How are you?

KareBear, I have a question about a particular woman and I only want the reading to come from you. If you can, before the summer is over, will you think about giving me a paid reading on this woman: Nileen Namita.

She believed she was Queen Nefertiti in her past life and she spent reportedly over $300,000 to make herself look more like me/Queen Nefertiti!

I want to reference her in my book.

She said, throughout my childhood and teen years I had constant vivid dreams of this ancient queen. They were visions of incredible intensity–I could see where she lived, her servants, her rooms, even the food she ate–and although at first, I found the dreams frightening, I began to research what they meant.

"Aged 23 I underwent psychoanalysis with a counsellor. Slowly I began to realise that I was having these dreams because I am a reincarnation of Nefertiti."

I just want to know, why does she believe she was Queen Nefertiti and was she even around the Chief Queen Nefertiti?

Thanx,
Jarnalia (Honoring my Father)

To: 2xQueen2xGoddess
From: KareBear
June 2, 2017 at 12:32 pm

Thanks for your email :) This is a case of someone who was very close to a popular historical figure but was not them. This happens so much in past life work, as the person can have these memories, like Nileen talked about, and therefore they think they must be the central figure in those memories. But, more often than not, the person was near to the historical figure. In this case Nileen was the top servant for Queen Nefertiti. She held that position for nearly 10 years, and has memories of the rooms, food, other servants, clothing, even places Nefertiti travelled to and so forth.

It is unfortunate when someone tries to replicate who they think they were in a past life, as that is certainly not the purpose of living an incarnation now. Yes, we are meant to learn from what took place before, but we are not back to have a copycat life of who we thought we were. It is actually cases like this that give past life work a bad name.

Please let me know if there is anything else you wish to know about here. Thanks!

Blessings,
Karen

Readers, can you see how Nileen's false claims could have been counterintuitive and destructive to my own awakening? Here I am, discovering something truly unique to myself, and this information was furnished to me by three highly gifted intuitives. Then someone else is claiming the same information as their own? Listening to Nileen's story left me slightly confused! I certainly didn't want to be an imposter.

In the words of Paul Wall, *"First they steal your lighter, then they steal your style…forgot to pay their homage, they just reuse and recycle, man they lie so much they don't know the truth, but they swear to God on the Bible… legend stealers!"*[51]

Well, people, that's my story, at least two facets of it, and I hope you enjoy the rest of my family's resurrection.

[51] Kirko Bangz, "Cup Up Top Down," track 10 on Progression III, Universal Music Publishing Group, 2014.

The Sculptor, Thutmose

Thutmose was an artist of the 18th Egyptian Dynasty. He was thought to have been the official royal court sculptor in our reign and was known as The King's Favorite and Master of Works. Thutmose is mostly known for the iconic bust of Queen Nefertiti—me.

According to Ancient-Origins.net, Nefertiti's "bust was discovered in 1912 by a German archaeological team led by Ludwig Borchardt of the German Oriental Company. During the exploration of several parts of Amarna they discovered the workshop of the sculptor. According to Borchardt, the famous bust stood on the shelf for years, maybe even centuries, before it became so corroded that the sculpture fell down on the sand brought into the damaged house by the wind. It stayed like this until December 6, 1912 when the beautiful bust was found by archaeologists. When the group of researchers saw the incredibly beautiful face of the woman, they were speechless. Immediately they knew that this artifact would be one of the most famous ancient Egyptian treasures in the world."[52]

Even today, I marvel at my own iconic bust—it's breathtaking. I've read somewhere that my bust is the symbol for Egypt. And with that said, *here's to the Queen*!

---

[52] Natalia Klimczak, "The Unique Sculptures of Thutmose…and a Secret Love for One of His Muses?" Ancient Origins, March 27, 2016, available at ***https://www.ancient-origins.net/history-famous-people/unique-sculptures-thutmose-and-secret-love-one-his-muses-005606.***

Thutmose's Gallery

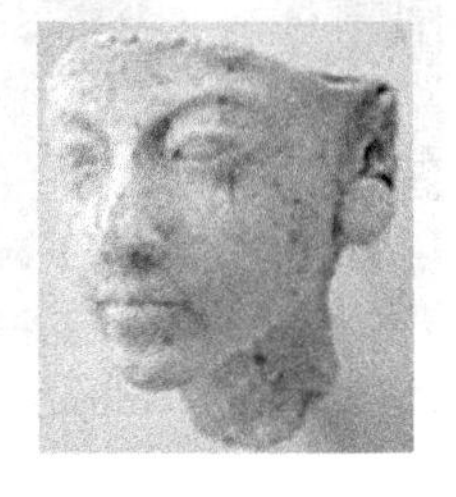

A plaster face of an old woman of Amarna.
Egyptian Museum of Berlin
A young woman thought to be Kiya of Amarna Egypt.
On display at Metropolitan Museum Art, New York
Portrait study thought to be Kiya.
Displayed at the Egyptian Museum of Berlin
Portrait study of Amenhotep III.
On display at Egyptian Museum of Berlin
Plaster portrait study of Pharaoh Ay.
Egyptian Museum of Berlin
Statuette of (me) Queen Nefertiti rendered in lime stone.
Egyptian Museum of Berlin
Plaster portrait study thought to represent (me) Queen Nefertiti.
Egyptian Museum of Berlin
Granite statue of (me) Queen Nefertiti.

The Iconic Bust of Queen Nefertiti

(Thutmose the Sculptor's most notable piece.)

In 1996, a French Egyptologist discovered in Saqqara a decorated rock cut tomb of the "head of the painter in the place of truth," Thutmose. This tomb dates back to the time shortly after the Amarna Period.[53]

With the powers vested in me, I resurrect the official Egyptian sculptor, Thutmose, declared by my husband Pharaoh Akhenaten as the King's Favorite and Master of Works. Today, he has incarnated as…

[53] Natalia Klimczak, "The Unique Sculptures of Thutmose…and a Secret Love for One of His Muses?" Ancient Origins, March 27, 2016, available at *https://www.ancient-origins.net/history-famous-people/unique-sculptures-thutmose-and-secret-love-one-his-muses-005606*.

Ivory

That's right, my old friend from middle school. Yep, the one who showed up in the lobby in my first fully conscious out-of-body experience, and who took me up past the three closed doors, then into the fourth door labeled Egypt. The same guy who I believed "busted" on me the day I played hooky from school, which in turn caused me to get kicked out of my mother's house.

Ivory, I'm still a little sour with you for destroying my life at that time. However, I can't prove you were the culprit who called my mother on the telephone that night, but you were the only one who would have done that shit to me! As of today, I'm going to release the malice I have for you in my head because it was you who showed up and took me up and into Egypt. Therefore, I thank you for assisting me and awakening me to my true self.

An Open Reading for Ivory

From: 2xQueen2xGoddess
To: Golden Rose
June 21, 2017, at 4:10 PM

Hello Golden Rose,

I have a question for you today that I'm dying to ask.

Back in 2011, I was led to Egypt through a door by an old classmate named Ivory in my OBE/dream state. Once I entered through the door, I was in a room, and in this room there were Egyptian artifacts. I picked up a few artifacts and looked at them, then I placed them back. I believe they were on shelves. Fast forward to this day and time, 2017. Now that I am writing a book on my relationship with Egypt, I ran across the word Ivory, as it was the color of the material that was used by the sculptor Thutmose.

I am wondering, and this is a total gamble on my end, was my old classmate Ivory, who led me up to Egypt's door, the famous Egyptian sculptor Thutmose of the 18th Dynasty? The sculptor Thutmose is known for my/Queen Nefertiti's iconic bust. If yes, could Ivory have led me into his workshop for me to discover me?

Thank you,
I am the Queen of the Nile, Jarnalia

From: GOLDEN ROSE
To: 2xQueen2xGoddess
June 23, 2017, at 2:36 PM

Hello Jarnalia,

Thanks for having another reading with me.

I am getting a yes on this!

I hope this answers your question today!

GOLDEN ROSE

Ivory (Thutmose the Sculptor), today you know me as Jenell, but as the dormant Queen Nefertiti, I would like to thank you for the most breathtaking sculpture known to man. Your work has sustained centuries, and still the replica of me stands vigilant. Ivory, just think how many lifetimes we've incarnated since that time and still, today, in the 21st century, you and I are still known for your ancient sculpted masterpiece.

Ivory, we should fly out to Berlin, Germany, and pay a visit to the Neues Museum. Once there, we should take a photograph together with Queen Nefertiti's perfection. How about it?

Ivory, someone owes you BILLIONS, buddy!

Pharaoh Kheperkheperure Aye/Ay of the 18th Egyptian Dynasty

"Everlasting are the Manifestation of Ra" and "Aye, Father of God"

Father: Yuya

Mother: Tjuyu

Wife: Queen Tey and my daughter, his granddaughter, Queen Ankhsenamun

Offspring: Two daughters: Queen Nefertiti and Queen Mutnedjmet

Other Notable Relatives: Queen Tiye, possibly sister or cousin

Reign: 4 years

Buried: WV23[54]

Before I start Pharaoh Aye's overview, in my research I've noticed Aye's name is spelled both with an E and without an E; therefore, I will use both interchangeably throughout his story. Pharaoh Aye was the penultimate pharaoh of the 18th Egyptian Dynasty and my father.

[54] Jenny Hill, "Ay (Aye)," Ancient Egypt Online, available at *https://ancientegyptonline.co.uk/ay/*.

Prior to him seizing the role of pharaoh, he was a powerful, influential and significant vizier to Pharaoh Akhenaten and the famous King Tutankhamun. He served under both pharaohs collectively for over 25 years. Aye was one of two viziers serving under King Tut. He was already an elderly man, so he was referred to as Grand Vizier Aye among the two appointed viziers.

King Tut inherited the throne from his father, Akhenaten, at a very early age, around eight or nine years old. Think back to when you were that age, what would you have known about ruling an empire? Sure, King Tut probably shadowed his father's footsteps, but we all know a child cannot govern an empire without the guidance of some experienced counsel by his side. It is said that Ay was the power behind King Tut during his reign.

While serving under my husband, Akhenaten, my father had been first a troop commander, then a regular overseer of horses, then he was promoted to the overseer of all the horses of the majestic, which was the highest rank in the elite charioteering division of the army, which was said to be just below the ranking of general.

On Aye's tomb is a list of titles that provides evidence of his many roles in Egypt. He was Fan-bearer on the Right Side of the King, Acting Scribe of the King, beloved by him, and God's Father. The title Fan-bearer on the Right Side of the King was a very vital position of high status, as he had the ear of the ruler. In Ay's final title, he was God's Father. Ay is mostly associated with this name and he later incorporated it into his royal name, Kheperkheperure Ay, when he became pharaoh.[55]

Ay's Family Origins

Pharaoh Ay's origins are a little unclear. This would be due to the other vizier, Horemheb, who campaigned to destroy everything Amarna once Pharaoh Ay died. I came across articles that stated Ay was the cousin

[55] "Ay," Wikipedia, available at *https://en.wikipedia.org/wiki/Ay.*

to Queen Tiye, who was the daughter of Yuya and Tjuyu. While some accounts state he was possibly the son of Yuya and Tjuyu. Ay was believed to be a native Egyptian from Akhmim and Yuya was from Akhmim as well. Yuya served as a member of the priesthood of Min at Akhmim, and he and his wife were both superintendents of herds in this city. Yuya was an influential nobleman at the royal court of Amenhotep III (Jay-Z), and Aye likely followed in his father's footsteps, finally inheriting his father's military functions upon his death. Aye and Yuya shared physical traits that makes them look alike and even had similar names and titles.[56]

Pharaoh Ay's Egyptian Nuclear Family

Pharaoh Aye had two daughters, me, Nefertiti, and my sister, Mutnedjmet. My father married Tey and she later became a queen. Queen Tey was given the title Nurse of the Pharaoh's Great Wife. The mother of Nefertiti would be expected to have the royal title Mother of the Pharaoh's Great Wife, and if Ay was the father of Nefertiti, then Tey would have been her stepmother. Was Queen Tey my birth mother or not? You know, it doesn't matter, because guess what, I've found her too! I have reincarnated and brought forth the truth and light of ancient Egypt's past.

Aye and King Tut, and a Family Scandal

King Tut was just a boy when he ascended to the highest position in Egypt, pharaoh. He was guided by two powerful viziers who provided him counsel, Grand Vizier Ay and Vizier Horemheb. During King Tut's reign, he made his half-sister his wife—my daughter Ankhesenamun. Then, tragedy struck, and the young pharaoh passed away at the tender age of 18, leaving his wife/half-sister Queen Ankhesenamun a widow.

[56] "Ay," Wikipedia, available at *https://en.wikipedia.org/wiki/Ay.*

King Tut and Queen Ankhesenamun did not produce any living heirs. In the event of the king's death, Tut had designated the commander of the army, Vizier Horemheb, to be his successor. This is also known as the "idnw," or Deputy of the Lord of the Two Lands.

What happened next was downright scandalous. Grand Vizier Ay outmaneuvered the chosen successor, Vizier Horemheb, by marrying King Tut's widow, putting himself in the highest position of Egyptian society before Vizier Horemheb could assume his role as pharaoh. Today, as I write this, I say gross to this type of incest, but on the other hand, my father Pharaoh Ay just seize the opportunity when it presented itself, that's all.

Aye as Pharaoh

As grand vizier under Tut, Ay was able to gradually reinstate the old religious practices of polytheism, reversing Akhenaten's decree of monotheism. Not only that, but Aye was noted for being the mastermind of moving the Royal Court from Amarna back to Thebes.

As pharaoh, Ay continued to reinstate the old Gods. He went back to his homeland of Akhmim and built a rock cut chapel and dedicated it to the local deity there, Min. Min is the brother of Horus, he appears to be literally the color black, and he is the god of fertility. If you were to pull up his image on the computer, you will see that he has a total boner. No laughing, he's a god, an Egyptian deity!

Pharaoh Aye first constructed his own tomb in Amarna, however, today, a new tomb was built for him in the West Valley of the Kings in Thebes. My father, Pharaoh Ay, also constructed a mortuary temple at Medinet Habu for his own use. The Medinet Habu is a temple that was designed to commemorate the reign of the pharaoh by whom they were constructed, as well as for use by the pharaoh's cults after death.

Pharaoh Aye did not produce any male heirs, and he realized that he needed to appoint a successor to carry out order in Egypt. So, in his fourth year, Aye crowned Nakhtim to be his successor.

Aye/Ay's Mummy

> "The mummy of Ay has never been recovered. The time during his rule is shrouded with mystery and there are many factors that could point to why his mummy can't be located. The most notable suggestion is that Horemheb could have had it destroyed to ensure that Ay did not get Afterlife as previously stated. Until the mummy of Ay can be located, or until we obtain other information about the life and reign of this pharaoh, the suggestion of murder and seizing of his throne through ill means will always surround this pharaoh."

Inside Pharaoh Aye's Tomb[57]

There appears to be physical evidence of damage to the tomb after Aye was buried, and great efforts were made to deface his image and chip away his name. My father's sarcophagus was once on display at the Cairo Museum, and since the restoration of Pharaoh Aye's tomb, The Supreme Council of Antiquities placed the sarcophagus back inside the tomb and added modern lighting.[58]

---

[57] "The Pharaoh Ay (Aye)," Kingtutonline, available at *http://kingtutone.com/pharaohs/ay/.*

[58] "The Pharaoh Ay (Aye)," Kingtutonline, available at *http://kingtutone.com/pharaohs/ay/.*

With the powers vested in me, and with great honor, I resurrect my father, Pharaoh Aye/Ay from his tomb (WV23). Today, he has incarnated as...

Tupac Amaru Shakur

The Most Quoted Emcee of the 20th and 21st Centuries, June 16, 1971—September 13, 1996

In this incarnation, Pharaoh Ay was Tupac Shakur. Pharaoh Tupac Shakur was an international rap superstar and an advocate and speaker of inequality in the black community. He was known and loved by the world, and he died at the age 25. Interestingly, 25 was the same amount of years he served as a vizier in ancient Egypt.

The first time I saw my father again was in the 1991 music video for *Brenda's Got A Baby*. I didn't experience anything out of the ordinary while watching the video, I was completely caught up in the lyrical content of the song and the video that followed. It was based on a true story and the message was deep as hell. At that time, I didn't know girls were out there living like that. However, I did notice that cute little baby girl he was holding and that big ass Nefertiti charm on his chain, but my processes weren't ready for that information just yet.

21 Years Later

It was my birthday and Thanksgiving Day too in 2012, and I had received an unbelievable, amazingly intangible birthday present. It came to me as I was watching *Poetic Justice* on the Bounce TV channel. As a teenager, I'd seen *Poetic Justice* many times, however, on this particular day I was seeing this movie with a different set of eyes; it must have literally been my third eye. As I watched the scene with Lucky (Tupac's character) standing in the doorway and holding his daughter on his hip, I was sitting directly in front of the television. I became spellbound by what I was witnessing on the television screen. On this day, my subconscious mind had tapped into some type of encoded recognition, because at that moment, I recognized something within Tupac that screamed Egypt. My inner voice asked, "*Was Tupac Queen Nefertiti's father, Pharaoh Ay*?" I leaped up and quickly walked to my bedroom and jumped on my computer. I proceeded to do a little light research on Tupac Shakur's biography. I was probing around for any significant clue from his current incarnation that would allude to a past life connection to Egypt and it didn't take me long to find something of significance.

My clever brain had interpreted the encryption immediately! It was within his middle name Amaru.

Now, if you flip the U and make it an N, you have Amarn. Now, add an A behind the N. You now have Amarna. *Aha*! It is important to remember that Pharaoh Aye/Ay was the penultimate pharaoh of the 18th Egyptian Dynasty and Tupac Amaru Shakur carried Pharaoh Akhenaten's city, Amarna, in his middle name. Now, it is speculated that Tupac Amaru Shakur was not his birth name, but the name of the Inca Revolutionary sure did fit the right pharaoh. In any event, I solved the puzzle. However, I just needed to have my findings verified by one of my clairvoyants. Finding my father, Ay, was just the right frosting on my imaginary birthday cake.

A few hours later, I received some immediate confirmation to my findings. First Lady Michelle Obama, Queen Tiye, appeared on the *Steve Harvey* talk show. For me, this was instant confirmation of my earlier discovery. Later that night, two individuals paid me a visit on my birthday/Thanksgiving, one was a gentleman visitor by the name JayDee. JayDee is a fineass brother, who has made it impossible for me to get a little bit of touch and love from. Well, it just so happens that JayDee's middle name is Shakur! How about that?! I then took my suspicion to the Angel & Guides.

Pharaoh Ay was the father of me, Queen Nefertiti. In this lifetime, he wore his daughter's bust on his chest and it read *2DieFor* underneath it! There is no doubt that I was his daughter! He was so proud to be my father that it even carried over thousands of years later in this lifetime. So, let the record show "Fan-Bearer on the Right Side of the King" has everything to do with his daughter being Queen Nefertiti, and Ay as the father-in-law to Akhenaten.

From: 2xQueen2xGoddess
To: Angel & Guides
11/28/12 at 7:46 AM

Hello, Angel & Guides.

How are you all?

I really miss you!

11-22-12 was my birthday! Originally, I wrote this to you on my birthday, but a very depressing individual came to see me and stayed for a good while. Ironically, the individual who came to see me, their middle name is Shakur, which is the last name of the person I'm asking you and the guides about today. So, I see that visit as confirmation of my suspicion before I could reach out to you and the guides for verification.

I think I may be on to something today (11-22-12). It came unexpectedly as I was watching an old movie called Poetic Justice. My mind has pointed out something most fascinating, and so:

I want to ask if Tupac Amaru Shakur aka 2Pac a notorious gangster rapper of this lifetime–who is now in spirit–was/is he Pharaoh Ay, Queen Nefertiti's father?

Thank You very much,
Queen Nefertiti

From: Angel & Guides
To: 2xQueen2xGoddess
11/29/12 at 7:42 AM

Hello and a belated Happy Birthday!

Boy 2Pac definitely has the energy to fit into that role. His energy in that lifetime was very powerful–intimidating–stern. He has little tolerance and doles out punishment harshly. He is one of those that may very tenderly bring you closer only to snap your neck. Wow is he unforgiving.

If you challenged him mentally, he respected that and would do whatever he could in his power to further your efforts.

But deceive him and there would be no mercy. So, he loved stimulating ideas and conversations. Very bright. Way ahead of his time. Very much an intellect who contemplated the stars and worlds beyond. So, his energy definitely takes to that role.

Good to hear from you!
Angel

After this reading, I sent a copy over to my trusted clairvoyant KareBear for her to confirm or deny this other reader's report. She also returned with a yes!

An Open Letter to My Ancient Egyptian Father, Tupac

What an amazing discovery!

I thank you for honoring your past life daughter in this lifetime. That is, by tattooing an effigy of Queen Nefertiti's iconic bust on your chest. It served as a significant clue when I was supposed to decrypt its meaning at a much later time. After I found you, every online forum I participated in and all my closing signatures on my emails, I always signed *Honoring Tupac*. You honored me; therefore, I'm honoring you now.

By the time I understood everything, I wanted to visit your memorial statue out in Stone Mountain, GA, only to realize that the park was closed. I was very heartbroken. Then I thought I could visit with your mother someday! But that didn't work out in my favor either.

Many, many years ago, my uncle was away and mailed me some of his personal belongings that he had to get rid of. Among the items I received was your doubled cassette tapes *All Eyes on Me*. Now many years later, I would have never believed that I would be writing a book about my life, my self-discoveries, and reincarnation, let alone naming you in my personal revelations. Not to mention naming one of my chapters after your doubled cassette tapes. Speaking of your music, my favorite three songs by you are: *Still, I See No Changes, To Live and Die in LA,* and *Hit Em Up*.

Damn, it breaks my heart to know what I know, and be unable to see you, touch you, hug you, laugh with you, or call you on the telephone and ask advice from an ancient grand vizier who was once my father. I honestly feel like I've missed out on knowing such a ***remarkable man*** this time around! Pac, had you known me in this lifetime, you would have adored me because I'm a great gal! When I used to talk to Livie Lux (Vizier Amenhotep-Huy) on the telephone, he would say to me, "You're going to be a Shabazz," and I would bellow in reply, "I'm a Shakur!"

Father Ay, I have a confession for you. When I was a teenager, I had a huge crush on Suge Knight. Can you believe that? If I was your daughter this time around, what would you have said about my teenage crush? Lol!!! When I was in second grade, I had a boyfriend named Damion, and we remained friends throughout high school. By the time we were in middle school, everyone said that Damion resembled you. I really didn't see it. When I was in middle school, I pierced my nose like yours, but only for a day. Because Mom Dukes would have gone ballistic had she seen that!

I was such a big fan of the movie *Friday After Next*, in fact, I would watch it day in and day out. However, once I found out you were Pharaoh Aye/ Ay, I stopped watching the damn movie altogether. The homosexual innuendos about you, now that shit wasn't funny to me at all! That scene is completely disrespectful to the essence of your pharaoh status. Ice Cube, Sekhmet says shame on you with her claws!

Tupac/Pharaoh Ay/my father, I love you till infinity and beyond, and may the future hold us in the same unit again.

Your Daughter Forever,
Queen Nefertiti (Jarnalia)

Images of Then and Now

I will be the first person to stand up and profess that you do not always look like your past life self. Shit, look at me! I'm cute and all, but I do not look anything like my old self as Queen Nefertiti and I'm sure that's what you were thinking when you read my overview as Queen Nefertiti, right?

However, I can't help but bring your attention to the identical features of Pharaoh Ay and Tupac, because there is a striking resemblance between him then and now.

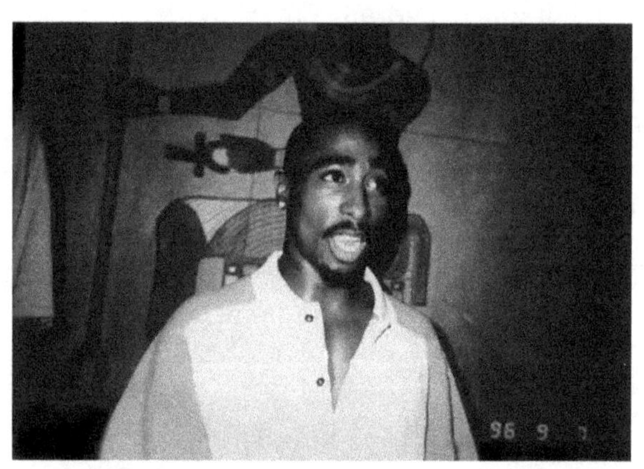

Tupac/Pharaoh Aye/Ay, was captured standing in front of a replica of an ancient Egyptian Wall.

This is Pharaoh Ay performing the opening of the mouth ceremony for King Tutankhamun, a scene from Tutankhamun's tomb.

By all means, my intent is not to be disrespectful with regards to this next image below. The image below was taken of Tupac when he was in a very fragile state in his life. I believe Tupac was leaving the hospital after being shot multiple times. My reason for showing you this image is to describe to you how my mind saw this picture for the first time around 2012 or 2013. Look at how Pac's hospital head dressing is very reminiscent of Pharaoh Ay's khepresh, an Egyptian royal headdress. Even his hands look like they're in the same upward position.

This was my dad! ❤

After resurrecting Pharaoh Aye/Ay, my dreams started directing my attention to his other daughter and Queen Nefertiti's sister, Mutnedjmet (Mut).

Honoring My Father Pharaoh Ay

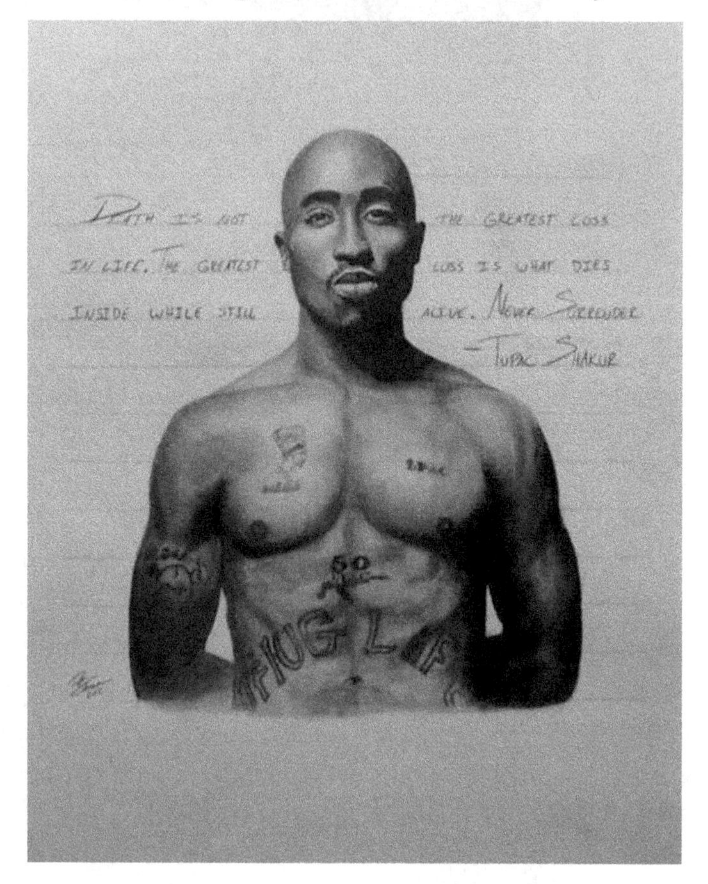

DEATH IS NOT THE GREATEST LOSS IN LIFE.
THE GREATEST LOSS IS WHAT DIES
INSIDE WHILE STILL ALIVE.
NEVER SURRENDER
-TUPAC SHAKUR

Queen Mutnedjmet Great Royal Wife and the Last Queen of the 18th Egyptian Dynasty

The Sweet Mut or Sweet Mama

Father: Pharaoh Aye/Ay

Mother: Queen Tey

Husband: Pharaoh Horemheb

Offspring: 1 pre-mature still born

Other Notable Relatives: Queen Nefertiti's sister

Reign: 13 Years

Buried: Saqqara Capital of Memphis, in Pharaoh Horemheb's unused Memphite Tomb

Mutnedjmet (Mut) was the daughter of Pharaoh Aye/Ay and Queen Tey, and she was Queen Nefertiti's sister. My sister! There's evidence of this in Pharaoh Ay's Tomb that mentions a woman by the name of Mut who is identified as *Sister of the Pharaoh's Great Wife.* Again, researchers doubtfully consider Queen Tey as my mother due to her title as Nefertiti's wet-nurse. In fact, the researchers speculate that Queen Tey could have very well been the birth mother to Mutnedjmet.

Just like her big sister, Mutnedjmet became a queen too. As strange as it may seem, Sweet Mut married Pharaoh Horemheb, King Tut's selected idnw.

Queen Mutnedjmet was not Pharaoh Horemheb's first wife, she was actually his second wife, after his first wife died. Queen Mut's royal title was Great Royal Wife of Pharaoh Horemheb. In addition to becoming the Great Royal Wife, she was also identified as Hereditary Princess, Great King's Wife, Great of Praise, Lady of Grace, Sweet of Love, Mistress of Upper and Lower Egypt, Songstress of Hathor and Songstress of Amun.

Queen Mutnedjmet and Pharaoh Horemheb did not have any living children. According to my research, Mutnedjmet is shown in reliefs accompanying her three eldest nieces, my daughters, Meritaten, Meketaten, and Ankhesenpaaten.[59]

Queen Mutnedjmet succumbed to death soon after year 13 of her husband's rulership. My sister was in her mid-forties when she died. Evidence of this was found in Pharaoh Horemheb's burial chamber on a wine jar in Saqqara at Memphis. Additionally, Queen Mut was buried with her infant. Egyptologists hypothesized that due to the nature of the mother and infant paired burial, Queen Mut died in childbirth. She gave birth to a premature still-born infant. Equally important, Queen Mutnedjmet's mummy showed that she had given birth multiple times. With all the attempts, Queen Mutnedjmet and Pharaoh Horemheb never produced any living heirs to the throne. Inside Pharaoh Horemheb's unused Memphite tomb, Queen Mutnedjmet and her infant were buried alongside the pharaoh's first wife, Amenia.

Queen Mutnedjmet and Pharaoh Horemheb went down in ancient Egypt's history as the last king and queen of the 18th Egyptian Dynasty. There are several monuments, statues and inscriptions that have been left behind in their honor.

---

[59] "Who was Mutnodjmet?" Temple of Mut, *https://templeofmut.wordpress.com/2007/03/01/who-was-mutnodjmet/.*

This 3,300-year-old artifact is of Queen Mutnedjmet. It was possibly defaced by Pharaoh Horemheb's adversaries. The vandals cut off Queen Mutnedjmet's nose and her eyes are gouged out.

With the powers vested in me, and with great honor, I resurrect Pharaoh Aye and Queen Tey's daughter, and my sister, Queen Mudjnedmet (MUT) from her Memphite Tomb in Saqqara. Today, Sweet Mut has incarnated as...

Jada Pinkett

Okay, you mutherfuckers, now you all can stop attaching Jada to the girl Tupac let get away! I'm here to tell you all she was his second ***daughter*** in the 18th Egyptian Dynasty and my sister! Let's get the shit right, got dammit! Jada is Will's woman! Now that I have straightened some, let's get on with my discovery.

It comes as no surprise to me that Tupac and Jada have chosen to reincarnate together, by keeping their kindred spirits alive and well. In one distant lifetime, they were father and daughter, and in this lifetime, they incarnated as platonic BFFs, aiding and supporting each other throughout the many stages of their personal growth. Before their individual fame as teenagers, they grew up together in Baltimore, Maryland and both went to the same performing arts school. Jada and Pac appear to have gone down two different paths to achieve their career goals, and yet both stood vigilant on the world's stage, Hollywood. Now, you may be asking how I discovered this.

My Intuitive Dream

(One of the most bizarre experiences I've had in my dream state.)

I remember sitting in the middle of a very long brown bench. I was very much aware that I was at a church and I was early. The two pews in front of me were empty, reserved for the family. I realized that I was at someone's funeral! I found out rather quickly who's funeral it was.

As I write these words that you are now reading, I'm suddenly aware that I am not back in my bed in Virginia Beach. This was my second out-of-body experience since Ivory took me up for my grand reveal. From my left, Will Smith came up to me. He was standing in the pew in front of me with his two children and they were really small. He stopped, then slightly bent down and kindly told me to come and sit with the family. He then pointed in the direction where the family was sitting. I looked over and saw that the family was sitting off to the right of the church in shorter pews. The sun was shining through the church's stained-glass window in that section. This is when I became aware that I was at Jada Pinkett-Smith's funeral! *WTF*?! My higher awareness knew that Jada had died from some sort of heart failure, though it was not verbally expressed.

I remember it as if I really had attended Jada Pinkett-Smith's funeral in this reality that I'm writing from.

Not only that, but there was another baffling dream experience that I encountered. A second before waking up, I was given a name! As I rose out of my slumber I said aloud, "Angela Davis."

What?!

A month coasted by and I saw my sister Jada on television with Angela Davis. This was bizarre and puzzling as hell! I immediately wondered if I was talking to Jada in the dream state.

I wondered if Angela Davis was Queen Nefertiti's un-named mother from ancient Egypt. I had to run to my clairvoyant and ask them what the hell was going on.

From: 2xQueen2xGoddess
To: Angel & Guides
Sent: Tuesday, March 12, 2013, 10:41 AM
Subject: Question 1

Hello there, Angel.

Is there something that I should know about Angela Davis, her name was said to me upon waking from my slumber. Angela Davis in this life had some association with the Black Panther Party. The mascot of the middle school I went to was a black panther.

As I study Pharaoh Aye/Tupac, in both lifetimes he is associated with panthers and black panthers.

On my own, I figured out that Jada Pinkett Smith was/is Queen Nefertiti's sister Mutnedjmet.

However, after hearing Angela's name, a month goes by and she is taking pictures with Jada Pinkett-Smith promoting a movie called Free Angela Davis and All Political Prisoners, produced by Jada Pinkett-Smith. I'm like what?

In my research, I know Queen Tey was not the mother of Queen Nefertiti, only her wet- nurse, a breastfeeding stepmother, and maybe she was Mutnedjmet's mother.

What should I know about Angela Davis as it pertains to me? Is she Queen Nefertiti's mother? Or, are Jada Pinkett-Smith and I communing in the dream state?

Please help me!
Thanks

From: Angels & Guides
To: 2xQueen2xGoddess
03/12/13 at 1:09 PM

I definitely get that Jada is communing with you. Her energy knows you can see the bigger picture. You have definitely worked with each other in past lives on noble causes. I also get that you have the strength of a panther. Quiet, observing, until threatened or those you love are threatened. I feel you also had a pet black panther while you reigned. He alerted you to dangers and you telepathically communicated and he was a very valuable asset to your kingdom. You found him as a cub and nurtured him until he died a natural death.

You and Jada have similar strengths and were probably sisters. I can see the two of you standing tall with swords against your enemies. You were ruthless and triumphant. It's interesting because Angela's energy isn't really coming through for me. It's more about Jada. But I can see her in the role of Queen Nefertiti's mother. Her energy is aloof and she really doesn't want me to delve there so I am not getting a lot of info about those two. But Jada comes through loud and clear.

Many blessings,
Angel

Jada is my sister 😀! I was searching and reaching to find Queen Nefertiti's mother, who would have been titled ***Mother of the Pharaoh's***

Great Wife and/or the other probable title ***Mother of Pharaoh's Great Daughter***. Initially, I assumed Whitney Houston was our mother Queen Tey. However, it turned out she wasn't. As a matter of fact, she was a Nubian queen.

I forwarded this reading to KareBear to see what she had to say about my reading. KareBear concurred and added, yes, this is true about Jada! She also explained to me that Angela Davis and I did experience a past life together, however, it is not connected to my time in Egypt. As of today, I still do not know the full details of our shared connection.

Many things came out of my reading with Angel & Guides. For one, I had a loyal pet panther. How interesting is that? Secondly, Jada and I were allies and we courageously fought our enemies with swords. Jada, with all our femininity today, sis, we could perhaps have been men in that lifetime! Third, my question was answered, Jada and I are communing on a deep subconscious level. This notion would prove to be true as I began writing this very chapter.

Another Open Reading for Jada

From: 2xQueen2xGoddess
To: Golden Rose
May 3, 2017, at 6:39 AM

Good Day, Golden Rose.

Well, I had a similar reading done once before about this same question, but it was quite confusing to me.

I know without a shadow of a doubt that Jada Pinkett was my sister, Queen Mutnedjmet, when I was Queen Nefertiti. How many lifetimes did we have together?

Thank You,
Queen of the Nile Jarnalia

From: GOLDEN ROSE
To 2xQueen2x Goddess
May 4, 2017 at 4:23 PM

Hello Jarnalia,

Thanks for having another reading with me. I hope that I can help again.

With regards to Jada, I am getting that you shared 4 lifetimes together, and this was also confirmed by my Pendulum. I also get that Jada Pinkett was your sister in the lifetime as Queen Nefertiti.

So I do hope this helps to answer your questions today. ♥

Sincerely,
GOLDEN ROSE

Jada, now that's four lifetimes we shared together!

One day, after our first reading, I visited a florist. As I walked around, I wondered how many lifetimes Jada and I had shared. When I walked out of the florist, there in the parking lot was a car that had your name on it, with three Roman numbers behind it. I thanked the Universe for answering my question expeditiously and snapped a picture of it. Isn't that just grand?

J, you know what I think, I think that you've had a representative of me working with you the entire time you were starring in *A Different World*. Let me explain what I mean. In middle school, I was told several times that I looked like Kaneesha from the movie *Lean on Me*. I didn't know who they were talking about because I had never seen the movie. I asked my mom to get me the movie for Christmas that year.

Finally, I got my hands on the movie, and my first impression of Kaneesha was she didn't look like me at all, and I actually thought she looked like my mom. As I continued to watch the movie, there was a scene where Kaneesha had on a pink robe, her hair was wrapped in a towel and she smiled. At that moment, I instantly saw my infectious smile and face. My 13-year-old self said, "I do look like her!" J, I am Karen Malina White's doppelganger. Even today someone will tell me that I look like the girl from *Malcolm and Eddie*.

Jada, did you work with Charmaine closely on *A Different World*? On a good day for me, because I'm very moody, my personality mimics Charmaine's character's ludic persona on *A Different World* and I talk just as fast too. J, as shown above, you have had a representative of me around you during that time in your life. Smile!

An Example of Us Communing in Dream State

Jada, when you appeared on the *Howard Stern Show*, you said you and Tupac shared a kiss just to see if there was any chemistry. I believed you specified that it was disgusting. I jumped up and shouted at my laptop, "*Because he was your father*!" When the show was over, I promptly searched for the *Howard Stern Show's* email address, and I found it too. At that moment, I became frantic because I needed to divulge this enlightenment to you. So, I emailed the *Howard Stern Show* expressing to them that I needed to get in contact with you, Jada. Can you imagine what it's like to possess sacred wisdom that has to be specifically addressed to a very precise individual, but you're at a disadvantage? It's nerve-wracking, I tell you! I even wrote Oprah a 42-page letter expressing this very issue, my issue, and I titled it *The Observer's Conundrum*. Although I never heard anything back from Ms. Harpo.

You know, J, I don't remember what year that was, when you appeared on the *Howard Stern Show*, but it was this year 2017, when I heard you profess a statement on the *Arsenio Hall Show* that led me to believe we are definitely communing in dream state and/or you have received my message telepathically.

Let me explain. On this particular day, I was beginning this chapter right here. I stopped typing briefly to listen to some music on YouTube and float around the house. First, I pulled up my song by Busta Rhymes,

Put Your Hands Where My Eyes Can See, and I started cleaning the bathroom. Next, I played Mr. Cheeks's *Lights Camera Action.* Then, I finished up with Lil Kim's *The Jump Off.* Once I finished cleaning the bathroom, I sat back down and got back on YouTube and watched an old interview clip with Faith on the *Wendy William's Show.* Faith was talking about how big her son was now and I wanted to see it for myself. It just so happens that I saw a video thumbnail of CJ Wallace and I clicked on it.

I watched the video for a few seconds until I noticed another video featuring CJ Wallace. In that video, CJ was talking about how he was playing his father in an upcoming Biopic called *All Eyes on Me.* I was wowed because I didn't know someone was making a biopic of our father Pharaoh Aye, who is known as Tupac today.

Damn, it showed that I titled our family's resurrection chapter correctly! I then saw a little thumbnail that I couldn't make out. It said, 'Jada Pinkett-Smith (Tupac Was Like a Father)' and immediately I clicked on that video. You were on the *Arsenio Hall Show* and explained that Pac treated you as someone who he wanted to see succeed without trying to get into a physical relationship with you, and in the process of you succeeding, he would be your protector. Me discovering your interview on the *Arsenio Hall Show* was no coinkydink. I was guided to this video by the Universal Forces, or my higher self, to confirm to me that our souls are communicating on a much deeper level and that I'm on the right track by writing out my truths.

I looked to see when this video was published, and it was published just two months before I started writing this chapter. The YouTube channel belongs to a YouTube member by the name: The Art of Dialogue. It just so happens this YouTuber's channel has an animated image of Michael Jackson's *Remember the Time* video, which is a picture of Queen Nefertari with Ramesses. Again, no coincidence, it's all Egyptian related.

My family reunited, and it feels so good!
Ancient Egyptian royalty, reflecting back to me my own greatness!
Thank you, family!

Father and daughter of ancient Egypt
Pharaoh Aye/Ay and his daughter Queen Mutnedjmet

I love this picture so much, and by the same token, I harbor just as much jealousy when I see them in pictures together. I fret because I wasn't around during these times. Can someone out there infuse me into this picture somehow, just so that I could feel better? Jada, it looked like I was the star in our father's eyes during our reign in the Egyptian lifetime and in this incarnation, it looks like you were the star.

Jada, I think the first time I saw you was in *A Different World*, but I remembered I really favored you in *Tales from the Crypt: Demon Knight* and I rented the movie often. I'm so proud of you for standing up and speaking on behalf of our father and who he was in this lifetime. If the shoe was on the other foot, I would have done the very same thing.

I often wonder, Jada, what it would have been like if I grew up in Baltimore with you two. How would you two have treated me? Or what if I would have been your little sister or even a classmate under you two, would I have been part of the clique? In any one of those probabilities, I just keep seeing you two being overly protective of me.

Jada, one day in the future, will you reminisce with me over when you and dad were growing up without me in the storyline? I would love to hear those stories. Did he try to dictate your life like he was your father? Jada, when I see you cry because you miss Pac, I cry because I miss you two and I missed out on my past life father and past life sister's reunification. Honestly, I feel left out. However, I wasn't too far away. I was just one state away in Norfolk, Virginia.

Jada, I love all the qualities that I see in you, the fight, the might, your proactive approach when it comes to shit that ain't right in your book. The way you'll pounce on someone's ass; it's the same approach that I would take! If we were lawyers, could you see us litigating together, advocating together on some noble causes? They would have coined a phrase for us two ladies. We were Pharaoh Aye's daughters in one lifetime and fellow warriors in another. J, after your initial shock and awe with the context of this book, can I anticipate your support again?

Hopefully, Jada, I've enlightened your heart and mind. And the message that I want to bring home to you is: it is important to realize when you lose someone to death, in that state of being it is not the end of a friendship or love. And you do see the departed again. However, that love will emerge in an entirely new role, in another incarnation. Jada, this is true for your children, your husband, your parents, your grandparents, your teachers, your classmates, your neighbors and even pets. With that being said, surely, if you and I have been together in four other incarnations, then it's certainly possible that you've been with your best male friend Tupac Shakur in another lifetime outside of the 20th century incarnation. I have shared and provided you with one outside of this current incarnation and I took you back to ancient Egypt, specifically, the 18th Dynasty when he was your father.

Now, it would behoove you to go and seek the truth for yourself! I urge you to go out and try to prove this hullabaloo wrong and prove that I've made all this nonsense up. If you find that I am on to something, come back and tell me of the other two lifetimes that you and I shared. I would be very much appreciative of that. For I can only tell you of five truths that are within me, that I know to be true because they're a part of me and it's my truth that just so happens to include you: 1. Tupac was Pharaoh Aye/Ay in ancient Egypt 2. He was your father in that lifetime 3. You were his daughter, Mutnedjmet 4. I was his daughter too and I was your older sister Queen Nefertiti.

Queen Jada, my sister, in my opinion, I believe you and I have served our past life father well in this lifetime. We have bridged Tupac's past and his present. We have honored our father greatly! Jada, I profess this to you, my love, to the farthest corners of the Universe, you will always have me as your ally, sis. Queen Mutnedjmet, I love you, my sister, and I have a gift for you. Just like I found you, I present to you my fifth truth, your husband then is also your husband now.

Your sister then and now,

Queen Nefertiti/Jarnalia Jennings

Pharaoh Horemheb
The Last Pharaoh of the 18th Egyptian Dynasty

Horus is in Jubilation

Father: Unknown

Mother: Unknown

Wife: Queen Mutnedjmet and Non-Royal Amenia

Offspring: 0

Other Notable Relatives: None

Reign: 14 years or possibly 26/27years

Buried: KV57[60]

Horemheb was born a commoner and his parentage is unknown to Egyptian historians. Although it is known that Pharaoh Horemheb did not come from a pedigree of Egyptian royalty. It is believed that

[60] Joshua Mark, "Horemheb," Ancient History Encyclopedia,April 22, 2014. available at *https://www.ancient.eu/Horemheb/.*

Horemheb could have been from Herakleopolis Magna or ancient Hnes (modern day Ihnasya el Medina) since his coronation text formally credits the god Horus of Hnes for establishing him on the throne.

Vizier Horemheb

In Horemheb's earliest career in the Egyptian military, he served as the royal spokesman for Egypt's foreign affairs, Vizier and commander in chief to Pharaoh Tutankhamun. He guided the Egyptian army to war against Hitties and personally led a diplomatic mission to visit the Nubian governors. This evidence can be found in the tombs of the Viceroy Huy. [61]

Vizier Horemheb, Grand Vizier Ay and King Tut

When King Tut ascended to the throne, he was left with his father's two most influential viziers as his counsel. As King Tutankhamun matured, it was believed that he started ruling Egypt in his own way. As a result, he no longer needed the support of his two viziers in making executive decisions. However, in the end, King Tut appointed Commander and Chief Horemheb as his apparent heir through the idnw, or deputy of lords of two lands upon his death. [62]

The designation of the idnw had no significance to my father, Grand Vizier Ay, as he outwitted his co-vizier Horemheb by marrying his own granddaughter, Ankhsenamun, King Tut's widow. This strategy guaranteed Ay the throne. Horemheb would later take the throne from Pharaoh Ay's designated idnw Nakhtim, to become the last pharaoh of the 18th Egyptian Dynasty and he married Pharaoh Ay's daughter Mutnedjmet.

---

[61] Joshua Mark, "Horemheb," Ancient History Encyclopedia,April 22, 2014. available at *https://www.ancient.eu/Horemheb/.*

[62] "Tutankhamen," History.com, available at *https://www.history.com/topics/ancient-history/tutankhamen.*

Pharaoh Horemheb and the Reform

Upon further review, I have decided to reference Margaret Bunson, to explain the transformations that transpired throughout ancient Egypt when Pharaoh Horemheb finally took the throne. Pharaoh Horemheb's internal reforms set the tone for the 19th Egyptian Dynasty.

Horemheb ascended the throne c. 1320 BCE and, according to the historian Margaret Bunson, "marked his reign with extensive programs to restore order and rebuild Egypt's decimated shrines. Tributes flowed into the land during his reign and lesser city-states and nations sent delegations to keep cordial relations with him. He was called `stern' by contemporaries." Claiming that the gods, specifically Horus of Hutsenu, his patron god, had chosen him to bring balance back to the land, Horemheb instituted a strict orthodoxy concerning traditional religious practice.

He returned the temple properties to the rightful priests, lands which Akhenaten had confiscated during the Amarna Period. He also dated his reign to the death of Amenhotep III in 1353 BCE, thus erasing the Amarna Period and its aftermath. His reign was also marked by building programs, including restorations and the start of additions to Karnak, Nubian shrines, a temple to Ptah and tombs at Memphis and Thebes."

Horemheb destroyed Akhenaten's city of Akhetaten and moved the capital to Memphis. The monuments, temples, and stele that had been erected by his predecessors were torn down and "used as fill in constructing new buildings. Horemheb proclaimed that all reference to the religion of Aten be obliterated. So successful was he in this goal that later Egyptians believed he was the successor of Amenhotep III and had simply continued that king's policies. Akhenaten, Tutankhamun, and Ay were forgotten by history so completely that it was not until they surfaced in excavations in the late 19th and mid-20th centuries that it was known they had ever existed."[63]

---

[63] Joshua Mark, "Horemheb," Ancient History Encyclopedia,April 22, 2014. available at *https://www.ancient.eu/Horemheb/.*

Horemheb's official titles include "Hereditary Prince, Fan-bearer on the Right Side of the King, Chief Commander of the Army, the attendant of the King in his footsteps in the foreign countries of the south and the north, the King's Messenger in front of his army to the foreign countries to the south and the north, and the Sole Companion, he who is by the feet of his lord on the battlefield on that day of killing Asiatics."[64] All evidence can be found spelled out in his Saqqara tomb.

Family

In Pharaoh Horemheb's lifetime, he had two consorts, but not at the same time. When Horemheb was a general, he was married to Amenia. Amenia and General Horemheb did not produce any children in their union. It is believed, that Amenia died during the reign of Pharaoh Ay, but her cause of death is unknown. As pharaoh, Horemheb married my sister Mutnedjmet and made her queen. Pharaoh Horemheb and Queen Mutnedjmet tried several times to conceive an heir, yet each time it was unsuccessful. Queen Mutnedjmet died in childbirth in her husband's thirteenth year of reign. Both of Pharaoh Horemheb's wives and stillborn child were laid to rest in his Memphite Temple at Saqqara.

Successor

With no heirs, Pharaoh Horemheb designated Paramesses to be his successor upon his death. Horemheb had a few reasons for selecting Paramesses, but mainly he used a little rationale in his decision making. One of the reasons for selecting Paramesses was based on his display of loyalty. Equally important, Paramesses had heirs. A son and grandson who could continue on the royal succession. The 19th Egyptian Dynasty would be ruled by these known successors (whose names should be read in your best Nacho Libre voice): The Great Ramesses I, Seti I, and Ramesses II.

---

[64] Anneke Bart, "Horemheb," Ancient Egypt, available at *https://mathstat.slu.edu/~bart/egyptianhtml/kings%20and%20Queens/Horemheb2.html.*

Inside Pharaoh Horemheb's Tomb KV57

With the powers vested in me, I resurrect Queen Mutnedjmet's husband, Pharaoh Horemheb, from his tomb in KV57. Today, Pharaoh Horemheb has incarnated as...

Willard Smith

"The Freshest Pharaoh of Bel Aire"

Will, you ain't no prince!

You are a goddamn pharaoh! Now, how accurate was that "***Gettin' Jiggy Wit It***" video, Pharaoh Will?

All that I can say about myself is, *Wow, "go, go Gadget"* eyes!!!

To my readers, are you asking, how I came to this conclusion?

Well, basically, I made two big discoveries in one. Once I found my sister Queen Mutnedjmet/Jada, I wondered who her husband could be? I took two good looks at a picture of Pharaoh Horemheb's bust. As I examined the image, I actually saw Mr. Shabazz (Vizier Amenhotep-Huy) because this is exactly how he looks in this current incarnation. However, shortly thereafter, my intuition immediately saw Will Smith's face.

For years I just carried on assuming that Will Smith was Pharaoh Horemheb without anyone else's opinion on the matter, until now. For the sake of this book, I moseyed on over to Golden Rose to have two readings done, with one specifically on my Egyptian suspicion as it related to Will Smith.

To Jada & Will,

I am truly happy for your reunification. Yesterday, you two were the last king and queen of the 18th Egyptian Dynasty, and today you have reemerged as a Hollywood power couple. It's so befitting of the Smith family!

An Open Past Life Reading for Will

From: 2xQueen2xGoddess
To: Golden Rose
May 3, 2017, at 6:39 AM

Good Day, Golden Rose.

I just wanted to confirm that Will Smith, Jada's husband now, was Pharaoh Horemheb in ancient Egypt. My intuition told me so, but I never had it confirmed by any other reader.

Thank You,
Queen of the Nile Jarnalia

From: GOLDEN ROSE
To: 2xQueen2x Goddess
May 4, 2017, at 4:23 PM

Hello Jarnalia,

Thanks for having another reading with me. I hope that I can help again.

With regards to Will Smith, it was confirmed by my pendulum that he was Pharaoh Horemheb in ancient Egypt.

So, I do hope this helps to answer your questions today. ♥

Sincerely,
GOLDEN ROSE

An Open Letter to Will Smith

Will, in 1988, I was 10 years old and I lived on Bland Street. One day, in the "summertime" I hopped on my bike and rode it up the street to Punnies Record Shop on Sewells Point Road. I went in and purchased your double vinyl album *He's the DJ, I'm the Rapper.* This was my first and only doubled vinyl album that I owned in my lifetime. When I returned home, I rocked the entire album and I loved it. But Will, listen, I was always home alone, and I was afraid of Freddy Krueger. On your album, your song *Nightmare on My Street* scared the bejesus out of me that day! I remembered that so clearly.

Will, check this out. I had a BFF named Sharon and she attended Norfolk State University before me. Sharon had a boyfriend who was from Philly, and he lived on the Norfolk State Campus as a student. Sharon told me her boyfriend Chuck talked non-stop about his big brother Charley, to the point it was getting on her nerves. She said Chuck exalted his big brother by talking about how cool he was and how he did all these fun things because he was your best friend. I even met Chuck once at Sharon's house.

If you know who I am talking about, look at how closely I was connected to you. This is a great example of six degrees of separation. During that time in my life, I had no concept of reincarnation! The only thing Egypt I knew of was the names Queen Nefertiti and King Tut and *Walk Like an Egyptian* by The Bangles. Now just imagine if I had knowledge of our story earlier on.

Will, please excuse me for my unsolicited analysis of your love life but look at how your life today parallels Pharaoh Horemheb's life. Pharaoh Horemheb had two wives, back to back and both wives were buried in the same tomb. In comparison, you had two wives, back to back and you created a united front or harmony among the two wives this time around. Smooth, brother, real smooth, Pharaoh Will! Will, I wouldn't be surprised if your first wife this time around was your first wife in ancient Egypt when you were just a general.

Will, my favorite songs by you are *Summertime* and *Miami*! Now, I've never been to Miami, but you certainly have inspired me to want to go.

Oh, Pharaoh Will, I see you got yourself two male heirs to the throne this time around. Congratulations!

Will, I remember seeing an interview you gave, where you mentioned that your dad had called you in the wee hours of the morning, just to have a heart to heart conversation with you. I can't recall what you said verbatim, but I think you explained that your dad was just amazed at how lucky you are in life. If I may, this is what I would say to your father, knowing what I know.

Mr. Smith, with all due respect, sir, I know my story sounds cock-eyed, but I'm here to tell you that your son was an Egyptian pharaoh of the 18th Egyptian Dynasty. In this lifetime, Will and his queen only came back to reclaim what's rightfully theirs, and that is sovereignty.

Pharaoh Will, I harbor no ill feelings toward you for destroying everything my pharaoh husband, my pharaoh son, and my pharaoh father worked so hard to institute along with your guidance for the betterment of Egypt and its continuation.

However, Will Smith/Pharaoh Horemheb, I do have some questions for you. You are in the hot seat, buddy!

If we as Egyptians believed in *reincarnation and the afterlife*, did you think we wouldn't come back to civilization and not remember our Golden Time of Day? You didn't expect anyone to notice how you scratched out our names from the storyline and you made the Egyptian history look like it went from Jay-Z and Michelle directly to you and Jada. No, no, no, that's Egyptian blasphemy! If nobody else remembers themselves, I'm certainly glad I was pushed to remember the players. I found you, and I see what you did, Pharaoh Horemheb.

Now, this leads me to my next question. How did you really feel about Barack Obama II as president?

Lastly, I learned this word from you somewhere along the way: rhetorical. Therefore, my last question is a rhetorical question. I would really love to know how you felt about Jada's and my past life father Pharaoh Aye, seeing as how he pulled the wool over your eyes so long ago when it came to the idnw by marrying King Tut's widow. If I were to make an assumption about how you felt about Tupac, I would guess there was a lingering sense of betrayal. I could be completely wrong, but it's just my opinion, that's all.

Pharaoh Will, if you ran for president and won, you just might have a positive effect on the United States of America. However, don't look for me to cast a ballot, brother-in-law.

Ancient Queen of the Land,
Jarnalia Jennings, *the Egyptian Resurrector*

Queen Tey
Great Royal Wife
of the18th Egyptian Dynasty

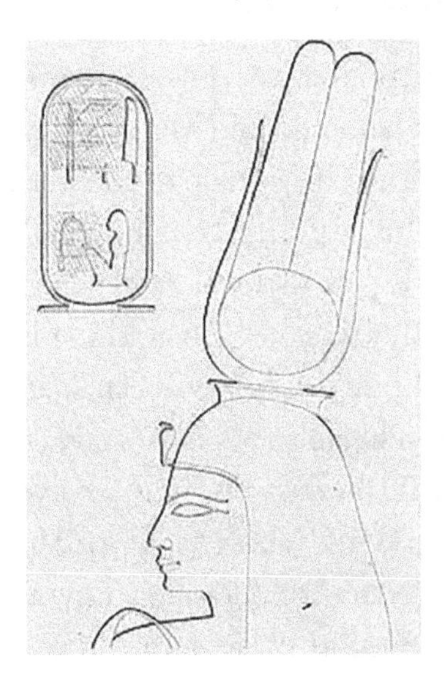

Father: Unknown

Mother: Unknown

Husband: Pharaoh Aye/Ay

Offspring: Queen Nefertiti and Queen Mutnedjmet

Other Notable Relatives: None

Reign: 4

Buried: WV23

Queen Tey was born a commoner and her parentage is unknown. Tey married my father, Ay, before his ascension to the throne. Once my father seized the Egyptian throne, my mother's status was raised greatly as well, and she became a great royal wife. That's right, Queen B status! Queen Tey went down in history as Hereditary Princess, Great of Praises, Lady of The Two Lands, Great King's Wife, his beloved, and Mistress of Upper and Lower Egypt.[65]

Nurse of The Pharaoh's Great Wife

Tey and Ay had two children and possibly a son. Their children were Nefertiti (me, Jarnalia Jennings) and Mutnedjmet (Jada Pinkett-Smith). After closer examination, Egyptian historians have concluded that Queen Tey was not actually Queen Nefertiti's biological mother because Queen Tey's official Egyptian royal title was *Nurse of the Pharaoh's Great Wife*. If Queen Tey was the biological mother of Queen Nefertiti, then her official royal title would have been *Mother of Pharaoh's Great Daughter*. Therefore, Pharaoh Aye must have been married prior to his matrimony with Tey and this unidentified wife must have birthed Nefertiti before dying. Grand Vizier Ay married Tey and she would have nursed his daughter Nefertiti. Although Egyptian historians believe Queen Tey is the birth mother of Mutnedjmet, it is theorized Queen Tey and Pharaoh Aye could have possibly been the parents of Nakhtim, Pharaoh Aye's apparent successor.[66]

Great Royal Wife "As Can Be Seen"

There are several depictions of Queen Tey from the Amarna Period. One can be found on walls of Pharaoh Aye's unused tomb. There is a scene where Pharaoh Akhenaten and Queen Nefertiti are dressed in their royal garbs and they appear with their children at a window—this scene is known as the "window of appearance."[67]

---

65 Joyce Tyldesley, "Chronicle of the Queens of Egypt:From Early Dynastic Times to the Death of Cleopatra," 2006.

66 Joyce Tyldesley, "Chronicle of the Queens of Egypt:From Early Dynastic Times to the Death of Cleopatra," 2006.

67 Anneke Bart, "Nefertiti," Ancient Egypt, available at *https://mathstat.slu.edu/~bart/egyptianhtml/kings%20and%20Queens/Nefertiti-inscriptions.html.*

In the illustration below, the royal family is throwing out rewards to the viziers below. The two individuals reaching out to receive the gifts are Grand Vizier Ay and his wife Tey.

Grand Vizier Ay and Tey

There is evidence that depicts Queen Tey on wooden boxes that are inscribed: "For the true scribe of the king whom he loves, troop commander, overseer of cavalry, and Father of the God Ay." And the text mentions: "The much-valued one, the sole one of Re, appreciated by the Great Royal Wife, the mistress of the house, Tiy."[68]

Lastly, Tey is depicted on a rock chapel that is dedicated to the fertility god Min in Akhmim.[69]

This shouldn't come as a surprise, considering Pharaoh Aye journeyed back to his homeland Akhmim and constructed a rock chapel in honor of the local deity there. The fertility god Min—yes, the one with the boner. Pharaoh Aye wanted to also dedicate a depiction of his favorite queen at the same rock chapel. An illustration of the rock chapel can be found at the beginning of Queen Tey's overview.

68 "Tey," Wikipedia, available at *https://en.wikipedia.org/wiki/Tey#cite_note-8.*

69 Aidan Dodson and Dyan Hilton, *The Complete Royal Families of Ancient Egypt*, Thames and Hudson, 2004, p.157.

Queen Tey's Resting Place

Egyptian historians assume Queen Tey was buried with her husband Pharaoh Aye in WV23 because there was evidence of female DNA present.

With the powers vested in me, and with great honor, I resurrect my mother, Mutnedjmet's mother and Pharaoh Aye/Ay's wife, Queen Tey, from her tomb in WV23. Today, Queen Tey has incarnated as...

Celestine Ann Beyince

Mrs. Tina, you were the Great Royal Wife of Pharaoh Aye/Ay. Your name was Queen Tey and you are from the 18th Egyptian Dynasty too! Mrs. Tina, today, your ancient Egyptian family is here as well. Tupac was your past life husband, Pharaoh Aye/Ay! Jada Pinkett-Smith was your past life daughter, Queen Mutnedjmet! And I too, Jarnalia Jennings, was your past life daughter, Queen Nefertiti!

Are you screaming, "*WHAT*?"

It took me quite a while to find you, Mrs. Tina.

My Intuitive Dream

(This dream came through on December 1, 2016)

I was in front of my neighbor Larry's hallway in the community where I currently live right now. I was standing on the sidewalk and there standing in an empty parking space near the curb was Mrs. Tina, and she asked me a question. I was directly facing her and standing directly behind me on the sidewalk was my aunt who I call Mama. Mrs. Tina asked me about a little boy who was running around outside unsupervised like a wild hyena. I believe I answered her question by telling her what I knew about the rambunctious little boy running about.

When I woke up, I wondered why I was dreaming about Beyonce's mother.

About 10 days later, I was doing some automatic writing with Dorrian, and I happened to ask him about the dream because it featured a well-known face. Without delay in written transmission, Dorrian shared his wisdom with me in full detail. I then did a little investigative work on Mrs. Tina's background. Within a few short weeks, I went knocking on Golden Rose's email door for a reading. For if what Dorrian had shared with me was certainly true, then that meant Mrs. Tina and Tupac Shakur were married in an Egyptian lifetime!

My Open Reading for Mrs. Tina

From: 2xQueen2xGoddess
To: Golden Rose
12/26/16 at 11:04 PM

Rose, Good Day.

On December 1, 2016, I dreamt I was standing in front of my neighbor's hallway on the sidewalk and standing in an empty parking space was Tina Knowles (Beyonce's mother) right in front of me, then my aunt, Mama, was standing directly behind me. I was positioned in between these two women.

Now, there is great significance in me standing in front of Larry's hallway; it has considerable meaning. When I woke up, I wondered why I was dreaming about Beyonce's, mother Tina Knowles?

A few days later, I was talking to Dorrian through automatic writing and I happened to ask Dorrian why I dreamed of Tina Knowles, Beyonce's mother.

Dorrian surprisingly told me that Tina Knowles was the Queen's mother!

I asked which Queen; (redacted) or Nefertiti?

And Dorrian said Queen Nefertiti's mother, and she was Queen Nefertiti's wet nurse, Queen Tey.

So, I went to Wikipedia to see if I could find any telltale signs and I found three immediately. First, her middle name is Ann, and my current mother's name is Diane, but my aunt, Mama, calls her sister Ann.

Secondly, Tina Knowles is known as "Momma Knowles," but I found out it's not spelled Momma Knowles, it's spelled, MaMa Knowles. This is the same name as my aunt who was standing behind me in the dream with Tina.

Third, it stated that she launched her clothing line, House of Dereon, in 2004 and went on The View with her daughter to promote, I'm guessing a new clothing line called Miss Tina, on November 22, 2010. Well, that was on my birthday. Ironically, I watched this on YouTube not too long ago. Ha!

So, I just want to know if Beyonce's Mother, Celestine Ann Beyonce Knowles, is Queen Nefertiti's mother and/ or wet nurse Queen Tey?

Thank You,
Queen of the Nile, Jarnalia

From: GOLDEN ROSE
To: 2xQueen2xGoddess
12/27/16 at 12:38 PM

Hello Jarnalia,

Thanks for having another reading with me. I hope that I can help again.

With regards to Beyonce's mother. I am picking up several overlays to her energy field. And so, I feel that her soul includes direct connections to Celestine Ann Beyonce Knowles, Queen Nefertiti's mother and/ or wet nurse Queen Tey. And really strongly Queen Nefertiti's mother. So, they are all intertwined in a way and not separated. I actually see about ten overlays or lifetimes to her energy field all playing out at once. And so, I feel this is why you had the dream and were standing in an empty parking space, in front of your neighbor's hallway and having Beyonce's mother in front of you and your aunt behind. As if to signify past/present/future or otherwise ancestral connections in some way. All these lifetimes or connections being shown to you as one, in parallel realities or timelines. So that you could make the connections and connect the dots. So absolutely I see and feel this connection as you have been given an interpretation as accurate and filled with goosebumps! Which means it is a validation of your dream, discoveries and feelings about all of this to be authentic. And, how the connections made are very real, in order to get your attention. So that you can connect to the energies more. So, continue to pay attention to your dreams for more information and revelations. As going into next year there will be many more.

I hope this helps!

Sincerely,
GOLDEN ROSE

From: 2xQueen2xGoddess
To: Golden Rose
12/27/16 at 1:58 PM

This was great, fast, and appreciated, but what is an overlay?

Thx

From: GOLDEN ROSE
To: 2xQueen2xGoddess
12/27/16 at 6:07 PM

Glad you enjoyed it. An overlay is just a term for levels and layers of energy in the auric field connected to the soul.

GOLDEN ROSE

This was one pretty complex reading. All I wanted to hear was yes. I happened to mention the phrase "great significance" in my email to Golden Rose and I'd like to expound on that term and why it holds a dual meaning in my enigma of a dream.

You see, my neighbor Larry is the brother of JayDee, the guy who paid me a visit on my birthday, the same day I discovered that Tupac Shakur was Pharaoh Aye. Larry's hallway was of great significance in that point of reference linking Tupac Shakur to Mrs.Tina.

I was standing in the middle of Mama now and MaMa then! What if my Mama (aunt) now is a fill-in for my MaMa (Queen Tey) then? Another minor parallel that comes to mind, my father in this current incarnation had a long-term girlfriend whose name was Tina as well.

An Open Letter to Mrs. Tina

Did you ever have an inkling, that you were connected to ancient Egypt? Wow, Mrs. Tina, your progenies are always female winners! Your daughter this time around is known as Queen Bey. But, really, wouldn't that make you the original Queen Bey, Queen Tey?

Mrs. Tina, despite what the artifacts exposed, I am a victor! And as a victor, I have the power to rewrite history. You and I had a mother/daughter relationship in ancient Egypt. Therefore, this is my book and you will now go down as my past life Mother. So, let's give you a new title: Queen's Mother and Great Pharaoh's Wife.

Mrs. Tina, I would just love to take a picture with you and Jada. It would be a great honor to have my past life sister and my past life mother standing by my side in the same frame! I can envision it now. The caption would read: The Resurrection of Three Royal Queens of the 18th Egyptian Dynasty: Queen Tey, Queen Mutnedjmet and Queen Nefertiti.

How beautiful does that sound?

Thank you for feeding me infinite beauty, power and wisdom.

Your daughter of the Ancient Land,
Queen Nefertiti aka Jarnalia Jennings, *the Egyptian Resurrector*

Spiritual Lesson #5: Acquaintances

If you have old acquaintances such as old childhood friends, old classmates, old teachers or old neighbors who show up in your dreams out of nowhere and decades later, nine times out of 10 you probably are seeing into a past life, when the two of you were once again connected in another time and place. These dreams are not limited to just past life reflection, they also can let you peer into future lifetimes and/or parallel realities. But one thing is for sure, you better believe there is more to that current relationship than meets the eye. Real talk!

Spiritual Lesson #6

The soul is at total liberty in the process of selecting a physical body to host it. Your soul has the option to choose from an array of nationalities displayed in something similar to a physical costume catalog. For example, your soul could elect to be of African descent, Cambodian descent, Dutch descent, Iranian descent, Norwegian descent, Puerto Rican descent, Samoan descent, or even multiracial. In like manner, this could be coupled with making a selection from a sub-category similar to Fitzpatrick's Skin Types, where you can select from the fairest skin tone to the darkest skin tone within that nationality or ethnicity. Again, the choice is up to the soul.

Although you do not remember, we have been all colors of the human race, we've been both sexes and we all have probably hosted bodies with physical ailments too. One part of me would love to say that it's extremely sad that we have these superficial egos as humans and we have divided and separated ourselves from everything with an -ism, such as colorism, racism, and sexism. However, as a Jarnalia Jennings public announcement, we have played all the ugly parts too!

Remember the soul is going to choose all the conditions and all the circumstances it wishes to experience or achieve, and these specific conditions and circumstances will ultimately make up the human experience for the soul. We are spiritual beings having a human experience. So, what is the point? The soul is all about evolving on its spiritual path.

It may be hard to fathom, but the soul does choose to have physical or mental impairments if it wishes to experience life from that perspective. You may say, "Jarnalia who would want to have Asperger's Syndrome, Cerebral Palsy, Down Syndrome, Muscular Dystrophy, visual impairments, etcetera? That's nonsense!"

The soul chooses all the conditions it wishes to experience and achieve. On some higher level of consciousness, your soul wanted to have this experience for its own evolutionary soul growth. Not only that, but I've read that souls preview their selected lives before they incarnate into it.

In one of my favorite metaphysical books, the author states that her brother had chosen to be physically handicapped for the purpose of *teaching the family about love*! Ultimately, that's what it's all about: loving others and serving others as we evolve on our spiritual paths of evolution.

8

The Afterlife Is Now, The Resurrection Of the Nights Over Egypt Family

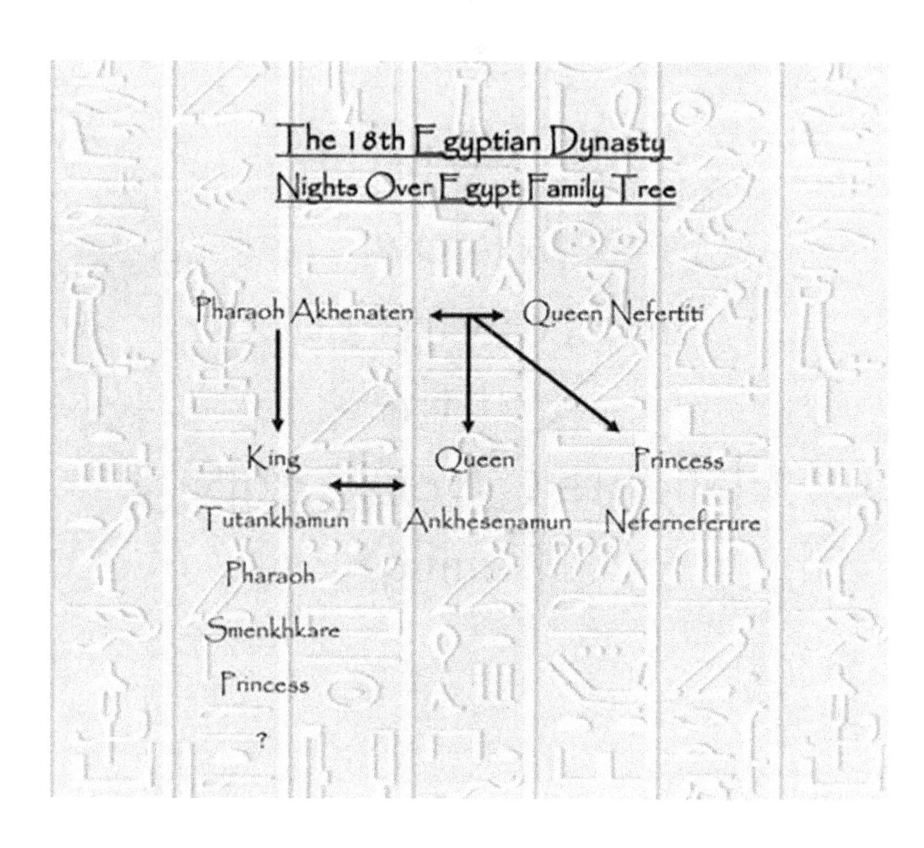
The 18th Egyptian Dynasty
Nights Over Egypt Family Tree
Pharaoh Akhenaten
Queen Nefertiti
King
Tutankhamun
Pharaoh
Smenkhkare
Princess
?
Queen
Ankhesenamun
Princess
Neferneferure

In the words of the Jones Girls,
"There's a star in the East over Pyramids at Giza,
There had once lived a girl, she ruled the world,
Then down the Nile he came with a smile,
he was a King, she was a queen under the moonlight,
Your eyes won't believe what you mind can't conceive."[70]

Nights over Egypt

Cynthia Biggs & Dexter Wansal, I love it!

---

[70] Jones Girls, "Night Over Egypt," track 3 on Get as Much Love as You Can, 1981.

Resurrecting Our Heirs

A stela of my husband Pharaoh Akhenaten, me,
Nefertiti, & three of our six children.

The Egyptian power couple, Pharaoh Akhenaten & Queen Nefertiti!

To My Pharaoh Akhenaten,

May these revelations enlighten you too!

Your Queen of the Nile,
Nefertiti

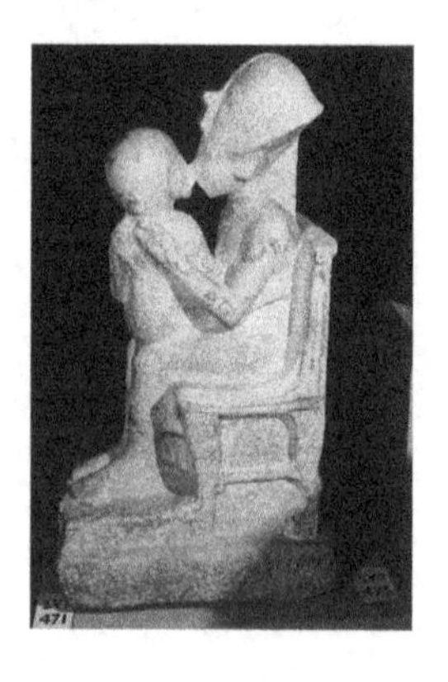

Boy Pharaoh King Tutankhamun of the 18th Egyptian Dynasty

"Living Image of Amun"

Father: Pharaoh Amenhotep IV/Akhenaten

Mother: Queen Nefertiti

Birth Mother: The Young Lady; his father's full sister, a daughter of Pharaoh Amenhotep III (Jay-Z) & Queen Tiye (Michelle O.)

Wife: Half Sister Queen Ankhesenamun

Offspring: 2 Stillborn

Other Notable Relatives: Grandparents: Pharaoh Amenhotep III & Queen Tiye, half-brother Pharaoh Smenkhkare, and six half-sisters from father.

Reign: 10 years

Buried: KV62[71]

---

71 "Tutankhamun," History.com, available at *https://www.history.com/topics/ancient-history/tutankhamen.*

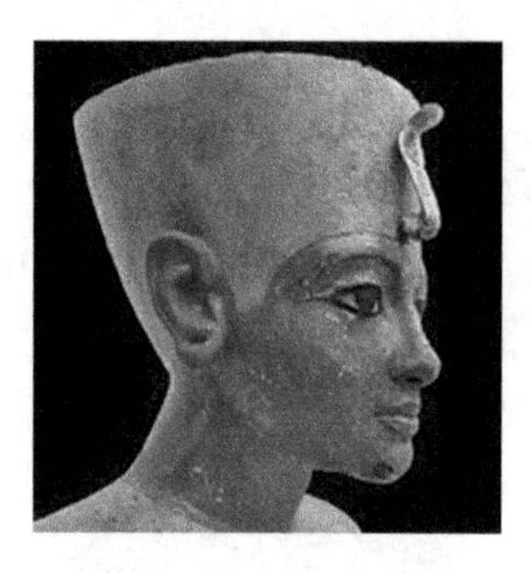

The Boy Pharaoh Origins?

Tutankhaten was the fruit of Pharaoh Akhenaten's loins. According to Egyptian historians, his birth mother is assumed to have been closely related to his father, Pharaoh Akhenaten.

Although Tutankhaten was not my birth son, he was still my beloved son.

King Tutankhamun ascended to the throne as the youngest pharaoh of the 18th Egyptian Dynasty. The boy pharaoh was only nine or 10 years of age upon his father's death. Once he became king, he took my daughter, Ankhesenpaaten, his half-sister, as his queen. Holy cannoli, now I wish I could remember this!

At the Beginning: Boy as King

Although the pharaoh was a young lad, he certainly had big shoes to fill, for this was the greatest role of his inexperienced life. He inherited two of his father's very powerful viziers: my father, Grand Vizier Aye (Tupac), and Vizier Horemheb (Will Smith).

In the beginning, King Tut's two viziers controlled Egypt through the boy pharaoh. In the third year of his reign, Tut overturned many of his father's mandates.

The boy pharaoh's first order of business was moving the capital back to Thebes, in Luxor. Where his father completely abandoned Thebes when he was pharaoh, King Tut would completely abandon our city Amarna. King Tut's second order of business was putting an end to the worshipping practices of Aten, the sun deity who enchanted his father and Queen Nefertiti. Under King Tutankhamun's new orders, he restored Amun as the supreme deity, then lifted the ban on the cult of Amun and restored the privileges back to the priesthood. Next order of business, the boy pharaoh-initiated building projects specifically in Karnak, in Thebes. Unlike his father, King Tut built many monuments and dedicated temples to Amun. Lastly, King Tut also restored the celebration of traditional festivals.[72]

In opposition to all things Aten, King Tut, changed his name too! Born Tutankhaten, which meant "*In the Living Image of Aten*," King Tut changed his name to Tutankhamun. With this new adjustment, Pharaoh Tutankhamun is now the "*Living Image of Amun,*" and reinforces the restoration of the supreme deity Amun.[73]

Even King Tutankhamun's wife's name was changed. Ankhesenpatten would now be known as Ankhesenamun. This was all to show an even more unified restoration to Amun.

Strengthening Relations

Although King Tut's restoration had many positive effects throughout the land of Egypt, it also had its disadvantages. The economy was suffering financially due to our reign (Pharaoh Akhenaten and me/ Queen Nefertiti). Akhenaten failed to maintain positive diplomatic relations with other kingdoms. In turn, this left our son King Tut, standing on his own merits to reestablish these positive diplomatic relations with other kingdoms. Despite a successful reestablishment with one kingdom, the young pharaoh was unsuccessful with other lands, and this resulted in war.

---

[72] "Tutankhamun," History.com, available at ***https://www.history.com/topics/ancient-history/tutankhamen.***

[73] "Tutankhamun (1336 BC–1327 BC)," BBC, available at https://www.bbc.co.uk/history/historic_figures/tutankhamun.shtml.

Here, in this famous painting, is of an older King Tutankhamun on his chariot at war.

The Death of a Young King!

Why did our son, King Tut, perish at the tender age of 18? Did my father, Grand Vizier Ay, have anything to do with it?

There are as many theories surrounding our son's death as there are boulders that keep the constructions of the pyramids erect!

One theory is that he died from adverse side effects of a mosquito-borne parasite that causes malaria, resulting in the pharaoh contracting multiple infections. Other theories suggest it was due to Kohler's Disease II or sickle cell anemia. Someone even thought King Tut died from complications due to his parent's incestual relationship. Assassination is even posited as a cause of death. Researchers think my father, Grand Vizier Aye/Ay offed King Tut in an attempt to steal the throne from him.

I am ordained by the gods to make this announcement. King Tut's immortal soul, immortal spirit, and immortal essence left that body in 1323 BC, then entered into another physically healthy body in the process called *reincarnation.* It is highly likely that this soul has incarnated on Earth several times since that lifetime as King Tutankhamun. *I'm sure of it*!

In 1922, there was an Egyptologist who I refuse to name in my book. This Egyptologist, let's call him HC. HC received the highest accolades for his part in the discovery of King Tutankhamun's tomb. Even today, when learning about King Tutankhamun's life, you are bound to come across his name, as if he was the Egyptian godfather to King Tut. To me, this is a disgrace to our son's legacy!

Once HC and his team discovered King Tut's tomb, this opened up the gate for our son's mummy to be dissected like a fetal pig. ***He was a Pharaoh! Where is your respect for the dead?*** And under these circumstances, it brings the greatest joy to my being to know that my burial markers are unknown.

To disturb the mummy of a god/pharaoh is the highest violation of the underworld. I perceive with every part of my being that this action is vile. It brings me great satisfaction to read that HC and his team received the grandest prize for their amazing treasure find. Each of them was rewarded with death!

As Sekhmet, the protector of pharaohs, and as Queen Nefertiti, the surrogate mother of King Tut, thou shalt not have disrupted the great royal tomb of King Tutankhamun. Unless you are ordained by the deities of the underworld, you should not have your paws on anything of the Egyptian dead. It makes me wonder what their life lessons were. To tamper with the resting place of an Egyptian pharaoh, make one of the biggest discoveries of history, then perish as a result!

Consequences for disturbing the Pharaoh

A chest of Anubis guarding King Tutankamun

I don't know if this image is authentic or if it's a replica, but a similar chest was discovered by HC & team in King Tut's Tomb.

"Curses after the Old Kingdom era are less common though more severe, sometimes invoking the ire of Thoth or the destruction of Sekhemet.[74]

"Zahi Hawass quotes an example of a curse: "Cursed be those who disturb the rest of a pharaoh. They that shall break the seal of this tomb shall meet death by a disease that no doctor can diagnose."[75]

To the writers of the movie *The Pyramid,* Danial Meersand & Nick Simon, you got Sekhmet's stamp of approval.

Now, let me get down to business!

With the powers vested in me, I resurrect the royal son, King Tutankhamun, from the Valley of the Kings (KV62). Today, he has incarnated as…

[74] David Silverman, "Ancient Egypt," p. 146, Oxford University Press US, 2003

[75] Zahi A. Hawass, "Valley of the Golden Mummies," p. 94–97, American University Press in Cairo Press, 2000.

Michael Jackson

August 29, 1958-June 25, 2009

***Yes, the King of Pop was the Boy Pharaoh*!**

I didn't dream this!

This insight was given to me.

At first, I thought King Tut was Nas! Yep, because of Nas's *I am* album cover. His face is merged with the image of a pharaoh. Then I saw a picture of Nasir rocking a phat King Tut pendant on a big-ass gold rope chain draped around his neck. Therefore, I ***assumed*** King Tutankhamun was *Nasty Nas*.

Puzzled by my own discovery, I was trying to arrange the pieces that were coming my way, so I ran over to KareBear to ask her if the rapper Nas was King Tut. When the verdict came back, it was shocking. She said *no*, in this incarnation, King Tut was *Michael Jackson*! This raised my suspicion about someone else who I thought may have played a major role in ancient Egypt who is closely related to Pharaoh Michael.

If KareBear had not given me this free insight, I would have gotten it on my own despite my assumption about Nas. I was watching *Celebrity Wife Swap* back in 2014 and the two celebrities were Jermaine Jackson and Daniel Baldwin. About nine minutes and 13 seconds into the show,

I saw an Egyptian temple in the background with Michael Jackson's bust in the center of the shrine. It was eyebrow-raising, and in an instant, I got really excited because I felt Michael Jackson knew who he was from ancient Egypt. I was also thrilled because KareBear is so on point!

The Music Video

When the *Remember the Time* music video came out, I must have been about 14 or 15 years old, and you already know I was parked in front of my television screen watching the world premiere on MTV! I felt the Egyptian theme was grand and I noticed that it was star-studded. I remember those women with the see-through hijabs, circling Michael Jackson and dancing with him. I thought that was neat. Oh, I do remember Michael Jackson kissing the queen. I thought, *Michael gettin him some—right*! All in all, I thought the dancing at the end was the best. I was mesmerized by the choreography! Everyone looked so good and in sync, I even remember trying to follow the dance steps. I sucked! This part of the music video is a feel-good moment for me.

The understanding wasn't there in my adolescent mind yet, so I had no clue of any connections. But after being awakened and enlightened, watching the music video again made my jar hit the floor! Pharaoh Barack, your son made a music video about us and our time in the 18th Egyptian Dynasty! How about that? King Michael tapped into a dormant past life memory, although the dynasty was one off.

Amazing!

I have my own theory.

What if this music video was the first essential key to resurrecting everyone, I've mentioned in these last three chapters, including myself, back in 1992? You know those latent memories lay dormant within our souls, playing opossum. They were just waiting for something to come along and stimulate them so they could redirect our attention inwards, to help us explore more of our true self. King Michael's *Remember the Time* video planted a seed within us all.

To all the pharaohs, queens and viziers I have resurrected, did you *Remember the Time* after watching King Michael's epic Egyptian music video? Where were you mentally in 1992? Was anything stirred within your beings after watching this video for the first time? What about the second time or anytime thereafter? Pharaoh Will, what about you, you also created an Egyptian themed music video.

In my opinion, the Universal Forces made sure someone of this dynasty "remembered our time". Those forces saw to it that "she" would summon them all and help them remember their royal Egyptian sovereignty. Not only was King Tut's/Michael Jackson's music video *Remember the Time* for us, the 18th Egyptian Dynasty, I'm guessing it was especially created for the 19th Egyptian Dynasty.

What do I think about the video in the aftermath of my enlightenment?

I was confused slightly because the Great Ramesses was a wrestling character on Nacho Libra! No, I'm playing! Ramesses the Great, was an Egyptian Pharaoh of the 19th Egyptian Dynasty. If you remember from Pharaoh Horemheb story, he brought in Paramessu as his successor. Paramessu was Ramesses's original name. Ramesses I had a son, Seti I, who had a son who was known as Ramesses II—*aka* Ramesses the Great. The succession of these pharaohs is chronicled in Egyptian Antiquities as the 19th Dynasty thanks to Pharaoh Will.

I assumed that Iman was portraying the role of Queen Nefertiti, and I thought to myself, *Well, she's definitely married to the wrong pharaoh*! I'm guessing after my reign as Nefertiti, other chief queens wore the same headdress as well. So, for the sake of this book, I will use the players from the 18th Egyptian Dynasty names for King Tut's music video plot. And for the record, I'm always bored! I even thought about titling this book *A Memoir of One Boring Life*, so Iman hit the nail on the head when she said that. I would love to have a baby lion seated next to me all the time; I just love big cats!

Next time, when you are watching the *Remember the Time* video, when you see Eddie Murphy as the Pharaoh, you should think President Obama as Pharaoh Akhenaten, and when you look at Iman the queen, think of my lovely face, QueenGoddess Jarnalia. So, let's have a little fun.

Let's re-enact the beginning of King Tut's video. Hold up, wait a minute, let me grab my son Beno to do the directing on the set.

Beno says: Action!

Queen Jarnalia: Pharaoh Barack, I'm bored! I want to be entertained (*I reach over and touch my husband's umm...hand*). Can my pharaoh find some way to entertain his queen, *Jarnalia*?

Pharaoh Barack: *(Pharaoh Barack raises his cup to his mouth and sips on his Cognac after the little servant girl Nileen refreshes his cup.)*

(Still silent, Pharaoh Barack obliges his queen with a clap to commence the start of some evening entertainment.)

Two performers are sent out.

The first unimpressive performer tosses around some darn sticks. Our servant girl Nileen seems to be entertained by this mess, but I'm not amused.

(I make a gesture indicating that I have had enough and audibly order death to this pathetic performer) ***"Throw him to the lions!"***

Then the second performer steps up, he is known as HC Pyro. He tries to impress me as well with his fire blowing, eating routine crap.

(Pharaoh Barack raises his eyebrow, as if he is questioning this performer's real intentions as the flames seem to be getting a little too close for comfort for my pharaoh.)

Queen Jarnalia: (so not amused, my body language shows that I'm slightly perturbed once more.) I ordered the guards, to decapitate the man with a precise motion of my hand across my neck. Bye Bye, HC!

To the Egyptian Announcer, Magic J. I'm merciless, I know. But you see, I am a gift from the gods and my role in Egypt is ***PARAMOUNT!*** Therefore, I need the equivalent in entertainment!

Pharaoh Barack: (Shouts out to the third mysterious participant) ***"So what is it you're going to do?"***

The mysterious man is dressed in all black. He throws out a handful of black magical granules and we all watch as they swarm into a cluster on the marble floor. Then this mysterious man stands within the band of the black granules and vanishes!

All eyes in the room widen with intrigue, including mine.

The granules convert into a golden pile of sorcery dust. And there, within this transformation, a shadowy man re-emerges as the golden boy, our son, King Tutankhamun/Michael Jackson!

Pharaoh Akhenaten, I dedicate the lyrics to you.

Do you remember how we fell in love, we were so young and innocent then?

Do you remember how it all began, it just seems like Heaven so why did it end?

Beno calls: *Cut*!

I know the answer to that question now. Life, or time, had to evolve, and that's why it had to end!

The Authentic Gift

When I was about eight years old, living on Bland Street, my grandma gave me quite an interesting gift. She gave me a spread that was autographed by Michael Jackson! Actually, it was the *Human Nature* album cover, but it was on silky material. She bought it for 100 bucks from someone who claimed that they got it in Hollywood.

Michael's autograph was on the bottom right of this picture in black magic marker. Today, honestly, I don't have a clue what I did with that spread. Was I supposed to hang it on the wall? Because I ended up keeping it on top of my comforter. I remember having a funny feeling about that spread. While in my bedroom listening to music, I had the face of Michael Jackson to keep me company, but it felt a bit weird. I was sensing something.

Little girl Jarnalia was overly concerned with the authenticity of the signature. I wanted to know if it was actually Michael Jackson's signature or not. In hindsight, there could have been many subliminal messages that I was receiving at that tender age, but my juvenile brain could not begin to understand anything outside of music, riding my bike and jumping off rooftops.

The Memorial Park

After having my memory restored on the true identity of King Tutankhamun in this incarnation, one day I was at the memorial park with my aunt Mama, and when my aunt visits the dead, she visits with everyone in her family and refreshes their vases with new artificial flowers.

On this particular day, we journeyed across the cemetery to pay our respects to her father, her brother, and her father's aunt's gravesite. My maternal grandfather's aunt Mary gave birth to 14 children and each of her children's names was printed on her tombstone. Mama and I moved on over to Aunt Mary's son-in-law's tombstone and his tombstone was similar to his mother-in-law's tombstone, flat and long. This relative's name was Perry and there displaced on Perry's full-length tombstone was a similar listing of his children's names, along with his grandchildrens' names. I stood there and read Mr. Perry's tombstone, and, lo and behold, there listed among the grandchildrens' names was Tutankhamun!

When I read this, I was shocked & amazed. Mr. Perry's grandson, Tutankhamun, who is living, would be my fourth cousin! At that moment, I felt that this was a confirmation for me, linking me to Egypt and Michael Jackson, and a signpost that I was on the right track. Next to Mr. Perry's resting place, to his left, his neighbor's name was Queen! Go figure! I told Mama, "I know who Tutankhamun was in this lifetime!" She looked at me like she always does, as if *I'm bout crazy as hell,* as comedian Terry puts it. With her look of bewilderment, I didn't speak any more of it. But isn't that interesting?

Opening of the Mouth Ceremony

The opening of the mouth ceremony was an Egyptian ritual for the dead. This funerary text was placed on the walls within the tomb of the dead and served as a survival manual to the dead, illustrating how to survive in the underworld and afterlife. It was believed that in order to survive the afterlife, our souls still needed sustenance like food and water. Therefore, the ceremony was conducted to help facilitate the opening of the mouth and eyes of the mummy. The ritual also provided a releasing of the person's ba (personality) from their body to seek out and be reunited with their ka (life force the pure essence of an individual), resulting in the forming of an akh (spiritual and immortal part of the soul.)[76]

Geez, where is Makalesi when you need her?

Here is an illustration of the ritual, from the walls of King Tutankhamun's tomb. It shows Pharaoh Aye/Ay conducting the opening of the mouth ceremony on Pharaoh Tutankhamun. Pharaoh Aye/Ay is using a tool called ritual adze.

---

[76] "The Opening of the Mouth Ceremony," Experience Ancient Egypt, available at *http://www.experience-ancient-egypt.com/egyptian-religion-mythology/egyptian-afterlife/opening-of-the-mouth-ceremony.*

And from my specs:

This is Tupac & Michael Jackson!

It is speculated that, when he was King Tutankhamun's grand vizier, my father poisoned my son King Tut! To put it in modern terms, Tupac poisoned Michael Jackson for the throne, however, there isn't any proof! It would be quite fascinating to know how Tupac felt about Michael Jackson and vice versa. My inquiring mind would like to know.

"I Bet You Remember!"

This is more accurate!
The 18th Egyptian Dynasty Pharaoh Akhenaten, Queen Nefertiti and son King Tutankhaten.

Queen Ankhesenamun Royal Chief Queen of the 18th Egyptian Dynasty

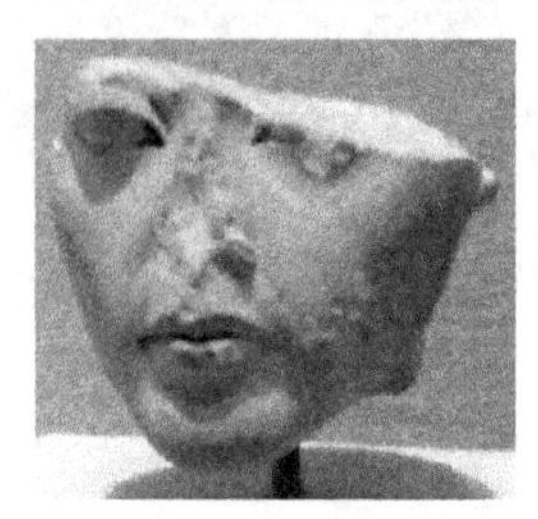

"Her Life is AMUN"

Father: Pharaoh Akhenaten

Mother: Queen Nefertiti

Husband: Pharaoh Tutankhamun (half-brother) & Pharaoh Aye/ Ay (her grandfather)

Offspring: 2 Stillborn

Other Noble Relatives: Sisters: Meritaten, Meketaten, Neferneferuaten Tasherit, Neferneferure and Setepenre. Grandparents: Pharaoh Amenhotep III, Queen Tiye grandparents and Queen Tey.

Reign: 9 years

Buried: Possibly KV21[77]

Princess Ankhesenapaaten was born into royalty around 1348 BC, the daughter of Chief Royal Queen Nefertiti and Pharaoh Akhenaten. Princess Ankhesenapaaten was the supreme couple's third born daughter out of six girls. She was born in Thebes, and her parents named her in honor of the sun deity Aten, *"Her Life Is of Aten."*

---

[77] April Holloway, "The tragedy of Queen Ankhesenamun, sister and wife of Tutankhamun" Ancient Origins, avialable at *https://www.ancient-origins.net/ancient-places-africa/tragedy-queen-ankhesenamun-sister-and-wife-tutankhamun-001555.*

From Princess to Queen

Princess Ankhesenapaaten's father, Pharaoh Akhenaten, died when she was around 12 years old. Once Ankhesenapaaten's brother, King Tut, became heir to the throne of Egypt, he married her, his half-sister, making her the Great Royal Wife of King Tut and a queen of the 18th Egyptian Dynasty. Queen Ankhesenapaaten's husband restored the exalting of the god Amun. Because of this, her name was changed to Ankhesenamun, which means "*Her Life Is of Amun.*"[78]

Queen Ankhesenamun and husband/half-brother King Tutankhamun conceived two daughters. However, both babies were stillborn. There is evidence of two stillborn girls within the tomb of King Tutankhamun, so it is assumed by the researchers that the stillborn babies belonged to him and Queen Ankhesenamun.[79]

The Queen's Great Loss

King Tut died at the tender age of 18/19, leaving Queen Ankhesenamun as a young, vulnerable widow. Even though King Tut had appointed a successor to the throne, this designation was unfulfilled, and the king's chair was up for grabs once again.

A Ball of Confusion

In the aftermath of King Tutankhamun's premature passing, Queen Ankhesenamun took action into her own hands. Queen Ankhesenamun placed a request to the king of Hittite, Suppiluliuma I, and this special request became referred to as Deeds of Suppiluliuma I.

Ankhesenamun told the ruler Suppiluliuma I that her husband has

[78] April Holloway, "The tragedy of Queen Ankhesenamun, sister and wife of Tutankhamun" Ancient Origins, avialable at *https://www.ancient-origins.net/ancient-places-africa/tragedy-queen-ankhesenamun-sister-and-wife-tutankhamun-001555*.

[79] Anneke Burt, "Queen Ankhesenamun," Ancient Egypt, available at *https://mathstat.slu.edu/~bart/egyptianhtml/kings%20and%20Queens/Ankhesenamun.html*.

died, and she has no heir to the throne. She asked the ruler to consider giving her one of his sons to marry because she did not wish to take any of her subjects as her husband.[80]

King Suppiluliuma I investigated the Egyptian queen's impromptu request. He must have determined that Queen Ankhesenamun's troubles were authentic. King Suppilulium I sent his son named Zannanza, to join Queen Ankhesenamum on the Egyptian throne. But before Zannanza could arrive in Egypt, he was killed.

Before the queen could blink, my father, Grand Vizier Aye/Ay, married his own granddaughter, *Queen Ankhesenamun.*

Gross!

This means Pharaoh Aye/Ay had two wives! Queen Tey and Queen Ankhesenamun, grandmother and granddaughter, and now *co-wives*! In the words of Big Momma: *"This sho is some freaky shit!"*

Queen Ankhesenamun gives her husband/half-brother King Tutankhamun a flower as an expression of love.

With the powers vested in me, I resurrect our royal daughter Queen Akhesenamun from the Valley of the Kings. Today, she has incarnated as…

[80] Anneke Burt, "Queen Ankhesenamun," Ancient Egypt, available at *https://mathstat.slu.edu/~bart/egyptianhtml/kings%20and%20Queens/Ankhesenamun.html.*

Janet Jackson

Ms. Jackson, if you're nasty!

Do you remember when I shared with you that on my birthday in 2012, while watching *Poetic Justice*, some extraordinary insight came to me about Tupac? After I investigated Tupac, I pulled up info on Janet Jackson. I happened to notice something strikingly reminiscent to my very own birthname—she and I have the exact same initials! Janet's full name is Janet Damita Jo Jackson, and my name is Jarnalia Denise Jennings. Janet just has one extra J, but it's all the same.

This revelation left me puzzled!

I knew without a doubt this was some sort of insight or clue for me. I did not know what to do with my newly discovered theory in that moment, so I just decided to scribble it down in my notes. At that time, I was only aware of a little of my Egyptian life—like who I was, and who the Obamas were as they related to my past life.

In addition to JayDee's visit on my thirty-fifth birthday, a girlfriend of mine came by to wish me a happy birthday and share some of her Thanksgiving plate with me that she got from someone else's house. You're not going to believe this, but this shit is true! My girlfriend's name was *Ms. Jackson*! Ms. Jackson and JayDee (Shakur) were both here on the same day, the day of my birthday, the same day I suspected Tupac was Pharaoh Aye, and the same day I realized that I had the same initials as Miss Janet Jackson.

In all honesty, this connection did not dawn on me immediately. It took me a few days to put two and two together, only because I do not call my girlfriend by her last name. The symbolism had to marinate a few days!

I immediately emailed KareBear back to share with her my other suspicion—that Janet Jackson was possibly one of Queen Nefertiti's daughters. After disclosing my behind the veil revelation to KareBear, she did not respond to confirm or deny my suspicion. I carried this revelation with me for five years before having it confirmed.

By this time, I had connected the dots and concluded that Janet Jackson had everything to do with my ancient Egyptian lifetime. They say the truth is stranger than fiction! To my very own amazement, I also concluded that the two main characters in *Poetic Justice* were once a part of my distant reality!

On a much deeper and existential level, Janet/Queen Ankhesenamun as Justice was playing out a story from another incarnation when she was once married to her own grandfather in a distant past life. Along the same lines, Tupac/Pharaoh Aye as Lucky was acting out from the same past incarnation when he was married to his own granddaughter. This is the ultimate reflection of *life imitating art*! Unbeknownst to John Singleton, he had it right!

I would like to take the time to say thank you to the late John Singleton for making this movie and having his hand in Michael Jackson's *Remember the Time* music video as well. Mr. Singleton, you also have been a guiding light in my understanding, thank you.

As disturbing as this image is to me, the truth of the matter is: this was Pharaoh Aye kissing his new wife, Queen Ankhesenamun! Ankhesenamun (Janet) is Tutankhamun's (Michael) widow, she is also our daughter (Nefertiti (Jarnalia) and Akhenaten (Barack), as well as, Aye (Tupac) & Queen Tey's (Tina) and Amenhotep III (Jay-Z) and Tiye's (Michelle) granddaughter! Today, their roles still play out as ancient truth in a 1993 fictional movie by John Singleton, starring Janet Jackson & Tupac Shakur in *Poetic Justice*.

Extraordinary, wouldn't you say?

An Open Letter to Janet

(Penny, I would have never burned you with an iron, for you are love, my love!)

Hi, Janet!

After reading my interpretation and the historical overview of the 18th Egyptian Dynasty's Queen Ankhesenamun and resurrecting her as you, I know for sure you are probably laughing your butt off and saying, "What the heck is this woman talking about?" And you'll probably throw the word crazy somewhere into that sentence!

Well, I'm talking about reincarnation, and how it relates to you in an ancient lifetime that you have forgotten all about. In that lifetime, I was much like Katherine is to you now. Now, just because you are older than I, by 11 years in this incarnation, does not exempt us from having a mother-daughter relationship over 3000 years ago. A good example of this would be a movie and book by Jenny Cockell called *Yesterday's Children*. Might I add, it's based on a true story!

Queen Janet, I would like to say, thank you for showing up and entertaining me this time around. I have really enjoyed your music over my lifetime. When I was 12 years old, my friend and I used to go to dances at Tarralton Recreation Center and I remember always looking for this special boy to dance with when your song, *Come Back to Me* was played. I must say, in some kind of way, I felt a small connection to you when that song was played.

Over the years, your music grew, you grew, and I grew too, and I can't single out just one of your songs that I favored over the others, because I have about 10 in my head that I would classify as my favorite. Especially your collaboration with Lisa Keith and Herb Alpert, *Making Love in the Rain*, such a beautiful melody. Moreover, I knew nothing about making love in the rain in the '80s, and as a 39-year-old woman today, I still don't! However, that song is still a hit in my book!

Queen Janet, all jokes aside, I'm sorry that I have to inform you through a book that Michael was your brother before this Jackson incarnation, but not only was he your brother then, he was also your husband in that ancient lifetime. Gross, I know! But there wasn't any other way for me to deliver this story of enlightenment to you. I can sympathize with you on having your life constantly exploited by gossip tabloids. Then, just when things seem to die down, another destructive story surfaces. In advance, I'm sorry for drawing any negative attention as it relates to our legendary past.

Janet, does my ancient story of remembrance bring you a little solace as it relates to your dearly departed? Even though you can't remember that lifetime, you and your brother Michael have never been apart, for death cannot sever the ethereal cords of love. This is the same love that has brought you two back together again. This time around as platonic brother and sister where you were able to just enjoy your brother as he was. Janet, Michael will always show up by your side again and again; *you can bank on that, my child*!

Whatever you felt when you played Justice in *Poetic Justice* with Tupac, you were tapping into a dormant emotion connected to ancient Egypt when Tupac was your elderly grandfather/ husband known as Pharaoh Ay. That's even grosser, I know. I see why you put up such a fuss behind the scenes about sharing a kiss for the movie.

Janet go and research your past life history, you've been through something, Queen. One more thing, not only do we share the same initials, I have the same beauty mark on the right-side of my face, right above my lip too!

To life, past, present, and future,
Jarnalia Jennings/Queen Nefertiti, *the Egyptian Resurrector*

Pharaoh Aye/Ay & Queen Ankhesenamun in the 20th Century

Look, Tupac even has on an Oakland A's jersey!

Wake up, people!

Michael Jackson & Janet Jackson when they were husband & wife in the 18th Egyptian Dynasty!

Pharaoh Smenkhkare of the18th Egyptian Dynasty

"Living are the Forms of Ra and Vigorous is the Soul of Ra-Holy of Forms"

Father: Unknown, but possibly Pharaoh Akhenaten

Mother: Unknown, but possibly Tutankhamun's Mother Young Lady 55

Wife: Queen Meritaten

Offspring: None

Reign: 1 year

Buried: Unknown

An enigmatic tale of a transitory Pharaoh of the 18th Egyptian Dynasty.

Very little is known about Pharaoh Smenkhkare due to the various campaigns to destroy everything Amarna after Pharaoh Akhenaten, King Tutankhamun, and Pharaoh Ay's Reign. Smenkhkare was one of two ruling pharaohs following the death of Pharaoh Akhenaten. According to Egyptian historians, this could be why Pharaoh Akhenaten did not have a successor, because a co-regency had been established after all. If a co-regency had been created, then Pharaoh Smenkhkare may have held equal power with Pharaoh Akhenaten.

Pharaoh Smenkhkare was married to Queen Meritaten, the first-born daughter of Queen Nefertiti and Pharaoh Akhenaten. This made Pharaoh Smenkhkare son-in-law to the royal couple. Or, Pharaoh Smenkhkare could have very well been Pharaoh Akhenaten's off-spring.

An abundant amount of evidence left behind proves that Smenkhkare was a pharaoh. In 1845, the identity of Pharaoh Smenkhkare emerged from within the tomb of Meryre II, Queen Nefertiti's superintendent and the overseer of two lands. Within his tomb, Pharaoh Smenkhkare and his wife Queen Meritaten are described with their royal titles as Great Royal Wife, as they are rewarding the owner of the tomb Meryre II. There was also a vase from Tut's tomb which bears both Akhenaten and Smenkhkare's names, a single wine docket, rings bearing his name, a vase hall named Smenkhkare Hall because a number of bricks stamped Ankhkheperure, and a linen shawl with his name on it.[81]

At some point, Smenkhkare either changed his name, or facilitated the role of a temporary pharaoh by the name of Neferneferuaten.

This is the bust of Pharaoh Smenkhkare and a plaster bust from the workshop of the sculptor Thutmose.

With the powers vested in me, I resurrect Pharaoh Smenkhkare from wherever his Egyptian royal corpse reposes. Today, he has incarnated as...

[81] Jenny Hill, "Smenkhkare," Ancient Egypt Online, available at *https://ancientegyptonline.co.uk/smenkhare/.*

NAS

His Father told him, "He'll Be the Greatest Man Alive!"

"Before we woke up in this country, [yes], we were kings and queens never porch monkeys." Yes, there was one specific empire in Africa called Amarna, where Nasir came from, representing these ancient books!

It made no sense at first. Not until I started researching and writing about King Tut's Egyptian history for this book. That's when I came across the name Smenkhkare. It took me four years to put two and two together when it hit me that Nas must be Tut's half-brother, Pharaoh Smenkhkare, and not King Tut himself.

Listed below is a partial reading from the Angel & Guides. As well as a full reading from KareBear and her input on what I received from Angel & Guides.

From: 2xQueen 2xGoddess
To: Angel & Guides
07/14/12 at 4:56 AM

Bonjour, Angel & Guides!

I have a hunch about someone walking this earth with me who is here for my/our entertainment. This has come to me in my dreams, through my research, & symbolism. As Sekhmet & Queen Nefertiti, I had a lifetime with this individual, so I believe I can personally ask about him.

Is Nasir Jones aka Nas, King Tutankhamun of the 18th Dynasty?

Thanks,
Queen Nefertiti

From: Angel & Guides
To: 2xQueen2xGoddess
07/16/12 at 2:53 PM

What an interesting question for me to look at! Love it!

You have done your research well, as Nas does blend with King Tut. Nas feels older–almost like King Tut just a few years older. What is interesting is that I can usually feel some distance between now and then but with these guys, it's almost like he just stepped from one dimension into another without a lot of lifetimes in between. The energy is so strong and so direct it's quite fascinating to see.

Many blessings to you,
Angel

She was sensing a slight difference and never said yes! Well, here is what KareBear had to say about my question.

From: 2xQueen2xGoddess
To: KareBear
Sent: Wednesday, July 10, 2013, 4:25 PM

KareBear,

I appreciate your services.

You are truly gifted & I trust you to give me the final yea or nay!

Is Nasir Jones aka (Nas), King Tutankhamun of the 18th Dynasty?

TY

From: KareBear
To: 2xQueen2xGoddess
Sent: Friday, July 12, 2013, 2:46 PM

Hi Jenell,

I have put a short answer next to the question number/topic. Hope this helps you 😀

Have a great weekend!

Is Nasir Jones aka Nas, King Tutankhamun of the 18th Dynasty?

No, but he was one of Tut's half-brothers.

Blessings,
Karen

From: 2xQueen 2xGoddess
To: KareBear
03/24/18 at 2:10PM

Hello, KareBear!

How are you? Well, I'm about to tie the bow on this book and

I cannot close it without your input.

I have Nas down as Pharaoh Smenkhkare because you told me he was half-brother to King Tut. Do you agree with this?

Thanks

From: KareBear
To: 2xQueen2xGoddess
03/27/18 at 12:06 PM

Hi Jenell,

Yes, Nas was 👍

Thanks,
KareBear

An Open Letter to Nasir

Pharaoh Smenkhkare, I am here as the Egyptian Resurrector this time around. I have assembled the horn players with the banners and all, to bestow you with an honorary Egyptian celebration announcement. Initially, Nas, in the very beginning of my Egyptian research, Wikipedia had Smenkhkare (your former self) listed under as a possible son of Amenhotep III's and his wife Queen Tiye (Michelle O). As of the time of this writing, someone has placed you under Pharaoh Akhenaten's Wikipedia page as a possible offspring of his.

Nasir, do you know what this means?

It means you were beefing with your ancient grandpops!

You were King Tut's half-brother! Now, in my opinion, this leaves only three possibilities to how this was possible. However, each of these possibilities still leads back to "J" being your past life ancestor. Here are the three possibilities (A). You were Pharaoh Akhenaten's offspring, (B). You were King Tut's mother's offspring; (Young Lady 55) or (C). You were conceived by both A&B! Whichever way (a), (b), or (c), Pharaoh Amenhotep III; (Jay-Z), was the father to both Young Lady 55 and Pharaoh Akhenaten; which still makes him your past life royal grandfather! *Pharaoh Nasir, from my perspective this is hilarious*!

Nas, just like I extended my gratitude to the others throughout my memoir, I am going to extend you the same. Thank you for showing up and entertaining me throughout this lifetime. In addition, thank you for leaving me little clues about yourself along the way. *Wink*! Having said that, I overstand that you didn't need for me to go and validate your Kingliness; granted you already knew that. Be that as it may, I would have to say, Mr. Jones, you needed me and my enlightenment, considering I'm rubbing elbows with the gifted KareBear, who informed me about your true self. Therefore, I have the knowledge to inform you on which king you really were among the (I'm guessing) 15 pharaohs of the 18th Egyptian Dynasty, just in case you thought you were your brother Pharaoh Tutankhamun.

King Nasir, when I was sitting up here writing this last chapter, I wanted to play your song *It Ain't Hard to Tell*, so I went and pulled it up on YouTube. Once the song started to play, and I was about to rock out to it, I had to pause for a sec because I thought it sounded like Michael Jackson's *Human Nature*. I was completely intrigued! I stopped your song and pulled up Michael's *Human Nature* on YouTube, just to make sure that's what I was hearing. I concluded, yep that's what I was hearing alright. Did someone say I'm late? No, I'm not late! I probably recognized it back in the '90s, but I'm getting younger by the day now and I had completely forgotten that's where the sample came from. The parallels in the track caught me completely off guard knowing what I know today. I say that to say this, Nasir when you were laying down your lyrical content over that *Human Nature* track, that was no accident. That was by divine design. Even if that's a sample you've always wanted to use, or it was sprung on you, do you see the significance of that connection? This is how the Universal Forces work or you might say (ARM LEG LEG ARM HEAD)! Either way, I still put respect on it!

Pharaoh Nasir, hopefully from my story you can tell that I'm genuinely into beats and instrumentals. My favorite instrumental by you is *You're the Man* and I was rocking that joint right before I moved to Jacksonville. This track happens to be very therapeutic for me, it helps me to get things right in my head. As far as copping to a favorite emcee of all times, I would have to confess that you would be one of three. Well, I've been the biggest fan of *The Grand Wizard; Slick Rick the Ruler,* since I was 10 years old. He is # 1 in my book! Nas, don't fret, you're #2! And, for the hip-hop readers, I'm torn between Ghost and Fab at my #3 spot!

Nas, my favorite song by you is *Life's a Bitch* featuring AZ. By the way, is AZ single?

Peace, Love & Respect,
Jarnalia, *the Egyptian Resurrector*

P.S. *Nas, if I ruled the world, indeed we'll walk right up to the Sun hand-in-hand*!

"It Ain't Hard to Tell"

Princess Neferneferure of the 18th Egyptian Dynasty

She is pictured on the left
"Beautiful of the Beauties of RE &/or Most Beautiful One of RE"

Father: Pharaoh Amenhotep IV/Akhenaten

Mother: Queen Nefertiti

Other Noble Relatives: Sisters: Meritaten, Meketaten, Neferneferuaten Tasherit, Ankhesenamun and Setepenre. Paternal grandparents: Pharaoh Amenhotep III & Queen Tiye. Maternal grandparents: Pharaoh Aye & Queen Tey.

Buried: Amarna, possibly Tomb 29

Princess Neferneferure was the fifth daughter born to Queen Nefertiti and Pharaoh Akhenaten in Amarna in the seventh year of his reign. In a fresco from the king's house in Amarna, she is depicted sitting on a pillow along with her sister Neferneferuaten.[82]

In the depiction below, Princess Neferneferure is seen with her two sisters—Setepenre, to her left and Neferneferuaten Tasherit to her right—in year 12 of the Durban. Neferneferure is holding a gazelle in her right hand and a flower in her left.

[82] "What Happened to the Three Youngest Armana Princesses?" The Aten Sequence Books, available at *http://atensequence.blogspot.com/2013/06/what-happened-to-three-youngest-amarna.html*

Princess Neferneferure's image was also captured on a small box bearing her name on its lid found among her half-brother Tutankhamun's possessions. The item was labeled (JdE 61498); this tag hits very close to home. Ra's name was "written phonetically" within Neferneferure's name instead of symbolized by a circle and a dot.[83]

With the powers vested in me, I resurrect our royal daughter, Princesses Neferneferure, from her tomb of Amarna. Today, she has incarnated as...

[83] T.G.H. James, *Tutankhamun*, Barnes and Noble Books, 2002.

Karen Malina White

With our stunning similar facial features, you would think Charmaine should have been the first person I zeroed in on a long time ago. When I began writing this book, I had no inkling that Karen and myself were linked together in another lifetime. When I wrote the letter to Jada, I still had no clue that Karen was connected to ancient Egypt.

So, when was the turning point?

As I was writing Malia's story, I mistakenly misspelled her name one too many times. I accidentally added N, making it Malina. While adjusting my many mistakes, I thought to myself, *That's my twin's middle name.*

Is she a daughter too? Am I overlooking her?

She never showed up in my dreams.

But she did! Karen Malina showed up in between the story of the two brothers!

My Intuitive Dream

I had a dream on October 18, 2015, about two guys and come to find out they were brothers in a past life. Today, you all know these two then brothers quite well through the mainstream media. I saw myself take on the role of the sassy, fast-talking Charmaine from *A Different World.* As a matter of fact, Charmaine was there too, paired up with Dwayne Wayne! Quite honestly, I don't even remember watching *A Different World* around the time of that dream. In that dream, Charmaine and Dwayne Wayne were in the dream behind me, they actually cut in for a few seconds. When I woke up, I thought it was a little odd that they had cut in but thought no more about it.

I was running out of money and I didn't want to pay $20 for a reading and be wrong. After four years, I went back over to eBay to see who was out there in the Metaphysical Corner. Honestly, I wasn't too impressed by the individuals who had listed their services. I felt that these people were younger, unseasoned and they were trying to be a little resourceful in their spare time. In my quest, I found an icon that said

Psychic Reading, Yes or No for a $1.95. I thought, *Shit, I've got a dollar ninety-five to blow if I'm wrong*! I proceeded to email my question.

My Open Reading

From: 2xQueen2xGoddess
To: Seaside Ash
July 21, 2017

Hey, I have a question.

Should Karen Malina White's name be included in chapter seven?

Thank You

From: Seaside Ash
To: 2xQueen2xGoddess
July 21, 2017

Hello!

I have an answer to your question "Should Karen Malina White's name be included in chapter seven?"

The pendulum swung in a clockwise circle and then immediately swung North and South. This seems to be a double affirmation the answer is yes.

Your card to explain your situation better: Queen of Cups

Meaning: Emotional security, calm, intuitive, compassionate.

Some relevant information:

The Queen of Cups is nurturing, caring, compassionate and sensitive. She is a good wife and a loving mother as she is emotionally secure and can connect on an emotional level with others. She is admired for her fairness and honesty and is warm-hearted. Often a healer, counselor or psychic, this is a woman who seems to know what is wrong even before you open your mouth. She seems to have exactly the right solution to problems relating to relationships, emotions, and feelings. She easily tunes in to what you are feeling and is able to help you make sense of it in a sensitive and compassionate manner. As such, her intuition is very strong, and she has a unique talent for being able to pick up on emotional energy. The Queen of Cups can manifest as a person in your life or as a part of yourself. She often appears as a mature female. No intuition is more powerful than that of the Queen of Cups. She is the pure force of water, and her connection with the subconscious is rivaled only by the High Priestess. She is often like a mirror, reflecting the hidden depths of others back to them, so they can see their own mysteries for themselves. Thus, the Queen of Cups indicates that you need to trust your intuition and listen to your inner voice. Trust the sensations and the feelings you are getting from your outside environment.

My input: The answer seems to be a clear yes. Twice even! I am unsure what relevance the card holds to you as I do not know your circumstances. I hope you enjoyed this reading; I wish you happiness and success in the days that follow!

-Ash

Had I known that the yes or no response was going to be revealed by tarot cards, I would have selected another reader's services. I'm not into the tarot stuff. However, the tarot card response hit the nail on the head. I could really relate to the meaning behind the Queen of Cups card and it was a double yes! As a result, I took my discoveries to someone who could help me figure out who's who out of Queen Nefertiti's girls.

An Open Letter to Karen Malina

Karen Malina, you were Queen Nefertiti's daughter in an ancient lifetime! That's something else huh?

Karen, I would love to meet you in the future and for you to meet my mother. As you can see, the Universal Forces would not allow me to complete this chapter, Nights Over Egypt, without the mentioning of your name.

I enjoyed watching you on *A Different World* and hearing your voice on *Proud Family*. Recently, I had a fine ass Puerto Rican gentleman over at my house who told me "You look like the girl from *Malcolm and Eddie.*" I laughed! I thought, at that time, the sole reason was our past and present connection to Jada/ Queen Mut, but I see now that wasn't the only justification for our resemblance.

Karen, when you played on *A Different World* alongside Jada, you were working with your distant past life aunt, Queen Mutnedjmet! When you worked alongside Will in *Fresh Prince of Bel Aire*, you were working with Pharaoh Horemheb!

Did you vote for Obama? If so, you voted for your ancient past life father, Pharaoh Akhenaten!

That means when you were watching First Lady Michelle on TV, you were watching your ancient past life paternal grandmother. Did you glimpse into the life of Malia as one of the first daughters of the White House? If so, you were glimpsing into the life of your ancient Egyptian past life sister's current life experience and you were peering into your past life family's life in the now.

I know you so loved Michael Jackson like the rest of us. Well, he was your half-brother, King Tut, in the 18th Egyptian Dynasty! His sister today, Janet, was your sister also in that ancient lifetime.

Karen, did you know Tupac personally?

If you ever interacted with him in any way, you were in the presence of your ancient Egyptian maternal grandfather, Pharaoh Aye/Ay. The famous mother of the Queen of Dance Music, Mrs. Tina, was your ancient maternal grandmother, Queen Tey! Oh, did I fail to mention that Jay-Z was your paternal grandfather in ancient Egypt? Yep, he was! It all sounds completely crazy, right? Trust me, *I know*! Beno calls it "my crazy talk," but crazy as it is, *it's my truth*!

Karen, that small box found in your ancient past life brother's possessions tagged JdE61498, it has a small meaning to me. I'll tell you in person what it symbolizes.

I am all smiles, my daughter!

Queen Nefertiti, *the Egyptian Resurrector*

An Open Past Life Reading for Janet, Malina, & Malia

From: 2xQueen2xGoddess
To: GOLDEN ROSE
On Tue, Jul 25, 2017, at 6:58 AM

Good morning. As I write this, there is an AOL pop-up box off to the right-hand side with Barack & Michelle–the constant symbolism in my life!

Golden Rose, I need your help once more.

I believe 3 of our daughters are here in the 21st century (Pharaoh Akhenaten & Queen Nefertiti's girls). Could you help me again? If you can, could you tell me if I'm right or wrong? And if I'm right, could you help me place the right name to the right girl?

First, I firmly believe that Janet Jackson was one of Queen Nefertiti's & Pharaoh Akhenaten's daughters and I believe she was Ankhesenpaaten, who later changed her name to Ankhesenamun. Yes?

Second, I believe without a shadow of the doubt that Malia Obama was one of Queen Nefertiti's & Pharaoh Akhenaten's daughters, but which daughter was she?

Third, there is an actress named Karen Malina White. I believe she was also one of Queen Nefertiti's & Pharaoh Akhenaten's daughters, but which daughter is she?

Here are the names of our royal princesses:

Meritaten
Meketaten
Ankhesenamun
Neferneferuaten Tasherit
Neferneferure
Setepenre

Thank you for your help,
Jarnalia Jennings (Queen of the Nile)

From: Golden Rose
To: 2xQueen2xGoddess
Jul 26, 2017, at 2:50 PM

Hello Jarnalia,

Thanks for having another reading with me. I hope that I can help again.

1. With regards to Janet Jackson, I get that she was one of the Akhenaten's daughters in a past life, and as well Ankhesenpaaten came in the strongest of the 6 children for her energy. So happy to share this with you today.

2. With regards to Malia Obama, I get that she was also one of the 6 children and for her, Meritaten came in the strongest as a connection for past life.

3. With regards to Karen Malina White, for her, I got that Neferneferure was the strongest energy for past life connection or embodiment.

So, I hope this helps to answer your questions today.

Sincerely,
GOLDEN ROSE

I sent this reading to KareBear and she agrees with everything, except she feels that Malia O did not play the role of Meritaten: "I feel that she was another undisclosed child/child out of wedlock."

KareBear's insight is law to me and I would never take her official rulings with a dismissive wave of the hand. KareBear's feedback left me extremely sad and I still questioned why Malia carries my name with her.

Malia Obama

Initially I thought I had the honor of putting Malia O. down under as Meritaten; a daughter of Pharaoh Akhenaten and Queen Nefertiti. This revelation revealed itself at the very beginning of my Egyptian enigma. Well, it turns out that there is some discrepancy with her role here.

One summer day in 2012, I went out to retrieve my mail. Just like any other day, I was a little intrigued to see who had corresponded with me. I pulled my mail out of the mailbox, and as I was inspecting my mail, I happened to take notice to the distinctiveness of the font style that was used for my name in the recipient's section on the letter. The R and N happened to be too close together, which made the two characters look like one solid letter M. In that instant, I noticed an eye-catching similarity in my name that paralleled with Malia Obama's name. As I was walking back to my apartment from the mailbox, I pondered if Malia Obama was part of this storyline too. By this time, I knew who Barack and Michelle were in Egypt's past. I couldn't believe I had taken notice of such an extraordinary phenomenon within my name. I had never paid it any attention beforehand.

When I got back inside, I rifled clumsily through my filed records, finally unearthing an older piece of mail that I had saved years ago. Sure enough, it was written in the same font. Just as I suspected, the lowercase R appears too close to the lowercase N, making it look like an M. I was sure that Malia Obama must have been one of Queen Nefertiti's daughters. It seemed to equate to a mother passing her name to her daughter, or a father sharing his full name with his first-born son but tacking on Junior or II to the end.

When typing my name in a default font such as Arial, you do not see the M fusion with the R and N. However, when you change the font to Papyrus, one of my favorites, it's a different story. Here is my name typed out in the Papyrus font style:

Jarnalia.

See look how the R and N look like an M?

Now, cover up the Ja with your finger. What name do you see?

Compelling, right?

Not only do I carry Janet Jackson's initials within my name, but through an optical illusion, I also carry Malia's name. I thought, "Wow she has placed herself in the midst of the right family unit once again." Malia has reunited with her father, Pharaoh Akhenaten, now known to the world as Barack Obama II. Except for this time around, her once grandmother, Queen Tiye, was now her mother, Michelle Obama. Malia has greatness on her side! Even without having any clairvoyants confirming my assumption just yet, I was certain Malia was one of Pharaoh Akhenaten and Queen Nefertiti's six Egyptian princesses.

I wanted to know if Sasha had a part in Pharaoh Akhenaten, Queen Nefertiti's, and Meritaten's Egyptian royal family. So, I ran over to Angel & Guides.

Dear Sasha,

Please forgive me if you took any offense. I wasn't trying to reject you from your own family, I was only trying to make a final analysis about Queen Nefertiti's past life family from my own perspective. Sasha, your family today was also Queen Nefertiti's family in a *very distant* and ancient lifetime. You have chosen very powerful and wonderful parents to guide you throughout this lifetime. Sasha, in my search for my own truth, believe it or not, I have a reading just for you as well.

An Open Reading

From: 2xQueen2xGoddess
To: Angel & Guides
Sent: Wednesday, November 28, 2012, 8:47 AM

Hello, Angel and Guides!

How are you all?

I really miss you!

I internally know for a fact, but I have not had it verified, that Malia Obama was one of Pharaoh Akhenaten & Queen Nefertiti's 6 daughters. However, my question is: Was Sasha Obama one of the six daughters of the pharaoh & queen in that lifetime as well?

Thank You Very Much,
Queen Nefertiti

From: Angel & Guides
To: 2xQueen2xGoddess
11/29/12 at 7:42

It is hard for me to hold Sasha's energy in that role. I can get her to go there but her energy fades away. It is almost like she was more of a great friend of one of the daughters but not a daughter herself. I can see her energy in that lifetime, playing at what appears to be a royal place like a palace but she just doesn't seem to live there. And yet she is very close to a female about the same age as her. She could have been a cousin possibly, but I just don't get that she's one of the daughters.

Good to hear from you!
Angel

In light of this emailed reading, I could now exclude Sasha as one of Queen Nefertiti's past life daughters and focus more on my assumption about Malia. And for the record, KareBear agrees that Sasha was not one of Nefertiti's and Akhenaten's daughters.

Again, at that time, I had not officially inquired about Malia's role as one of Queen Nefertiti's young princesses yet. But I knew without a shadow of a doubt that she once was a daughter of this chief queen and it would be five more years before I would have it confirmed or denied.

An Open Letter to Malia

Dear Malia,

I once overheard from one of the media outlets that you were choosing a career as a film director. I said to myself, Yep, that's my daughter alright. Ever since my son Beno, was seven years old, he himself has wanted to be the same thing, a film director.

Malia, can you believe you once lived in ancient Egypt and your parents today were once rulers of that ancient Egyptian dynasty! Although they were not a couple during that lifetime. It's funny, you see, because your father was my husband (Pharaoh Amenhotep IV/Akhenaten) and your mother this time around was your father's mother in that distant lifetime! Not only that, but when your mother was playing the role of Queen Tiye, she was actually married to Jay-Z, who was then Pharaoh Amenhotep III, and they ruled for 39 years. Your dad today was one of their sons in that distant lifetime in Thebes.

Malia, I am very disheartened that you were not my daughter Meritaten. Even though you were not my blood child, I still except you with open arms just the same as your brother King Tutankhaten. This still makes you kin to everyone.

Queen Janet and Princess Karen Malina were your past life half-sisters, and King Michael and Pharaoh Nasir were your past life brothers. You see, young lady, we are all connected!

As a result of me discovering my own true essence, I discovered all of you in the process, and this book is a true testament of my time delving into Egyptian antiquities and seeing behind the veil.

What did I discover while wearing my French pith helmet, tan blouse and knickerbockers held up by a stained brown leather belt, with a pair of 6.5 natural leather camel boots on my feet and toting my archaeologist satchel? I discovered that Egyptian antiquities are all about us!

XOXO,
Queen Nefertiti, the Egyptian Resurrector

In Memory of:
Prince,
Michael Jackson,
Tupac,
&
John Singleton

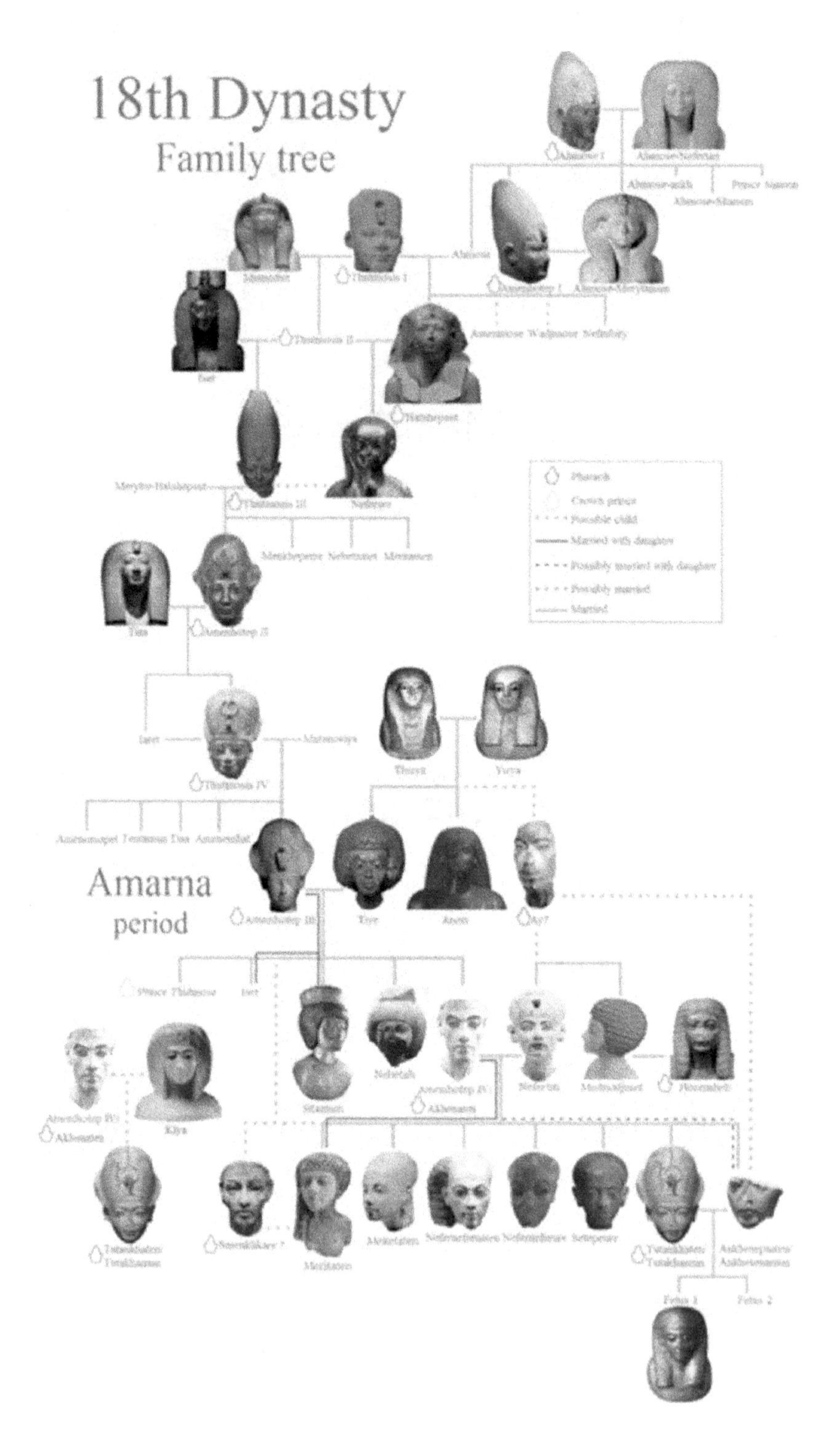
18th Dynasty
Family tree
Amarna
period

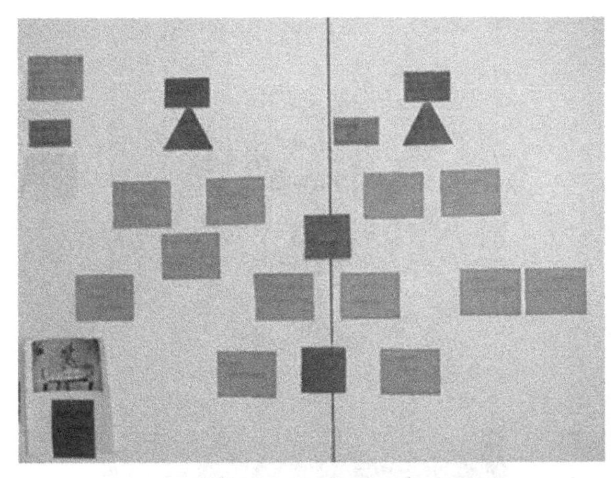

Getting organized.
The 18th Egyptian Dynasty Resurrection.
One was wrong (Meritaten) and one was discovered in the process (Neferneferure).

I do agree with you, Mr. Hemmitt!
However, you must remember that
your soul has been all the races.
"Reincarnation is about the soul." –KareBear

Between my ear and eye, can you see a backward L engraved on my face?

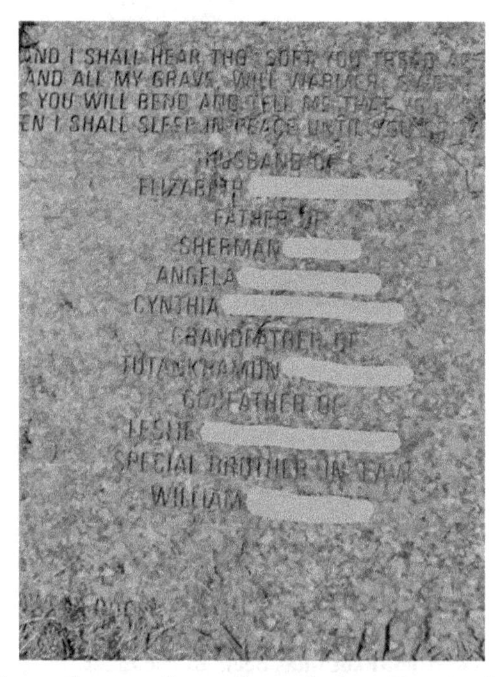

This is the tombstone of one of my relatives. Engraved on it is a list of names and his relationship to them. Look whose name is scribed fifth from the bottom under the list of grandchildren.

This is my relatives reposing neighbor, Queen! She's lying opposite of my relative. Here's the coinkydink, Mrs. Queen is next door to Tutankhamun! Taking into account what I already knew, the Universal Forces was bringing me some sort of confirmation.

One morning while working, I happened to notice these blank coloring sheets laid out for the clients to color.

Universal Forces answered me expeditiously!

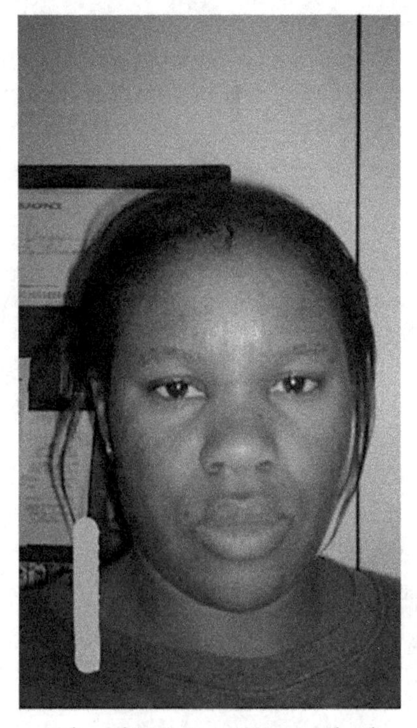

Yes, I know that this is one *very* rough photo of me.
This picture was taken the morning after my bathroom accident.

Bibliography

Bart, Anneke. "Amenhotep Huy." Ancient Egypt. Available at https://mathstat.slu.edu/~bart/egyptianhtml/kings%20and%20Queens/Amenhotep-Huy.html.

Bart, Anneke. "Horemheb." Ancient Egypt. Available at https://mathstat.slu.edu/~bart/egyptianhtml/kings%20and%20Queens/Horemheb2.html.

Bart, Anneke. "Nefertiti." Ancient Egypt. Available at https://mathstat.slu.edu/~bart/egyptianhtml/kings%20and%20Queens/Nefertiti-inscriptions.html.

Bart, Anneke. "Queen Ankhesenamun." Ancient Egypt. Available at https://mathstat.slu.edu/~bart/egyptianhtml/kings%20and%20Queens/Ankhesenamun.html.

Botnar, Katy. "Always Happy! Meet Pharrell WIlliams and his adorable family." Body Height Weight. September 2, 2017, available at https://bodyheightweight.com/pharrell-williams-family/.

Dodson, Aidan. "Crown Prince Djhutmose and the Royal Sons of the Eighteenth Dynasty." Journal of Egyptian Archeology. 1990.

Dodson, Aidan and Dyan Hilton. *The Complete Royal Families of Ancient Egypt.* Thames and Hudson. 2004.

Dorman, Peter. "Akhenaten." Encyclopaedia Britannica. Available at https://www.britannica.com/biography/Akhenaten.

Grajetki, Wolfram. *Ancient Egyptian Queens: a hieroglyphic dictionary.* Golden House Publications, 2005.

Hill, Jenny. "Ay (Aye)." Ancient Egypt Online. Available at https://ancientegyptonline.co.uk/ay/.

Hill, Jenny. "Ra." Ancient Egypt Online. Available at http://ancientegyptonline.co.uk/ra/.

Hill, Jenny. "Smenkhkare." Ancient Egypt Online. Available at https://ancientegyptonline.co.uk/smenkhare/.

Holloway, April. "The tragedy of Queen Ankhesenamun, sister and wife of Tutankhamun." Ancient Origins. Available at https://www.ancient-origins.net/ancient-places-africa/tragedy-queen-ankhesenamun-sister-and-wife-tutankhamun-001555.

Hutchinson Kim. "Soulmates: Soul Family, Soul Groups and Twin Flames." in5d. November 21, 2014, available at https://in5d.com/soulmates-soul-family-soul-groups-and-twin-flames/.

Jones Girls. "Night Over Egypt." Track 3 on Get as Much Love as You Can. 1981.

Kirko Bangz. "Cup Up Top Down." Track 10 on Progression III. Universal Music Publishing Group. 2014.

Klimczak, Natalia. "The Unique Sculptures of Thutmose…and a Secret Love for One of His Muses?" Ancient Origins. March 27, 2016, available at https://www.ancient-origins.net/history-famous-people/unique-sculptures-thutmose-and-secret-love-one-his-muses-005606.

Kozloff, Arielle. *Egypt's Dazzling Sun: Amenhotep III and His World.* The Cleveland Museum of Art, 1992.

Mark, Joshua. "Amenhotep III." Ancient History Encyclopedia. July 15, 2011, available at https://www.ancient.eu/Amenhotep_III/.

Mark, Joshua. "Horemheb." Ancient History Encyclopedia. April 22, 2014, available at https://www.ancient.eu/Horemheb/.

Mark, Joshua. "Tiye." Ancient History Encyclopedia. July 18, 2011, available at https://www.ancient.eu/tiye/.

Millmore, Mark. "Ancient Egyptian Gods and Goddesses." Discovering Egypt. Available at https://discoveringegypt.com/ancient-egyptian-gods-and-goddesses/.

O'Connor, David, and Eric H. Cline. Amenhotep III: Perspectives on His Reign. Ann Arbor: University of Michigan Press, 1998.

Sacco, Arianna. "Opportunity Knocks: the kingship of Ay." Ancient Warfare Magazine. Available at https://www.karwansaraypublishers.com/awblog/opportunity-knocks-the-kingship-of-ay/.

Schmitz, Leonhard. "Bacchanalia." Penelope University of Chicago. Available at http://penelope.uchicago.edu/Thayer/E/Roman/Texts/secondary/SMIGRA*/Bacchanalia.html.

T.G.H. James, *Tutankhamun*, Barnes and Noble Books, 2002.

Tyldesley, Joyce. "Chronicle of the Queens of Egypt: From Early Dynastic Times to the Death of Cleopatra." 2006.

Tyldesley, Joyce. Chronicle of the Queens of Egypt. London: Thames & Hudson, 2006.

Tyldesley, Joyce. "Nefertiti." Encyclopeadia Britannica. Available at https://www.britannica.com/biography/Nefertiti.

Woolf, Virginia. "Saturday 5 September." Woolf Online, available at http://www.woolfonline.com/?node=content/contextual/transcriptions&project=1&parent=41&taxa=42&content=6303&pos=7.

A Tribe Called Quest, Jazz (We've Got You), track 11 on The Low End Theory, Jive Records & RCA Records, 1991.

Akashic Records. Available at http://www.akashicrecordsofsouls.com/.

"Amarna: Egypt's Other Lost City (SECRET ANCIENT HISTORY DOCUMENTARY." Youtube Video, 47:41. Gracieladavina516. 2016, available at https://www.dailymotion.com/video/x3thir8.

"Amenhotep, son of Hapu." Available at https://www.britannica.com/biography/Amenhotep-son-of-Hapu.

"Ay." Wikipedia. Available at https://en.wikipedia.org/wiki/Ay.

"Eighteenth Dynasty of Egypt." Crystalinks. Available at https://www.crystalinks.com/dynasty18.html.

Leaders of the New School, Sobb Story, track 8 on A Future Without a Past, producers, 1991.

"Nefertiti." Biography.com. Available at https://www.biography.com/royalty/nefertiti.

"Pharrell Williams," Wikipedia, last edited May 9, 2019. Available at https://en.wikipedia.org/wiki/Pharrell_Williams.

"Pharaoh Akhenaten." Crystalinks. Available at https://www.crystalinks.com/akhenaten.html.

"Proof Found of Amenhotep III-Akhenaten co-regency," The History Blog, February 6, 2014 available at http://www.thehistoryblog.com/archives/29044.

"Provocative Yet Sacred: The Ancient Egyptian Festival of Drunkenness." Ancient Origins: Reconstructing the Story of Humanity's Past. February 3, 2016, available at https://www.ancient-origins.net/history-ancient-traditions/provocative-yet-sacred-ancient-egyptian-festival-drunkenness-005289.

"Questions and answers about Ramtha, JZ Knight," The Olympian, July 16, 2006. Available at https://archive.is/20130204080730/http://www.theolympian.com/689/story/50048.html.

"Sekhmet." Ancient Egypt Online. Available at https://ancientegyptonline.co.uk/sekhmet/.

"Soulmates, Soul Family, Soul Groups, Twin Flames." Poonam Bhartie KyronIndia Channel, LinkedIn. December 17, 2016, available at https://www.linkedin.com/pulse/soulmates-soul-family-groups-twin-flames-kryonindia-channel.

"The Canopic Jar." Encyclopaedia Britannica. Available at https://www.britannica.com/topic/canopic-jar.

"The Eye of Ra: How Sekhmet Became Hathor." Youtube. 5:01, LetItBeOnigiri, 2007. Available at https://www.youtube.com/watch?v=RDlfHTx-c0A&feature=youtu.be.

"The Pharaoh Ay (Aye)." Kingtutonline. Available at http://kingtutone.com/pharaohs/ay/.

"Thutmose (Prince)." Up/Closed. Available at https://upclosed.com/people/thutmose-3/.

"Tey." Wikipedia. Available at https://en.wikipedia.org/wiki/Tey#cite_note-8.

"Tomb of Ramose (TT55)." Egyptsites. February 7, 2009, available at https://egyptsites.wordpress.com/2009/02/07/tomb-of-ramose-tt55/.

"Tutankhamen." History.com. Available at https://www.history.com/topics/ancient-history/tutankhamen.

"Tutankhamun (1336 BC—1327 BC)." BBC. Available at https://www.bbc.co.uk/history/historic_figures/tutankhamun.shtml.

"What Happened to the Three Youngest Armana Princesses?" The Aten Sequence Books. Available at http://atensequence.blogspot.com/2013/06/what-happened-to-three-youngest-amarna.html.

"Who was Mutnodjmet?" Temple of Mut. https://templeofmut.wordpress.com/2007/03/01/who-was-mutnodjmet/.

Part II

The Revenants & The Entire History of Me

CPSIA information can be obtained
at www.ICGtesting.com
Printed in the USA
LVHW021452140820
663176LV00015B/142